'The growing battle over globalization was being won by those making the most money, at least until they lost on the streets of Seattle in late 1999. In a stunning, well-researched and outspoken analysis of this historic battle, Nicholas Guyatt has written not only a powerful analysis of these forces and their sometimes famous apologists, but raised fresh, fundamental questions about an entire range of US foreign policies that have deep roots in the American economic and cultural experience.'

WALTER LAFEBER, Cornell University, author of
Michael Jordan and the New Global Capitalism

'Nicholas Guyatt has done us a great service. With this book he has given us a succinct, bold and penetrating critique of the triumphalist ideology which insists on American domination of this and the next century. *Another American Century?* is both sweeping in its argument and rich in the evidence it produces to show the dangers to us all in the idea that our country has the right to impose its will on the rest of the world.'

HOWARD ZINN, author of
A People's History of the United States

'A cogent and incisive history of the present. Guyatt situates major debates about American foreign relations (the consequences of globalization, Washington and the United Nations, the role of the Pentagon after the Cold War, humanitarian interventions) in a concise but sweeping interpretive history going back to the Depression and World War II. In so doing he skewers a number of shallow and insubstantial foreign affairs pundits who may get a lot of media attention, but get few things right about the problems and perils of American foreign policy in a new century.'

BRUCE CUMINGS, University of Chicago,
author of *The American Ascendancy*

NICHOLAS GUYATT was educated at Emmanuel College, Cambridge, and Princeton University. He is currently completing his Ph.D. in Princeton's Department of History. He is the author of *The Absence of Peace: Understanding the Israeli–Palestinian Conflict* (Zed Books, 1998).

ANOTHER AMERICAN CENTURY?

The United States and the World after 2000

NICHOLAS GUYATT

PLUTO PRESS
Sydney

UNIVERSITY PRESS LTD
Dhaka

WHITE LOTUS
Bangkok

FERNWOOD PUBLISHING LTD
Halifax

DAVID PHILIP
Claremont

ZED BOOKS
London & New York

Another American Century? The United States and the World after 2000
was first published in 2000 by

In Australasia: Pluto Press Australia,
6A Nelson Street, Annandale, NSW 2038, Sydney

In Bangladesh: The University Press Ltd,
Red Crescent Building, 114 Motijheel C/A, PO Box 2611, Dhaka 1000

In Burma, Cambodia, Laos, Thailand and Vietnam:
White Lotus Co. Ltd, GPO Box 1141, Bangkok 10501, Thailand

In Canada: Fernwood Publishing Ltd,
PO Box 9409, Station A, Halifax, Nova Scotia, B3K 5S3

In Southern Africa: David Philip Publishers (Pty Ltd),
208 Werdmuller Centre, Claremont 7735, South Africa

In the rest of the world: Zed Books Ltd,
7 Cynthia Street, London N1 9JF, UK
and Room 400, 175 Fifth Avenue, New York, NY 10010, USA

Distributed in the USA exclusively by St. Martin's Press, Inc.,
175 Fifth Avenue, New York, NY 10010, USA

Cover designed by Andrew Corbett
Designed and typeset in Monotype Bembo by Illuminati, Grosmont
Printed and bound in the United Kingdom by Cox & Wyman, Reading

A catalogue record for this book is available from the British Library

US CIP data is available from the Library of Congress

Canadian CIP data is available from the National Library of Canada

ISBN 1 86403 129 8 Pb (Australasia)
ISBN 1 55266 036 2 Pb (Canada)
ISBN 0 86486 365 9 Pb (Southern Africa)

ISBN 1 85649 779 8 Hb (Zed Books)
ISBN 1 85649 780 1 Pb (Zed Books)

A Brave New Series

GLOBAL ISSUES
IN A CHANGING WORLD

This new series of short, accessible think-pieces deals with leading global issues of relevance to humanity today. Intended for the enquiring reader and social activists in the North and the South, as well as students, the books explain what is at stake and question conventional ideas and policies. Drawn from many different parts of the world, the series' authors pay particular attention to the needs and interests of ordinary people, whether living in the rich industrial or the developing countries. They all share a common objective – to help stimulate new thinking and social action in the opening years of the new century.

Global Issues in a Changing World is a joint initiative by Zed Books in collaboration with a number of partner publishers and non-governmental organizations around the world. By working together, we intend to maximize the relevance and availability of the books published in the series.

Participating NGOs

Both ENDS, Amsterdam
Catholic Institute for International Relations, London
Corner House, Sturminster Newton
Focus on the Global South, Bangkok
Inter Pares, Ottawa
Third World Network, Penang
World Development Movement, London

'Communities in the South are facing great difficulties in coping with global trends. I hope this brave new series will throw much needed light on the issues ahead and help us choose the right options.'

MARTIN KHOR, Director, Third World Network

'There is no more important campaign than our struggle to bring the global economy under democratic control. But the issues are fearsomely complex. This Global Issues Series is a valuable resource for the committed campaigner and the educated citizen.'

BARRY COATES, Director, World Development Movement (WDM)

TITLES IN THE GLOBAL ISSUES SERIES

Already published

Nicholas Guyatt, *Another American Century? The United States and the World after 2000*

Robert Ali Brac de la Perrière and Franck Seuret, *Brave New Seeds: The Threat of GM Crops to Farmers*

John Madeley, *Hungry for Trade: How the Poor Pay for Free Trade* (Spring 2001)

Oswaldo de Rivero, *The Myth of Development: An Emergency Agenda for the Survival of Nations*

Riccardo Petrella, *The Water Manifesto: Arguments for a World Water Contract*

In preparation

Peggy Antrobus and Gigi Franciso, *The Women's Movement Worldwide: Issues and Strategies for the New Century*

Amit Bhaduri and Deepak Nayyar, *Free Market Economics: The Intelligent Person's Guide to Liberalization*

Julian Burger, *Indigenous Peoples: The Struggle of the World's Indigenous Nations and Communities*

Graham Dunkley, *Trading Development: Trade, Globalization and Alternative Development Possibilities*

Calestous Juma, *Governing Biotechnology: The Global Biosafety Regime*

John Madeley, *The New Agriculture: Towards Food for All*

Lloyd Pettiford, *Sustainable Development: A Critical Reintroduction*

Harry Shutt, *A New Globalism: An Alternative to the Breakdown of World Order*

For full details of this list and Zed's other subject and general catalogues, please write to: The Marketing Department, Zed Books, 7 Cynthia Street, London NI 9JF, UK, or email Sales@zedbooks.demon.co.uk

Visit our website at: http://www.zedbooks.demon.co.uk

For Kristen

CONTENTS

ACKNOWLEDGEMENTS

This book was written in Princeton, Washington DC, and Cambridge, England, between July and December 1999. In the United States, I'd like to thank Wendy Cadge, Laura Fiske, Andrew Graybill, Sarah Igo, Drew Levy, Nina Paynter and Eileen Scully for reading the manuscript entire, and making many useful suggestions. Eileen Scully was instrumental in finding more readers for the manuscript outside of Princeton, for which I'm also grateful. For their help with specific queries, and/or their kindnesses to me as I put this book together, I'd like to thank Jeremy Adelman, Asli Bali, Ezra Block, John C. Culver, Michael D'Alba, Alec, Kelly and Mali Dun, Jennifer Ebinger, Philip Gourevitch, Kristen Harknett, David Kasunic, Jennifer Moorehead, Stefan Siegel, Emily Silverman, Todd Stevens, Simon and Eleri Tyler, and Chris Wren. Kristen Harknett and Andrew Graybill very generously gave their time to the thankless task of proof-reading, for which I'm very apologetic and grateful. Claire Minton offered very useful advice on indexing.

In England (or thereabouts), I am indebted to Robert Molteno at Zed Books for suggesting the project to me, and for his circumspection when I delivered twice as many words as I was supposed to. I'd like to thank my family for their continuing support. I'm also grateful for the encouragement and generosity of William Flemming, Conor Houghton, Robert Palmer, Edward, Nancy and Catherine Shaw, and Matt Thorne. Richard Serjeantson read the manuscript in its entirety, and allowed me to complete the book in his Cambridge rooms even as he succumbed to a grisly flu. Ben Jackson should have appeared here last time around, so now he has my apologies as well as my thanks. I'm grateful also to Lucy Morton and Robin Gable for their skill, generosity and attentiveness in setting the manuscript. Of course, all errors of fact or interpretation in the following remain my own.

FOREWORD

This is a short book on a very large topic: the present relationship between the United States and the rest of the world. It seems appropriate, then, for me to begin by recognising some of the book's deficiencies. Despite my title, this is not a work of prediction or prophecy; nor is it predominantly concerned with the events which may take place 'after 2000'. What I have tried instead to do is to sketch some recent American engagements beyond US borders, and to draw from these some general patterns of US foreign policy and its effects on the rest of the world – in economic, political, military and ideological terms. The collapse of the Soviet Union, the much-trumpeted 'end of history', and the supposed triumph of Western economic and political thought make this a propitious time for such a study, and so I have taken the liberty of focusing predominantly on the 1990s in what follows – and on the Clinton administration in particular.

One of the most important themes of this book, however, is that mainstream political debates in the United States and in many other parts of the world have become much more consensual in the past decade, since formerly left-leaning political parties (such as Clinton's Democratic Party) have embraced many of the policies of their right-wing rivals, especially in the economic realm. The Clinton administration therefore represents not a left-wing interlude in American history, but a reasonable reflection of current thinking across the political mainstream. This seems particularly the case when we focus on foreign policy and the international economy rather than social issues, an emphasis which I will adopt in the pages that follow. As we will see, Bill Clinton has scored notable successes in the export of American economic policies around the world, a fact which also shapes my focus. Finally, Clinton was elected to the presidency as a post-Cold War president, the first American leader since Franklin Roosevelt to shape his views of international affairs without having to counter the Soviet Union. His own rhetoric encouraged high expectations of the United States, and provides a useful standard by which to judge the actions of his administration.

I should note that this is not an account of the Clinton administration's foreign policy, but a broader attempt to assess the most important trends and moods which shape the US relationship with the rest of the world at the end of the twentieth century. Although I devote many pages to the activities and beliefs of government officials, I want also to address the interpretations and frameworks of American society more generally. This is obviously a difficult endeavour; but I hope to offer at least a sense of wider American perspectives – in business, in the media, in the public at large – on the US role in the world. I also want to encourage readers to think about these issues not simply in the historical context, but with a view to the coming decades. I don't presume to answer the question of whether the twenty-first century will be 'American', but I think we should pause to consider more fully the terms and implications behind that question, and the triumphalist mood in which many Americans have already offered responses in the affirmative.

In February 1941, ten months before the United States entered the Second World War, Henry R. Luce, the millionaire publishing magnate, contributed an article to his own *Life* magazine on the state of the nation. Luce argued that Americans had failed, in the first four decades of the twentieth century, to recognise the extent to which their country now controlled the destiny of the world, and that the course of human history had therefore taken an unfortunate turn:

> Consider the 20th century. It is not only ours in the sense that we happen to live in it but ours also because it is America's first century as a dominant power in the world. So far, this century of ours has been a profound and tragic disappointment. No other century has been so big with promise for human progress and happiness. And in no one century have so many men and women and children suffered such pain and anguish and bitter death.[1]

Of course, Luce looked to the great wars of his time in reaching this assessment; but his was not a pessimistic vision, or a call for his readers to set their horizons more modestly. On the contrary, Luce argued, the greatest problem facing the world was that America had yet to accept fully its responsibility to assert ownership of the twentieth century. Americans had been isolationist, overly reluctant to reach out to the peoples of the rest of the world. Luce provided a series of better models for American engagement, then presented them to his readers as a challenge to be taken up:

> America as the dynamic center of ever-widening spheres of enterprise, America as the training center of the skillful servants of mankind, America as the Good Samaritan, really believing again that it is more blessed to give than to receive, and America as the powerhouse of the ideals of Freedom and Justice – out of these elements surely can be fashioned a vision of the 20th Century to which we can and will devote ourselves in joy and gladness and vigor and enthusiasm.

Hence, argued Luce, it was time for Americans to think in terms of the title of his article – to embrace 'The American Century'. Six decades later, Luce was hailed as a visionary for exactly this insight – the realisation that the Americanisation of the twentieth century would mean the Americanisation of the world, a process which has advanced – more or less consistently – ever since.[2]

In his State of the Union address of January 1999, President Bill Clinton echoed Luce's words as he encouraged Americans to reach for the 'next American century'. At the end of the 1990s, Luce's coinage was treated by politicians and commentators either as a properly triumphant statement of American achievement in the years since World War II, or as a simple and uncritical description of the one hundred years since 1900.[3] It could easily be forgotten that Luce's original article was the subject of some controversy around the time of its first appearance, not least because it seemed excessively pro-American and inappropriately nationalistic, even at a time of war. Franklin Roosevelt's vice-president, Henry A. Wallace, explicitly addressed Luce's 'American century' in a speech delivered in 1942, which was widely reprinted and distributed during the war. Wallace's objections to Luce were clear and direct:

Some have spoken of the 'American Century'. I say that the century on which we are entering – the century which will come out of this war – can be and must be the century of the common man. Perhaps it will be America's opportunity to suggest the freedoms and duties by which the common man must live.... No nation will have the God-given right to exploit other nations. Older nations will have the privilege to help younger nations get started on the path to industrialization, but there must be neither military nor economic imperialism. The methods of the nineteenth century will not work in the people's century which is now about to begin.[4]

Wallace was especially disturbed by some of the more nakedly self-interested and commercial elements of Luce's article, including Luce's urgent anticipation of the 'tremendous possibilities' for world trade. In proposing a 'people's century' to set against Luce's vision of global Americanisation, Wallace expressed his hope that the post-war order would diverge from the status quo, and his belief that only a more equitable global arrangement could peacefully harness the enormous social and political forces of the developing world.

I want to recall this debate between Luce and Wallace because it offers an important political and ideological distinction between 'Americanisation' and 'internationalism', which was largely absent across the four decades of the Cold War. For Luce, the US had an opportunity to exploit its power and predominant status in the winning of new markets abroad, and the expansion of American political and cultural influence. Wallace, on the other hand, argued for a US responsibility towards the developing world, and (most importantly) for the right of poorer countries to determine their own path of development, with American assistance but without submitting to American imperium. The Cold War seriously disrupted Wallace's own career, and the international politics he hoped to create; but at the end of the Cold War, nearly fifty years after Luce and Wallace argued these positions, a more internationalist rhetoric again emerged in American political life. The end of the Soviet Union promised a substantial peace dividend; the new Democratic president, Bill Clinton, pledged in 1992 to strengthen the United Nations and to put the US in its service; and advances in technology and communications promised to link the world more closely together than ever before, uniting even its most poor and remote regions with wealthy nations like the United States.

This book tells the story of this proposed internationalism, and of the emergence in the post-Cold War period of a new wave of 'Americanisation'. Bill Clinton's triumphant inauguration in 1999 of the 'next American century' is a useful starting point for our investigation, and each of the chapters that follow is headed by an epigraph from Clinton's 1999 State of the Union address. My hope is to test Clinton's rhetoric (and, by extension, the idea of another 'American century') against the historical record from recent years, whilst trying also to describe shifts in American thought and action beyond the Clinton administration and Washington, DC. The book is arranged in four chapters, each dealing with a separate aspect of the US relationship with other nations – and covering, broadly speaking, economic, political, military and ideological engagements with the rest of the world.

Chapter 1 deals with the influence of the United States on the global economy since 1945, paying particular attention to the establishment of the International Monetary Fund and World Bank, the quest for new markets for American products overseas, and the eclipse of government management of the economy in favour of a more free-market approach. This last development, I argue, has been especially marked since the global debt crisis of 1982, and has had particularly serious effects on the developing world. Moreover, despite the apparent absence of government from the free-market model, the evidence suggests that the US has very strongly pushed this particular economic configuration, putting the substantial resources of the American government behind the drive to remove other governments from the management of their national economies. To give a better view of how this has worked in practice, I offer three examples of the effects of American economic policies abroad: the Mexican peso crisis of 1994/5, the ongoing efforts to create a US–Africa free-trade agreement, and the American-led attempt to rebuild the Russian economy after the collapse of the Soviet Union.

Chapter 2 focuses on the American relationship with the United Nations, particularly in the context of Bill Clinton's 1992 promise to strengthen the relationship between the US and the UN. I trace the emergence of the 'international community' in American rhetoric, and assess the US interest in complying with the rules of such a community by exploring the American response to two major multilateral initiatives in the 1990s: the effort to create an International Criminal Court, and the international campaign for a ban on the use of landmines. I also examine the American commitment to peacekeeping operations in the past decade, looking in detail at the failed intervention in Somalia in 1993, the disastrous avoidance of engagement during the Rwandan genocide in 1994, and the confused policy over Bosnia before the US-led Dayton Accords of 1995. These various episodes suggest a highly selective and self-interested American 'internationalism', which has certainly contributed to the deterioration of American relations with the United Nations, and the effective eclipse of that body less than a decade after it was fêted by Clinton and other American officials.

Chapter 3 considers the fate of the US military in the wake of the Cold War, and explores the ways in which Pentagon planners and government figures have managed to sustain high levels of military spending even after the collapse of the Soviet Union. In this chapter, I examine the doctrine of 'rogue states', which has been used to justify increases in the US defence budget, as well as the efforts to preserve a strong 'Western alliance' by enlarging NATO (again, despite the Soviet absence). From this analysis, I contend that the current rates of military spending in the USA are excessive – and I try to offer some reasons why they persist by looking at the relationship between the Pentagon and major American corporations. In the final section of this chapter, I offer a more extensive discussion of US military action abroad, taking as examples the 1991 conflict in Iraq (and the subsequent attacks on that country) and the 1999 NATO campaign in Kosovo. I am interested here in the place of military action in a broader scheme of American foreign policy, and particularly in the relationship between the actual conduct and outcome of military operations and the post-Cold War rhetoric (usually internationalist) of the American government. In conclusion, I look at the threat of terrorism, and the likely alienation (and radicalisation) of American adversaries abroad, especially those who have been personally affected by US military action.

Chapter 4 moves in a rather different direction, and tries to offer a broader context in which to consider the material discussed in the earlier chapters. Although it is extremely important to make some reckoning of US conduct abroad, we should not lose sight of the

greater challenge as observers of American policy – to understand
not only what has happened, but how and why these events have
occurred. This final chapter attempts to answer these questions at
least provisionally, by looking in detail at different bodies of American opinion, and at the different contexts in which opinions are
expressed. In the first section of the chapter, I offer a brief summary
of the state of academic thinking in the US on foreign relations, as
well as an account of the relatively privileged surroundings of these
'experts'. The second section pushes beyond the government, universities and think-tanks to examine the wider constraints in the US
on the formulation of ideas about foreign policy. I examine the
pressures on politicians to take a particular line on foreign questions;
the constraints and biases of the mass (and predominantly corporate-
controlled) media in the US; and the perspectives and awareness of
the American public.

My hope in this is to get past an interpretation of American
foreign relations that collapses every event and problem into a simple
frame – be it economic or political. Although big corporations and
wealthy individuals in the US exert a strong influence over American
foreign policy, the process by which the United States acts abroad is
complicated and multifaceted. Alongside the straightforward observation that the US might act directly to rein in the interests of its
wealthy minority, I want to give a sense of the many different factors
which have contributed to some of the more unfortunate or destructive American policies abroad. This fuller understanding of
American thinking and action is vital to any redirection of US foreign
relations, and to persuading the majority of US citizens that another
American century is not a desirable outcome.

NOTES

1. Henry Luce, 'The American Century', *Life*, 17 February 1941. The
   essay is reproduced, along with a number of responses from historians,
   in *Diplomatic History* 23, no. 2 (1999): 159–71. Subsequent references
   are to the *Diplomatic History* reprint.
2. It's worth noting that Luce was hardly the first figure to suggest that
   the twentieth century would be strongly influenced by the United States,

or that the process of 'globalisation' would entail, in large measure, an 'Americanisation' of the world outside the USA. For a much earlier view, see W.T. Stead, *The Americanization of the World; or, The Trend of the Twentieth Century* (New York: H. Markley, 1902). Luce also noted in his own essay that 'there is already an immense American internationalism', citing jazz, Hollywood movies and 'American machines and patented products' as evidence of the extent of US influence. Luce, 169. For a recent scholarly account of this pre-World War II 'Americanisation', see Emily S. Rosenberg, *Spreading the American Dream: American Economic and Cultural Expansion, 1890–1945* (New York: Hill & Wang, 1982).

3. Bill Clinton, 'State of the Union Address', Capitol Hill, Washington, DC, 19 January 1999. More recent paeans to Luce's 'American century' are detailed in the Afterword. President Clinton himself endorsed the phrase even before his 1999 address – see his remarks at the 75th anniversary celebration for *Time* magazine, Radio City Music Hall, New York City, 3 March 1998: 'Tonight, *Time* has paid tribute to the time it not only observed but helped to create – the stunning years your founder, Henry Luce, so unforgettably called the American Century.' The mission of *Time* magazine, in the view of its managing editor, Walter Isaacson, continues: 'To the extent that America remains an avatar of freedom, the Global Century about to dawn will be, in Luce's terminology, another American Century.' 'Luce's Values – Then and Now', *Time*, 8 March 1998.

4. Henry A. Wallace, 'The Price of Free World Victory', address before the Free World Association, New York City, 8 May 1942; reprinted in Leland M. Goodrich, ed., *Documents on American Foreign Relations, Vol. IV: July 1941–June 1942* (Boston: World Peace Foundation, 1942), 62–9. This essay was printed in a variety of mass editions, including (along with other pieces by Wallace) Russell Lord, ed., *The Century of the Common Man* (New York: Reynal & Hitchcock, 1943).

CHAPTER I

THE US AND THE
GLOBAL ECONOMY

When you come right down to it, now that the world economy is becoming more and more integrated, we have to do in the world what we spent the better part of the century doing here at home. We have got to put a human face on the global economy.

William Jefferson Clinton, 1999 State of the Union address[1]

For much of the twentieth century, the United States economy was the largest in the world. Consequently, the gradual development of a global economy, highly integrated and diversified, has depended on American guidance and direction. At the close of the century, the global economy was dominated by American corporations and by standards and institutions largely shaped by the US. Meanwhile, the recent financial crisis which swept through Asia, Russia and Latin America has raised serious questions about the stability of the international system.

In this chapter, I want to ask two questions: how has the US shaped the world economy since 1945? And how equitable and stable is the current global arrangement? In the first section, I will take a broad perspective on these questions; in the second, I want to look in more detail at three examples – Mexico, Africa and Russia – to see the ways in which US economic policies play out across the world. In conclusion, I will elaborate some of the established features of the global economy, and the substantial ways in which its 'human face' has been disfigured.

THE GLOBAL ECONOMY SINCE 1945

The Depression and the case for regulation

Looking back across the twentieth century, two events stand out as crucial to the course of the world economy: the Great Depression of the 1930s, and the Second World War which followed it. The Depression was pivotal in demonstrating that economies needed regulation and prudence as well as enterprise and daring. In 1929, a boom in stock-market speculation and international bank lending precipitated a collapse of confidence and of financial institutions on an unprecedented scale. Companies and banks in the US went bust; loans were called in around the world, bankrupting more companies and banks outside the US; and ordinary people lost their jobs and their savings, plunging below the poverty line. Although every country had experienced the boom–bust cycle at some point, the size and duration of the Great Depression suggested to the US and other governments that something had to be done to prevent a repeat of this disaster. As President Franklin D. Roosevelt ministered to the immediate needs of the US population, therefore, his administration also set in motion a series of financial reforms and restrictions with a view to the long term: banks would be limited to particular regions and particular kinds of lending; bank deposits would be insured by the government to protect savings; speculators would be constrained in their gambling. The net result was a US economy in which government played a large role, and advocates of 'free markets' and unfettered financial activity were marginalised.[2]

If the Depression revealed the dangers of rampant speculation and overlending, World War II suggested the need for global cooperation across a raft of issues, especially the economy. Although the war was conventionally presented as a conflict of ideas, a battle between fascism and freedom, the underlying economic and imperial tensions between the combatants were readily apparent. The United States emerged from the war as the strongest economy in the world, and made provisions even before the end of hostilities for an international economic framework, a road map for the global economy which would contain future ambitions and tensions. An international conference held in Bretton Woods, New Hampshire, in 1944 largely established the rules and institutions by which the post-war economy would be managed. Currencies would be pegged, with some provision for occasional adjustment; the new International Monetary Fund (IMF) would step in to make emergency loans to any countries having trouble maintaining their currency rate; and a World Bank would make loans to poorer countries to facilitate their development. In theory, these provisions should have ensured the stability of national economies and encouraged the progress of smaller nations, especially those struggling to emerge from the shadows of imperialism and colonialism. In practice, however, powerful obstacles stood in the way of achieving these aims.[3]

Was the Bretton Woods system an American invention? Did it advance US interests? We can answer both of these questions in the affirmative: the Bretton Woods conference took place under US supervision, and the models of economic development which emerged were strongly supported by the American government.[4] We should not forget that, as the Bretton Woods rules were put into place, the United States was entering a conflict with the Soviet Union which was both political and economic: the lure of socialism had generated a real enthusiasm for radical economic change in many countries, and the US was willing to intervene with force to uphold its vision of development rather than the socialist alternative. The post-war American government clearly felt that other countries should adopt the Bretton Woods system, and even used the CIA in Italy and Greece to destabilise those left-leaning parties which had alternative ideas of economic reform.[5]

We should be careful, however, to avoid seeing Bretton Woods as the first stage of an unbroken and unilateral American domination of the world economy. In the first instance, the conference itself depended heavily on the ideas of the British economist John Maynard Keynes, who had become the most prominent spokesperson for the view that governments had a big role to play in managing and encouraging economic growth.[6] Moreover, those ideas of government participation and regulation infused the discussions. Before 1930, there had been relatively little talk of the responsibility of governments to keep a close watch on their national economies, let alone the global economy which had come to assert a major influence on domestic conditions. After the Great Depression, however, it seemed irresponsible for a government *not* to control the financial markets, and to stand idly by as the ground for a future crisis was laid. The global economic breakdown had hit the US as surely as Europe and Latin America, and Bretton Woods suggested that every country had an interest in better-regulated and less risky financial activity in the future.[7] In this respect, at least, the original Bretton Woods agreement was very different from the arrangement at the century's end.

The idea of free trade had been tied closely in American minds to the quest for overseas markets for American products; after the Depression, then, US policymakers accepted the need for governments to regulate their economies in various ways, but maintained their interest in finding new markets overseas for American goods. After World War II, the US was especially well-placed to export its products, as long as it could find some way for the cash-starved economies of Europe and elsewhere to pay the bills. This was the context for the massive 'Marshall Aid' programme of 1948; and also for the inauguration of the General Agreement on Tariffs and Trade (GATT) and the International Trade Organisation (ITO), which sought to broker international agreements that would enable 'free trade'.[8] The phrase itself is a misnomer of sorts, and the idea of free trade certainly chafed with the Bretton Woods commitments to government intervention and management. Although the US correctly argued that protectionism and colonial privileges had contributed to the onset of the recent world war, the claim that free trade was to everyone's advantage was disingenuous. The US economy had finished the war in much better shape than its rivals in Europe and Asia, and so those governments felt the need to defend their own moribund industries against cheap American imports.[9]

Meanwhile, new nations in the developing world, and some older countries which had struggled in the transition to 'developed' status, toyed with the idea of more protectionism as a means of establishing their economic independence from Europe and America. Countries which were rich in raw materials were extremely sensitive to the changing price of their exports on the international markets, and were uncertain that 'free trade' would actually free them from the vagaries of price changes on the commodities exchanges. Many nations dissented from the US model of free trade and decided instead to encourage domestic industry and a protected domestic market. Given that American companies often had a substantial interest in extracting or harvesting commodities for export in these foreign countries, local decisions to concentrate on industrial development would frequently provoke a hostile reaction from the US government.[10]

In the decades following World War II, therefore, the US was alternately collaborative and coercive in its stewardship of the global economy. In its dealings with large, developed nations, the US upheld many of the Bretton Woods rules and collaborated to maintain the pegged currency levels which underpinned economic stability.[11] At the same time, however, the US promoted a model of 'free trade' which was unlikely to guarantee economic stability in poorer countries, and stood ready to intervene (sometimes militarily) in situations where a government or popular opposition threatened to secede from the international order. In Iran, Guatemala and Chile, the threat of communism was invoked by US policymakers to justify the enforced American rearrangement of those nations' economic policies. Under cover of the 'Cold War' with the USSR, the US was willing and able to impose its own model of economic development, disregarding the wishes of local people and occasionally killing them in the process.[12]

'Free markets', bank lending and the return of the speculators

As we will see, American advocacy of 'free trade' has been constant in the decades since World War II; the US perspective on government regulation of the economy, however, has changed dramatically, and has to some extent dovetailed with the argument for free trade. Originally, the Bretton Woods system tried to establish the conditions for stable economic development by fixing the value of currencies, and persuading nations both to help each other to maintain these values and to deter flows of money which might upset the balance. Until 1971, therefore, countries largely cooperated with each other (through the buying and selling of different currencies) to keep the various values in the right place. In addition, governments tried to limit capital flows emanating from private individuals or corporations; although companies could operate in other countries, they were not permitted to deal in currencies or financial instruments which might adversely affect the pegged values under Bretton Woods. Effectively this limited the amount of money flowing through the international system and made it easier for governments to maintain rates of exchange.[13]

In the 1960s, however, the stability of these currency values was seriously threatened. As memories of the Depression faded, governments in Europe and the US became more complacent about the activities of companies and banks, and increasingly tolerated the ingenious efforts of corporations to maximise their profits. Growing international trade was complicated by devious accounting procedures, by which a company might take advantage of a weaker currency in packaging a particular foreign sale or purchase. Meanwhile banks and financial institutions, especially those based in the US, exploited loopholes in domestic law to establish offshore branches. London became the centre of the 'Eurodollar' market, in which US banks offered dollar accounts and loans to foreign customers away from the supervision and regulation of the American government. Of course, this violated the cardinal principles established in the wake of the Depression; but it also brought large profits to some of the most powerful individuals and companies in Europe and America – ample compensation for the abandonment of that earlier prudence.[14]

As companies and investors tried to bend the rules and introduce renewed speculation into this system, the American economy ran into difficulties which also put pressure on fixed exchange rates. Under Bretton Woods, the various currencies were pegged to the US dollar, and the dollar itself was fixed to gold: in theory, every currency could therefore be exchanged for gold (via the dollar) at a fixed rate, which meant that the US had to ensure that the dollars in circulation were backed by its reserve holdings of gold. Tallying gold with dollars became harder in the 1960s as the Eurodollar markets put huge dollar sums beyond the control (or knowledge) of the US government. Additionally, the US escalation of its war in Vietnam put pressure on the entire American economy and sent its inflation rate creeping upwards. By the late 1960s, US dollars and US gold reserves were no longer in synch, and the administrations of Lyndon Johnson and Richard Nixon feared that a run on the dollar would force a devaluation and the end of the Bretton Woods system of pegged rates. The increasing appeal of speculation to wealthy Americans and Europeans, and the ballooning cost of the Vietnam War, ultimately destroyed the exchange-rate system. In 1971, Nixon closed the 'gold window' and allowed the dollar to 'float', to find its own value against other currencies without government intervention. The US dollar was devalued, and the pegged currencies began to float alongside it in the new international currency market.[15]

The demise of the pegged-rate system may seem a rather arcane detail in world history. Its effects have been profound, however, and have shaped the face of the global economy at the turn of the century. The breakdown of the exchange-rate system was a major blow to Keynes's original vision of a world economy managed by government cooperation. Moreover, the victory of the 'market' over government allowed (and even encouraged) riskier forms of investment and speculation to re-emerge from their long disgrace. In the mid-1970s, many of the surviving restrictions on capital flows were removed, and the legacy of caution left by the Depression was disavowed. Within a few years, enormous sums of money were moving around the world, largely outside the control of national governments; new forms of borrowing, lending, and especially of speculation were devised; and the profits of financial corporations depended increasingly on their foreign activities. US banks and firms led the charge, taking full advantage of this deregulation to expand their activities worldwide.[16]

Much of the speculation was initially confined to the developed world, and focused on stocks, government debt certificates and currencies. Developing countries, however, were slowly sucked into this new world of easy credit and private/corporate influence. In the 1950s and 1960s, developing countries relied principally on development loans and grants from specific countries or the World Bank to finance their various projects. Given the public-interest nature of most of these endeavours (electrification, damming, road building, and so on), the favourable terms of these development loans were properly tailored to the likely returns. Lending was specifically based on the premiss that these poorer countries needed assistance, and that they were unlikely to attract private banks or to repay loans at private rates. In the two decades following World War II, a combination of wariness on the banks' part and government regulation in the US and Europe kept private lenders out of the developing world.[17]

In the 1970s, however, the larger trends we have been tracking – government deregulation and an amnesia about the Depression – persuaded the banks, especially in the US, to look for business in the developing world. As inflation rates remained high in their traditional markets, banks were attracted to Africa and especially Latin America and the prospect of big loans at high interest. Developing countries, meanwhile, entered the bargain for various reasons. Some were run dictatorially and placed the interest of a ruling elite above the needs of the wider population; others were struggling to industrialise or to pursue their own development models without the assistance and approval of the World Bank. Developing countries previously faced difficulties in winning grants and loans from official sources for more redistributive or left-leaning programmes; many turned to private banks in the 1970s as a last resort, eager to implement their reforms and hopeful that they could somehow deal with the interest that these private loans would demand. The banks, meanwhile, competed with each other to offer loans to virtually any country which asked for them, even if that country's economic situation was already parlous.[18]

It would be hard to overestimate the loan bonanza of the 1970s and its influence on developed economies.[19] In the US, major banks like Citicorp and Bankers Trust were reaping almost 80 per cent of their profits from overseas transactions, and making cash advances that far outstripped their own deposits.[20] In the developing world, meanwhile, the loans had spiralled out of control, and the interest payments alone were forcing governments to borrow even more money. With the global economy largely idling in the 1970s, and given slow returns on investment in development projects, debtor governments edged closer to disaster. The banks, meanwhile, dismissed warnings of impending doom with the breezy claim that governments in the developing world could not go bankrupt, and that the debts would continue to be paid.[21] In August 1982, Jesús Silva Herzog, finance minister of Mexico, announced just the opposite: Mexico was indeed bankrupt, and would not be able to service its debts any longer. Thus began the 'debt crisis', and a series of US-led policies and decisions which have defined the current global economy.[22]

*From crisis to 'consensus': debt and development
in the 1980s and 1990s*

As the implications of Mexico's announcement sank in, commentators
and politicians in the US and Europe realised the scale of the problem. Some of the largest banks in the world had committed themselves well beyond their own reserves, and were now faced with the
awful consequences of these bloated bad loans. If companies and
individuals tried *en masse* to remove their deposits from the banks,
they would quickly exhaust the reserves and would force a collapse
of the banking system, returning the world to the disasters of the
1930s.[23] The recklessness of the banks' lending practices had brought
the global economy to the brink of another crash, and banks and
government officials had quickly to respond to the Mexican and
other defaults before the inevitable run on the banks. Of course, the
first step was for governments to assume the management of the
crisis, and for the banks to take a back seat as politicians worked on
a solution.[24]

The response of creditor governments was to avoid recognising
the disaster in its true depth and extent, and to follow a course of
action which denied the basic fact that many developing countries
were bankrupt. The longer developed-country governments and
banks could make it seem that the debtor countries were solvent,
the more chance they had of deferring a widespread panic and a
slump of confidence in the banks. The first principle of this creditor
response, then, was to keep at least some money flowing from the
debtors to the creditors. Loans were rolled over, interest payments
were postponed in part, and everything was done to deny the
suggestion that the loans were bad. In tandem with this, debtor
governments were ordered to find additional revenue for repayments,
even if the consequence of this was a series of budget cuts which
hit the poorest people in their societies. This two-track approach –
a postponement of some loans and a series of 'austerity measures' on
the part of developing-country governments to generate repayment
revenue – characterised much of the developing world in the 1980s,
and enabled the major banks in Europe and the US to stave off
panic on the part of their depositors. The developed world was
largely saved from bank failures and economic collapse, while

developing countries endured the destruction of their social infrastructure – including basic health care and education programmes –
and further impoverishment.[25]

Who managed the creditor response to the debt crisis? Ironically,
the private banks and individuals who had done the lending were
represented by the World Bank and especially the IMF, which
arranged the conditions for 'structural adjustment' of developing
economies and monitored the success of the accompanying 'austerity
measures'. The IMF was working under a double influence. In the
first place, developed-country governments were terrified of a widespread banking collapse, and obviously preferred to see the burden
transferred to the developing world rather than to accept the consequences of failing financial institutions. Second, the big private banks
themselves exerted pressure, threatening to pursue their own repayment arrangements with debtor countries even though this might
trigger a more widespread collapse of the global financial system.[26]

The US role in all this was substantial. US banks were heavily
involved in the bad lending; the American economy was especially
vulnerable to a banking crisis; and the US government enjoyed the
largest influence of any country over the World Bank and the IMF,
both of which have their headquarters in Washington. The debtor
countries, meanwhile, were largely helpless: if they followed the IMF
instructions, they would be forced to slash public spending and to
cut vital services on which the population depended; if they refused
the advice, and defaulted on the loans, they would be denied access
to credit, would have their foreign assets seized, and might collapse
altogether. The developing world's 'acceptance' of structural adjustment is hardly surprising given these dire options.[27]

The decision to impose structural adjustment in 1982 was pivotal
in many respects to the economic situation today. First, it established
a rhythm of developing-world poverty and economic constraint
which persists two decades later. Second, it averted the major global
depression, or even collapse, which would have followed the failure
of Western banks. Finally, it confirmed a drift away from Keynes,
who would not have seen the logic of 'austerity' and of government
abdication in the developing world or elsewhere. Just as Nixon's
1971 suspension of the 'dollar standard' had suggested the surrender
of national governments to the international market, so the adjust-

ment programmes of 1982 implied that government spending in the developing world was injurious to economic health. This seemed to vindicate those economists who had been arguing since the 1950s for the submission of all areas of government to free-market logic. A group of economists based at the University of Chicago had put forward the economic and political philosophy known as neo-liberalism – these theorists claimed that free trade (and especially freedom of capital movement) should be a primary goal of economic policy, along with tight governmental control of the money supply. Job creation, social programmes and welfare systems were substantially less important to the neoliberals, and were usually the first sacrifices to the new god of 'economic discipline' or 'austerity'. Neoliberalism had initially attracted little support in the heyday of capital controls and Keynes. As the older prudence and the memories of the Depression began to subside, however, the 'Chicago School' converted more economists and politicians to the neoliberal point of view. The debt crisis offered an opportunity to put these ideas into action, as well as a political emergency to strengthen the claim that free markets were the only way forward.[28]

In the 1980s, these free-market ideas came to prominence in Europe and especially the US, just as the IMF insisted on their implementation in poorer countries. Over the course of the decade, as free-market principles were selectively imposed in the developed world, the medicine of 'adjustment' was increasingly presented as an orthodox rather than an emergency measure in developing countries: 'austerity' was less a last resort than the first step to a new economic well-being. The relative decline in the economies of the developed world during the 1970s played a part in legitimising this new rhetoric of free markets; further deregulation of the financial industry, especially in the US, also encouraged the belief that private money could take over the responsibility of governments. American banks and investment firms led the way in financing new kinds of debt and stock in the developing world, resuming cash flows to heavily in-debted countries but concentrating their resources on privatisation and the operation of the private sector. Those countries which remained too poor to appeal to Western investors simply languished in 'austerity', bound to their debts and to IMF conditions and largely forgotten in their plight.[29]

In 1990, a British economist gave a name to the recent policies of neoliberalism and structural adjustment: the 'Washington Consensus'. This title reflected the fact that the IMF and World Bank are located in the American capital; but it also captured the distinctly American flavour of the 'Consensus'.[30] The turn towards free markets could not have occurred without the gradual deregulation of the US financial industry, and might have faltered without the intellectual backing of American economists and policymakers in the late 1970s and 1980s. Moreover, the power and reach of American banks is truly staggering, and their full-fledged support for the 'free-market' model has exerted a powerful influence on successive US presidents. The American financial industry has many reasons to love the 'Washington Consensus'. One of its conditions is that developing countries drop their controls on capital movements and open their doors to foreign investors and businesses. This has allowed US firms to move into developing-country markets and to cream off business, especially among the wealthier members of a developing society. Another plank of the Consensus encourages privatisation of state-owned enterprises (SOEs) such as power or telephone companies. This has also excited Wall Street by giving firms the opportunity either to buy into these SOEs at discounted rates, or to claim substantial commission fees for underwriting or consulting on the sale. Finally, developing countries have been forced to maintain convertible currencies, enabling European and American speculators to gamble against particular currencies in the international exchanges or the futures market. Although this gambling can have disastrous effects on the economy of a poorer country, it can also result in huge speculative profits for private firms or individuals, a higher priority from the perspective of Washington or New York.[31]

As we have seen, developing countries were largely offered the Consensus as a *fait accompli*, the only option in (economic) theory and in (political) practice. Those leaders who followed the IMF's direction, however, were offered some rewards. In the first instance, budget cuts hit the poorest in society, but had less impact on the middle and upper classes. In fact, many upwardly mobile members of developing societies profited from the cuts in state spending, since these provided business opportunities to the domestic private sector. The same is true of privatisation, which transferred public resources into private hands at discount prices. Alongside foreign investors, domestic elites bought into the former SOEs and began to run them as private monopolies, usually at a substantial profit. Their new-found wealth was also boosted by currency convertibility and the introduction of financial services from US firms – domestic elites could now choose to keep their money inside their home country, to transfer it to offshore accounts, or even to gamble against their own currency in the hope of personal gain.[32]

The consequences of the Washington Consensus, then, were wide-ranging. The IMF had certainly laid the ground for the world's biggest banks and corporations to capture new markets and profits; but it had also encouraged a widening gap between richer and poorer countries, as well as a divergence in the fortunes of rich and poor *within* developing societies as local elites were drawn into the Consensus. The US was in the forefront of all this, pursuing the Consensus in its foreign policy and strengthening its grip intellectually. By the 1990s, free markets were largely enshrined in American universities and business schools; moreover, the most privileged and powerful members of developing societies were dispatched to those universities and schools to learn the orthodoxy for themselves.[33] At the end of the twentieth century, political leaders throughout the world were routinely catalogued as 'Harvard-trained', as if their passage through American business programmes would underwrite the soundness of their economic thinking.

'TRADE, NOT AID': US VERSIONS OF 'DEVELOPMENT'

Perhaps the best examples of the significance of these economic changes come from the presidency of Bill Clinton, who was elected in 1992. Clinton represented the Democratic Party, the party of Franklin Roosevelt, which had been shut out of executive office since 1980 by Republican presidents Ronald Reagan and George Bush. Although Clinton told voters in 1992 that he was a 'New Democrat', and that he represented a new approach to economics and politics from his Democratic predecessors, he was not considered a neoliberal in his economic thinking. The free-market ideas of the Chicago School had traditionally been linked with the party of the right, and so Clinton's success raised the question of how far free-market thinking had gone within mainstream US politics. As it transpired, Clinton ultimately took free-market ideas to new extremes, confirming the 'New Democrats' in their break with their party's past. Although Clinton was reluctant to slash public spending and to privatise many government programmes, his stance on international trade was avowedly neoliberal: economies around the world should open to foreign investment; any remaining restrictions on capital flows should be lifted; and American goods and financial services should be sold freely around the world.[34]

To assist him in implementing this agenda, Clinton surrounded himself with advisers and officials who had spent considerable time designing or profiting from the Washington Consensus. Foremost among these were Robert Rubin, Treasury Secretary from 1995 to 1999 (and a key Clinton adviser from the beginning of his presidency), and Lawrence Summers, Rubin's deputy and eventual successor. Rubin had been chairman of Goldman Sachs, one of the world's largest investment banks, until he was asked to become a New Democrat.[35] The *New York Times* candidly noted that 'Mr Rubin had made a fortune on Wall Street' before working for Clinton, and quoted a Clinton administration official who stressed Rubin's 'very Wall Street view' in his new public office. Lawrence Summers, meanwhile, was a Harvard academic who had become chief economist of the World Bank in the early 1990s, working specifically to tailor 'austerity measures' and other conditions to developing-country loans.[36] To prevent his Treasury team from feeling lonely in a left-leaning Cabinet, Clinton picked a number of other Wall Street alumni for top jobs in his administration; and watched several advisers (including Rubin) leave public duties to return to the lure of high-finance and corporate derring-do, when they tired of public service or sought a higher return for their expertise.[37]

Although the US economy enjoyed a lengthy upturn under Clinton's direction, his efforts to shape the global economy were far less successful – the flagship North American Free Trade Agreement (NAFTA) between the US, Canada and Mexico was severely buffeted by the Mexican peso crisis of 1994/5; the Asian financial crisis of

1997 spread to other parts of the world in 1998, and had an especially disastrous effect on the struggling market economy of Russia; and large parts of the world continued to suffer under the burden of loan repayments and IMF 'adjustment', decades after the loans had been contracted. Given the concern of many American voters with their own economic well-being, these foreign events have had less of an impact within the US. I want in the remainder of this chapter to focus upon them, however, before concluding with a summary of current American thinking on the global economy and some consideration of the likely course of events in coming years.

Mexico: 'It's not a loan, it's not a bail-out'

To many observers in the early 1990s, Mexico seemed a textbook case of the benefits of the Washington Consensus. It had undergone a period of budget cuts and 'austerity', which had impacted heavily on poorer sections of society but which satisfied the IMF. In the late 1980s, the government of Carlos Salinas embarked on one of the largest privatisation programmes the world had ever seen, which also brought plaudits from the IMF and from foreign investors. Confidence in Mexico's 'progress' was so high that Bill Clinton invited Salinas to join NAFTA in 1994, binding the Mexican and US economies and promising jobs to Mexico and cheap labour to American companies. If the US had any doubts in the Mexican government, they were assuaged in a familiar manner: Salinas himself was 'Harvard-trained', and his finance minister, Pedro Aspe, boasted a doctorate from MIT.[38]

NAFTA went into effect on 1 January 1994, amidst general enthusiasm for the Mexican economic 'miracle' and happy prospects for the future. The causes of instability were already in place, however.[39] Mexico was still paying back its earlier debts, and was relying increasingly on continued loans and investment to cover its own current-account deficit. In the interest of avoiding a destructive devaluation, the Mexican government had in 1988 linked the peso to the dollar. By 1994, this linkage was only viable with continued infusions of foreign investment into Mexico. The Mexican government's anxiety about this weakness could have been remedied by a devaluation; but this might have upset the confidence of those same foreign investors, and have done more harm than good. It might also have antagonised poorer Mexicans whose savings would lose their value after the peso's fall: 1994 was an election year, and Salinas was especially keen to avoid such an unpopular measure if at all possible. His party's candidate to succeed him, Ernesto Zedillo, might have suffered at the polls if Salinas mismanaged the economy in his final months in office.

Salinas thus fell back on a series of risky strategies which might keep Mexico afloat. The government issued more short-term bonds, and tied $30 billion of them to a fixed dollar rate. These dollar-linked bonds, nicknamed *tesobonos*, were easier to sell but would be especially hard to redeem when they expired in December 1994, unless the downward pressure on the peso was relaxed. As the *tesobonos* bought Mexico time, Salinas's government put its hopes in the continued climb of the Mexican stock market, and a rise in the global price of oil, a major Mexican export. Meanwhile, Salinas could only hope that currency speculators would overlook the under-lying evidence of peso vulnerability: a concerted effort to bring down the currency would almost certainly succeed in this weakened climate.[40]

For all the austerity and restructuring, Mexico was still fretting over the price of oil on the international commodity markets and the prospect of speculators undoing its modest progress. Structural adjust-ment may have preserved Mexico's ability to borrow from the IMF and private banks, but it had hardly strengthened the nation's eco-nomic or political independence. Moreover, the growing number of super-rich within Mexico posed an additional threat. Between 1991 and 1994, the number of Mexican billionaires increased from two to twenty-four, a result of the huge profits made from privatisation and financial deregulation.[41] This domestic elite, however, had no particular loyalty to the government or to the peso. The loosening of capital controls in Mexico had encouraged the rich to set up dollar accounts in the US and Europe, and various offshore accounts in the world's many tax havens. This gave domestic investors and speculators ample opportunity to sell their Mexican stocks, to cash in their debt certifi-cates, and even to bet against the peso on the currency markets. Instead of mitigating Mexico's vulnerability to foreign capital, the Washington Consensus had deepened and domesticated the threat.[42]

In the final months of 1994, then, word of the peso's weakness circulated among Mexican elites, and encouraged many wealthy Mexicans to move their money out of the domestic stock and bond markets. Some even bet on the peso's fall, taking short positions on the currency markets and further aggravating the problem. The Mexican government had tried to offset the peso slump by selling its gold reserves, and managed to mask the extent of the crisis so effectively that Salinas's chosen successor, Zedillo, won the presidential election in August. As capital flight continued, however, it was clear that the new Zedillo government would be forced to devalue. Moreover, that devaluation would not make Mexico's December bond repayments any easier: the *tesobonos* holders expected to be paid in dollars, and the Mexican government was broke. Following the lead of domestic elites, American and European investors rushed for the exits, compounding the difficulties of the stock market and denying any foreign capital to the Mexican government. By January 1995, the Mexican economy was in free fall, with no obvious means of dealing with the crisis.[43]

Around this time, Robert Rubin, Clinton's new Treasury Secretary, was enjoying a fishing vacation in the Caribbean. A phone call from Clinton disturbed this tranquil scene, and Rubin was rushed back to Washington to engineer a response to Mexico's plight. Clinton's flagship economic project, NAFTA, would certainly be battered by a prolonged financial crisis in Mexico. Clinton had previously persuaded a wary US public that Mexico was a strong and stable partner; there was little evidence of this amidst the panic selling and devaluation of December and January. Rubin was well equipped to remind Clinton of another American interest in Mexico: many Wall Street firms were holders of debt certificates, including the *tesobonos* now due for repayment. How would these firms get their money back? How could the US deal with the inevitable instability that would follow Mexico's troubles?[44]

Rubin and Clinton initially proposed that the US sign loan guarantees for Mexico, which would enable the Mexican government to borrow $40 billion from private banks with the US acting as guarantor of the loans. This was good for Clinton, who told the nation in the January 1995 State of the Union address that the $40 billion package was 'not a loan, not foreign aid, not a bail out'.[45] It was also good for Rubin's Wall Street friends, who could advance more money to Mexico in the sure knowledge that the US, in the last resort, would pick up the tab. The only constituency that remained underwhelmed was the taxpayers, in spite of Clinton's reassurances. Many members of Congress had been sceptical of NAFTA, and this latest fiasco suggested that the benefits of the Clinton Mexico policy might be less compelling than the costs of engagement. Although Rubin seemed (by turns) serious and amiable, it was hard to avoid the conclusion that the US population at large was paying to rescue his super-rich colleagues in high finance: 'Why should Main Street bail out Wall Street?', asked one Congressman.[46]

Clinton and Rubin needed the support of Congress to pass their massive loan guarantees. Congress, in the second half of January 1995, made clear its serious reservations about the plan. What happened next was to have profound significance in ensuing years. Clinton took the unprecedented step of making a huge loan – not a guarantee – on his own authority. Uncovering a legislative loophole from Franklin Roosevelt's administration, Clinton circumvented Congress and put up $20 billion of US money for the immediate use of the Mexican government. In addition, Rubin confirmed the power of the US over the supposedly multilateral IMF by persuading the Fund to lend $18 billion on the same terms. This was a staggering sum, dwarfing previous 'emergency assistance' and setting a precedent for similar IMF 'rescue operations' in the following years. As the US Congressional representatives watched from the sidelines, open-mouthed, Clinton and Rubin matched the $40 billion they had previously sought in loan guarantees and, contrary to Clinton's earlier promise to the American people, engineered the largest bailout in US or IMF history.[47]

Even such a huge sum was quickly devoured in bond repayments and the effort to restock Mexico's dwindling reserves. Mexican financial elites were largely ecstatic: they made a great deal of money from their management of stocks and bonds and from currency speculation, and were mostly fleet-footed in getting their money out of the country. Wall Street had a mixed experience. Bondholders were eventually bailed out by the re-infusion of cash from the US and IMF; those who had traded heavily on the Mexican stock market, however, had to swallow some heavy losses. At least the big Wall

Street firms could take comfort in the prospect of more consulting and underwriting deals with the Mexican government, however. The rescue deal was conditional on even more austerity measures, a hardening of the adjustment regime for which Mexico was previously the poster-child. Although rich Mexicans and Wall Street emerged from the peso crisis in the black, ordinary Mexicans bore the brunt of the 'adjustment': inflation and unemployment increased; public spending was slashed; and social unrest, particularly in the southern state of Chiapas, continued to grow. This was the silent constituency which no one sought to 'bail out'.[48]

The US response to the peso crisis shaped the rules by which the global economy now operates: the IMF is prepared to advance massive loans to countries under speculative attack, with those loans largely underwriting investors who have become overexposed in that country, or who simply seek to cash out their winnings. It also reflected some of the uncomfortable realities of an economy in which private gain is unchecked by national loyalties or the claims of a broader public interest. The most striking aspect of the crisis is the sheer scale of money at stake, which seems even more daunting when we consider the speed and chaos of the peso's collapse. Although economists and politicians have subsequently stressed the weakness of Mexico's economic 'fundamentals' in 1994, and especially its reliance on foreign money to finance its deficit, the adjustment programmes following 1982, and the grander political reforms of the Washington Consensus, have encouraged precisely this dependence. A policy of deregulation and abolition of capital controls, lodestar of Clinton's 'New Democrat' perspective on the world economy, has been faithfully exported with disastrous results: any economy is vulnerable to capital flight and speculative attack, and the combination of weak capital controls, hot money and continuing economic instability make the developing world an especially attractive location for such profiteering.

Perhaps the biggest US achievement in Mexico has been to fashion parallel domestic elites which reliably implement these policies, come rain or come shine. One group consists of US-trained technocrats, who have imbibed the neoliberal elixir at elite US schools and whose dedication to the plan is consistent and dependable. These economic experts take their place in a broader techno-

cratic coalition which has been blooded in the US and which
reaches around the globe: having passed through US economics
departments and business schools, some technocrats stay on in
academia to teach and research the creed; some return to their
national governments to implement what they have learned; others
go to the IMF or the World Bank, liaising between the distant
points of this alumni network. Alongside the technocrats, the other
elite group consists of financiers and speculators. Once again, many
have been trained or employed in the US, and do business there
(often keeping their winnings in American dollars). We might expect, rather naively, that the technocrats and the financiers would
eye each other suspiciously across the first-class lounges and restaurants where they chance to meet; the financiers, after all, showed
little allegiance to the efforts of the technocrats in the midst of the
peso crisis. In fact, the reverse is usually true. Technocrats and
financiers, following Rubin's example, move effortlessly from one
side to the other, seemingly content to organise speculative attacks
on a currency or to manage a central bank. In the world of free
capital flows, financiers are too powerful to be shunned or criticised, and so we have seen a kind of inversion of national feeling:
if elites were once loyal to the idea of the nation, national governments are now loyal to elites – even if those elites have plundered a
country's resources and attacked its currency.[49]

The US Congress was correct, then, to suggest that the 1995
bail-out put Wall Street ahead of Main Street; but perhaps the most
profound development was not the rescue of Rubin's friends, but
instead the confirmation of powerful Mexican elites who can profit
from speculation even more dexterously than Wall Street firms. In
'emerging markets', the financial elite alternately helps to build and
destroy the handiwork of the governing elite, and the two groups
often transfer star players from one side to the other, confirming
their entanglement. As Mexico struggled to emerge from the crisis
after 1995, it seemed unlikely that the new president, Ernesto Zedillo,
would draw attention to the instability which accompanied volatile
capital flows, or mount an attack on local and international finance.
His Ph.D. thesis, written in the early 1980s at Yale University, argued
that Mexico's previous debt crisis should be blamed on the government rather than the banks which made loans. As long as the US,

the IMF and international financiers are ready to administer the 'assistance', this kind of confession seems set to continue.[50]

Africa: 'The sin of neglect and ignorance'

In March 1998, President Clinton left Washington for a two-week tour of Africa. The first US leader to visit the continent since Jimmy Carter, Clinton journeyed throughout the sub-Saharan region with a message of US humility and economic optimism. Although Clinton promised a new relationship between the US and sub-Saharan countries, he paused often to make reference to the previous state of this relationship. 'Perhaps the worst sin America ever committed toward Africa', he declared in Uganda, 'was the sin of neglect and ignorance.'[51]

US interest in Africa has waxed and waned since World War II. Given the ravages of colonial exploitation across the continent, economic development was both desperately needed and desperately difficult. Basic infrastructure was missing in most areas, and the threat of disease and famine compounded the problem. From the 1950s until the 1980s, the US viewed Africa (like much of the rest of the world) through a Cold War frame, and frequently lavished aid and loans on repressive regimes which would side with the US against the USSR. Given that American largesse was directed toward the governing elite which could vouchsafe this support, US presidents showed little interest in how the money was actually spent – and so basic development projects were ignored as dictators and their associates got rich. Coupled with the unwillingness of US business to extend its operations to Africa, this blunt Cold War strategy amply deserved Clinton's 1998 language: the US was ignorant of African politics and neglectful of the needs of its people. Worse, its channelling of loans and aid contributed to undemocratic rule across the continent, and a major debt crisis in the 1980s and 1990s.[52]

The debt burden hit Africa particularly hard. Even those countries which had thrown off their corrupt leaders had to foot the bills for former profligacy. Austerity measures were applied, under IMF direction, to economies which had skeletal public services in the first place. These IMF plans were intended to ensure that money kept flowing to service the debts; the plans were insensitive to the effect of the austerity measures on the population at large. By the mid-1990s, at least 40 per cent of Africans were living on less than a dollar a day, and the same proportion suffered from malnutrition and hunger. Even those governments which were interested in the welfare of their people faced daunting obstacles to development. Debt in sub-Saharan Africa had reached $250 billion and most countries were devoting more revenue to interest payments than to spending on education and health combined.[53]

The IMF, content to see money flowing out of Africa to service the debts, was sanguine about the side-effects of structural adjustment. Western campaigners and many African-advocacy groups, however, protested against the IMF's policy in the strongest terms. In 1996, these complaints finally forced a concession from the IMF. Responding to protesters' demands that the debts be written off, the IMF proposed the 'Heavily Indebted Poor Countries' (HIPC) initiative. The HIPC plan first identified the neediest countries, 80 per cent of which were in Africa. These countries were then required to pursue IMF dictates for six years, before being rewarded with a reduction in interest payments. Although the plan was introduced with much fanfare, it proved inadequate both in its qualifying terms and in its results. Six years of austerity measures promised a great deal of misery before any reward; the eventual payoff, meanwhile, made little more than a dent in the massive debt repayment provisions. Only two countries in Africa had qualified for any relief by 1999; one of these, Mozambique, was offered a cut in its repayment of $10 million a year, leaving $110 million outstanding as its annual fee – twice its annual health budget.[54]

In 1999, protest groups refocused media attention on the issue of debt. With the support of rock stars, religious leaders and even some economists, organisations like Jubilee 2000 demanded debt forgiveness to coincide with the millennium.[55] These campaigns were well organised and quickly gained popular support from the general public in developed countries. Debt was once again a political issue in the US and Europe, and the American government offered a new version of the HIPC plan in June 1999. The new proposal, however, shared many of the problems which had stymied the 1996 initiative. A very modest level of debt relief was again contingent on poorer countries' acceptance of IMF 'discipline'. Moreover, the major industrialised countries that would bankroll the relief programme could not agree on how to pay for it. One idea was to sell off the IMF's gold reserves, then invest that sum and use the interest to fund debt relief. The immediate effect of this announcement, however, was to impoverish many African countries still further by pushing down the market price of gold, a major African export. As Western leaders used the proposals to boast of their own munificence, Oxfam dismissed the new 'debt relief' plan as 'painfully inadequate'.[56]

Behind these proposals and counter-proposals lies a fundamental battle over debt and development. In the 1950s and 1960s, the US and other countries provided loans or grants to Africa for the establishment of public infrastructure. By the end of the 1990s, the idea of government-controlled services had fallen out of fashion with economists and politicians, and the market had been crowned as the legitimate provider of even basic needs like health and education. According to the neoliberal creed, Africa's problem was not the burden of debt, but the apathy of the international private sector. The solution to problems of development lay therefore in more austerity and adjustment, followed by the opening of Africa's borders to free flows of foreign capital. As the *Financial Times* put it in a revealing article on anti-debt campaigners, it was a 'myth' to believe 'that debt relief has to be good for poverty alleviation'.[57]

One might expect a progressive American government to be wary of neoliberal solutions. As we have seen, however, the Clinton administration has rushed to embrace free markets and free capital flows at every opportunity, exporting its enthusiasm around the globe. When Clinton visited Africa in 1998, and lamented the decades of 'neglect and ignorance', he had a genuine alternative in mind: a hefty dose of neoliberalism, specially designed to take advantage of Africa's new-found commercial appeal to US corporations. Speaking of the need for 'trade, not aid', he urged African leaders to put their hopes in budget reductions, privatisation and a new wave of foreign investment. The US would act as their partner in this, and would spearhead an investment drive which would more than compensate for reductions in the US aid budget, and the continuing burden of old debts.[58]

On his return to the US in 1998, Clinton followed up on his promises and encouraged legislation for a US–Africa economic agreement.[59] The plan, the African Growth and Opportunity Act (AGOA), was quickly dubbed 'NAFTA for Africa', and was rejected by the Senate later the same year. President Clinton, however, praised the Act in his 1999 State of the Union address, and it returned to Congress soon after.[60] The AGOA calls for Africa to abandon controls on capital movements, to reduce tariffs, to privatise SOEs, and to reduce taxes for business. It also requires qualifying countries to avoid 'gross' human-rights violations (whatever that means) and 'activities that undermine United States national security or foreign policy interests.'[61] In return for meeting these criteria, African countries would be given special consideration by US corporations and investors, many of whom are already excited at the prospect of acquiring monopoly concerns in Africa via privatisation programmes. AGOA also establishes a free-trade area, and envisages the delivery of African products (often made in US-owned factories) to the US with negligible tariffs. Although US labour unions are concerned at the possibility of a deluge of cheaply manufactured goods, American corporate leaders are intrigued by the prospect of a cheap African workforce. US investment firms, meanwhile, stand ready to pour short-term capital into the region, particularly as the Asian crisis of 1997/8 has dented confidence in other 'emerging markets'.[62]

The Clinton administration is dedicated to AGOA, and it seems likely to become law in 2000.[63] At this point, sub-Saharan Africa will split into two blocs: those countries which meet the US qualifications and enter into the agreement, and those that cannot or will not qualify. The future for the disqualified countries looks bleak indeed. The US has very deliberately undermined its aid budget and has rejected the idea of bilateral assistance – Clinton's 1998 tour made clear that trade was the way forward, and it seems unlikely that those who refuse to trade on US terms will be given aid as a consolation prize. Moreover, the non-qualifiers will suffer from the disruption of the existing trade network inside Africa. Because the qualifying countries will be locked into preferential trading with the US, it seems unlikely that any success they are able to attain will spread to former trading partners who have not qualified for the AGOA.[64]

Perhaps the only consolation for non-qualifiers will be the grim knowledge that qualifying nations have their own set of problems. American critics of the US–Africa trade deal have described a proposal 'that combines NAFTA's failed rules with cruel IMF dictates'.[65] This is a reasonable prognosis for those countries which agree to the US offer. Although US companies will create some new jobs, and neoliberal policies will enrich the higher echelons of society, the majority of Africans are unlikely to see any benefits in the short or medium term. In fact, the continued squeeze on public spending, and the supposed need for private rather than public investment, will probably worsen conditions for the poorest Africans.[66] Of course, the advocates of free markets have claimed that the long-term benefits of such policies will eventually redeem the decades of suffering. This argument seems hard to sustain, especially given the recent crisis involving Latin American 'success stories' and the flight of investment capital. As speedily as money hearkens to Clinton's call, it will leave Africa at the first sign of trouble, or of a more lucrative opportunity elsewhere.

Given sub-Saharan Africa's particularly severe poverty crisis, Clinton's recent corporate courtship of the region seems especially disingenuous. Alongside Clinton's protectionist opponents at home, who fear the loss of US jobs to cheap African labour, some Congressional representatives have lined up against the trade agreement on the grounds of its potentially destructive impact upon Africa. Jesse Jackson, Jr., a Congressman from Illinois, has even introduced alternative legislation which reverses Clinton's emphasis: instead of trade taking priority over aid, Jackson has proposed debt forgiveness and a substantial aid package as a first step to addressing poverty and disease across the continent.[67] Given the looming disaster of HIV/AIDS, which is devastating many African states, Jackson has justifiably argued that millions will die before any benefits trickle down to the poorest Africans. In response, the US Congress has proposed to delegate the African AIDS problem to a familiar friend: 'Corporate America,' pleaded one Congresswoman, 'we need you to band together, to use your resources to cement Africa's greatest resource, its people.' She went on to suggest that 'corporate America' should be given responsibility for funding a response to AIDS across the African continent, perhaps contributing to a fund for AIDS research and care. Since the African labour pool is substantially larger than the number of jobs corporate America has to offer, this faith in the private sector seems misplaced. Perhaps US firms will take a greater interest if they can successfully turn Africans into consumers of their products – a more distant prospect.[68]

Clinton's treatment of Africa has at least clarified US policy on aid and economic reform. If poorer countries could once expect a measure of assistance simply because of their poverty, the new US linkage of neoliberalism and development has extended 'market discipline' even to the world's poorest people. Simply to give out aid without insisting on austerity and open markets is to risk alternative modes of development; linking 'discipline' and 'austerity' to some kind of debt relief, however, gives the US the opportunity to shape African economies to its own preferences. This raises the question of whether African countries really want to become 'emerging markets', and returns us to Clinton's initial apology for the decades of US 'ignorance and neglect'. If US know-how can only offer an Africa of 'free markets' and continued social disaster, many Africans may hope, in spite of their current poverty, that the American 'neglect' continues.

Russia: 'I can't tell you exactly what happened'

In the summer of 1991, the Soviet Union was in its death throes. The US government, seemingly as surprised as anyone by the rapid collapse of its arch-enemy, faced the attractive but daunting prospect of assisting Russia and its former satellites in their transition from communism. With the discrediting of the old system, and even of those 'reformers' like Gorbachev who had tried to reconfigure the Soviet economy, the way was cleared for new faces and new ideas. Although some of the stars of the US policymaking establishment – such as Henry Kissinger – urged that the US keep its distance from the transition process, American politicians and economists could not resist the opportunity before them. A group of US academics met with aides to Boris Yeltsin in July 1991 to prepare a set of radical ideas that, they promised, would transform Russia's economy in five years or less.[69]

The US government became actively involved with the Russian transition in 1991, but promptly channelled many of its grants and assistance loans through a prestigious subcontractor: Harvard University. Harvard's Institute for International Development (HIID), comprising economists and development experts, petitioned to take charge of the US intellectual mission to Russia and was soon assuming awesome responsibilities in Moscow and St Petersburg. On the Russian side, this American involvement was not viewed with hostility, at least at first. Broad sections of the population could look at the fantastic wealth of the US and hope for direct aid, rather than loans and technical assistance. Russian elites, meanwhile, were impressed at the involvement of America's premier university, and susceptible to the HIID rhetoric about the necessity for radical change.[70]

The most prominent American economist in this mission to Russia was Jeffrey Sachs, an HIID professor who led the 'Harvard Boys' into Russia, and would later direct the Institute.[71] Sachs had already, by 1991, won repute as the evangelist of 'shock therapy', a programme of extreme economic reform which he had peddled throughout eastern Europe. In essence, 'shock therapy' called for a drastic and sudden reorientation of an economy, with immediate cuts in public spending and the suspension of government price controls to contain a country's deficit.[72] Appearing as part faith healer, part mountebank, Sachs was wont to pepper his speeches with memorable truisms which would reinforce the neoliberal message: 'You can't jump a chasm in two leaps' was a particular favourite, and rather revealing. Perhaps the chasm was too wide to be scaled with one leap? Sachs prodded the new Russian government to jump all the same.[73]

By 1992, Sachs and the HIID were receiving millions of dollars from the US government to fund the creation of Russia's new financial architecture. The Russian finance minister, Yegor Gaidar, was pushing through HIID-recommended reforms. Although price controls were lifted, the 'therapy' had disastrous effects; as the Harvard Boys implemented their reforms, prices soared out of control, leading to hyperinflation (which reached 2,500 per cent at one point) and the devastation of ordinary Russians' savings. Gaidar was discredited, and soon out of a job. Sachs and the Harvard Boys, however, merely switched horses to the new 'reformer', Anatoly Chubais. Reluctant to abandon their policies even after this disaster, and strengthened in their convictions that popular discontent should not affect the 'reform' process, the Harvard economists entered an alliance with the 'Chubais clan', a group of Russian economists and businessmen who were to mastermind extraordinary feats of larceny and corruption over the following years.[74]

Much of this corruption surrounded the second phase of 'shock therapy': privatisation. In 1992, the Supreme Soviet (precursor to the Russian parliament) voted for a voucher scheme which would widely distribute ownership in newly privatised SOEs. The initial privatisation programme was open to many forms of abuse, especially since the bosses who had previously managed Soviet industries were in a position to maximise their personal holdings in the various share issues.[75] The first privatisation wave, however, seemed a model of probity in comparison with the 'loans for shares' scandal of 1995/6. In brief, the Yeltsin administration gave away controlling interests in some of Russia's largest companies to wealthy bankers, in return for much-needed funds which would bolster the government in an election year. Although the deal was supposedly a temporary one, which would have allowed the government to buy back the shares after the 1996 election, government officials and Russia's emerging financial elite actually agreed in secret that the transfer of shares was to be permanent. In return for obtaining the shares at low prices in rigged auctions between colluding banks, the government extracted a pledge of support from the financial elite in the 1996 election. Tycoons like Boris Berezovsky thus threw their substantial influence (and their media empires) behind the Yeltsin campaign, stressing his democratic and economic achievements even as they engineered the least democratic and the most corrupt deal in post-Soviet history.[76]

In 1996, when the banks were obliged to sell the shares they'd acquired the previous year in another auction, another round of price-fixing ensured that Berezovsky and his colleagues obtained permanent control of many of Russia's largest companies for a fraction of their market worth. Berezovsky himself, appointed to Yeltsin's government in the wake of the 1996 election victory, made little effort to disguise what had happened: he told the *Financial Times* that, before the election, 'business realised that if business is not consolidated, we will not have a chance. It is not possible to have this [market] transformation automatically. We need to use all our power to realise this transformation.' Chubais, meanwhile, was the chief architect of this deal; or, as the *Financial Times* put it, the 'businessmen's conduit' to Yeltsin. Acting as the chief liaison between the Russian financial elite, the Yeltsin administration, and the series of international 'experts' and reformers who were supposedly overseeing Russia's transition, Chubais apparently decided that the promotion of private ownership justified any means necessary to obtain it, even massive theft.[77]

Since a small number of Chubais' colleagues and associates became rich, and very few ordinary people benefited from privatisation, this second phase of Western-inspired 'reform' discredited the idea of reform in general. Of course, this popular dissatisfaction merely encouraged Sachs and the Harvard Boys to strengthen Chubais further, while the new US President, Bill Clinton, praised Boris Yeltsin's expansion of executive power. By the mid-1990s, American diplomacy and 'technical assistance' (in the form of HIID directions) were dedicated to political and economic 'reform' which encouraged Yeltsin's autocracy and the Chubais clan's kleptocracy. As Sachs and others continued to boast of the linkage between economic liberalisation and democracy, a very undemocratic system appeared to be emerging in neoliberal Russia.[78]

The final element in the Russian disaster was an inevitable consequence of the corrupt means by which new fortunes had been created. Although the Harvard reformers and their Russian colleagues (led by Chubais) claimed that the new kleptocracy would at least ensure prudent management of the new wealth and newly privatised companies, the financial elite feared that its gains would continue to be vulnerable as long as they were held inside Russia. World Bank chief economist Joseph Stiglitz pointed out the danger in 1999:

> Consider the incentives facing the so-called oligarchs in Russia. They might well have reasoned: democratic elections will eventually conclude that their wealth was ill-begotten, and there will thus be attempts to recapture it. They might have been induced to pursue a two-fold strategy: on the one hand, to use their financial power to gain sufficient political influence to reduce the likelihood of such an event; but, assuming that that strategy is inherently risky, to use the other hand to take at least a significant part of their wealth out of the country to a safe haven.[79]

Thus, the 'free market' reforms had not only concentrated power and money in the hands of a tiny few in Russia, but had given them every reason to move Russia's wealth outside its borders altogether. In the process of converting Russian state assets into private property through a process of corruption and theft, the US-inspired 'reformers' actually invited massive capital flight which would further consolidate

Russia's financial crisis. This was the background for the crisis of 1997/8, as money haemorrhaged from the country into the private, foreign bank accounts of the kleptocracy.[80]

Who was to blame for this mess? The most obvious target for opprobrium was the neoliberal creed itself, particularly as it was inflected by the Harvard Boys. As we have seen elsewhere, the proponents of neoliberalism have tended to treat it more as a science, or even a religion, than as one rather extreme (and questionable) model of development. The folly of this scientific confidence was readily apparent in Russia, where some awareness of cultural and political experience might have clarified the means and goals of reform. Even though Harvard University boasted a number of famous Russian experts, the HIID made little effort to seek their counsel as it designed Russia's 'shock therapy'. In fact, to solicit country-specific advice might have undermined the claims of neoliberalism, by suggesting the importance of local variations and of human factors beyond economic logic and 'rational choice'. HIID representatives seemed interested in Russian history only when their policies lay in ruins — at that point, it was finally helpful to address uniquely Russian character flaws which could explain this exception to the global rule of neoliberal 'success'.[81]

Moving beyond Harvard to the broader US perspective on Russia, there was undoubtedly a triumphalism in the early 1990s which blinded policymakers to the reality of the US–Russian relationship. American claims of 'victory' in the Cold War fed an arrogance toward the extent of Russia's difficulties and the limited efficacy of American neoliberal 'solutions'. The Bush and Clinton administrations happily channelled cash to Harvard on the assumption that these academics must have the right answers, and that Russia could be made again in the likeness of the US. The flip side of this narcissism was the concern that the US continue to wage a 'Cold War' against the forces of reaction: Russia had been 'won' in 1991 but might still escape from the US, if sufficient attention was not paid to the (free-market) development of the former Soviet Union.[82] Richard Nixon, the disgraced former American president, regaled his successors, Bush and Clinton, with the warning that they not 'lose Russia'. Clinton seems to have been especially haunted by Nixon's admonition, up to and beyond the latter's death in 1994.[83]

Some of the blame naturally fell on Russian elites, who appeared ready to implement Harvard directions only in return for fantastic personal wealth. These Russians were encouraged in their plundering in two important respects, however. First, the economic programmes implementing 'shock therapy' were dependent on a strong-minded and powerful Russian government which could push them through, in spite of popular anxiety or protests over budget cuts; 'shock therapy' would therefore mandate substantial political authority for the 'reformers'. Although Jeffrey Sachs, Lawrence Summers and other leading Harvardians may not have intended to produce corruption, their strategy of instantaneous and massive 'reform' tacitly encouraged it. Believing that the goal of an 'adjusted' economy was more important than the means necessary to achieve it, the HIID's local operatives could hardly help but give in to the pilfering of Chubais and his associates. This strengthened the sense of Russian elites that the 'free-market transition' was in fact a free-for-all, a once-in-a-lifetime opportunity for personal gain.[84]

Unfortunately, this problem was complicated by the second encouragement to plunder: the Harvard operation had its own improprieties, and members of the 'reform' team may actually have participated in what ordinary Russians glumly called 'the great grab'. In the first place, the bulk of US money, disbursed by the Agency for International Development (USAID), had gone to Harvard without competitive tender. More seriously, questions arose about the extent of Harvard's official and personal involvement in the Russian economy. Harvard investment managers appear to have received preferential treatment in Russian privatisation auctions, since they were the only foreign buyers allowed to invest (save for George Soros). Two of the Harvard professors who administered USAID funds, meanwhile, were accused in 1997 of using their money and contacts improperly. One Harvard professor, Jonathan Hay, even helped his girlfriend to set up a mutual fund in Russia, which was somehow licensed by Hay's Russian counterparts ahead of much larger and established US competitors. USAID finally cancelled the HIID contract in 1997, citing evidence that Harvard professors were engaged in 'activities for personal gain'.[85]

The consequences of all this for ordinary Russians were severe. From the mid-1990s, the country was controlled autocratically by Yeltsin, the mafia and a group of business leaders attendant on Chubais, many from the old Soviet *nomenklatura*. The Russian parliament protested against Yeltsin's rule, but was largely unable to stop further 'reforms'. The government, unable or unwilling to tax the new elites, failed to pay the wages of remaining public-sector employees. The number of Russians in poverty increased from 2 million in 1990 to 60 million in 1999. Parts of Russia reverted to pre-cash systems of exchange, bartering goods and labour; and crime, violence and alcoholism reached unprecedented levels. Russian life expectancy slumped to 61, comparable with Indonesia, Paraguay or Egypt. One of the few policy initiatives to enjoy a modicum of democratic legitimacy was the brutal conflict with Chechnya, a diversion from the economic crisis which threw Russians back on older prejudices against nationalities and ethnic groups within the former Soviet Union. Although Yeltsin could hardly count on public support for his economic 'reforms', his 1999 offensive against the Muslim Chechens won some approval, especially in Moscow and St Petersburg. The price for this fleeting burst of popularity was paid in full, however, by Russian conscripts, Chechen fighters, and the civilians of Grozny, the capital of Chechnya, who suffered indiscriminate bombardment and Russian occupation.[86]

In spite of everything, the Russian economy did not collapse altogether. Wealthy Russians saw potential for further profits by manipulating the nascent Russian securities markets, and international investors, many of them ignorant of the true extent of neoliberal failure in Russia, saw the new stock exchange as a promising 'emerging market'. As the Russian government struggled in 1997 and early 1998 to roll over loans and to reschedule bond redemption, international investors created a speculative bubble which further enriched the *nomenklatura*. Financial managers in the US and Europe inflated the bubble with pension and mutual fund deposits, even as the Asian crisis of late 1997 suggested the inherent instability and danger of 'emerging markets' which were over-dependent on loans and foreign capital.[87]

The Clinton adminstration's response to Russia's difficulties was one of alarm. In 1998, as Russia was about to default on its loans, the US Treasury scrambled to engineer another bail-out. This time, unlike in Mexico, the money would be dispatched before disaster struck – a pre-emptive measure that was renamed a 'bail-in'. After much US prodding, the IMF announced a $22 billion package in July, and sent an initial $4.8 billion immediately to help the Russian government to restore the confidence of investors.[88] Strangely, huge dollar sums began to leave Russia as soon as the IMF money was transferred; and, to the horror of the US, the Russian rouble collapsed on 17 August, barely a month later. Something had gone terribly wrong with the 'bail-in', and the Russian economy – including the 'hot' stock market – crashed spectacularly. By 1 September, the value of the Russian stock exchange had fallen precipitously to around 10 per cent of its October 1997 value.[89]

Of course, the flight of international investors was hardly surprising just before and after the devaluation – the speculators were hardly likely to stick around when disaster seemed inevitable. A more interesting question concerned the first segment of the IMF loan, the $4.8 billion delivered in July, and the large sums that left Russia around the same time. Although the details were initially murky, it emerged in 1999 that Russian elites had basically used the loan to underwrite their own rush to sell roubles. Instead of building confidence and encouraging investors to stay in Russia, central bank officials used the money to prop up an unnaturally high rouble rate, and allowed (or even encouraged) wealthy Russians to convert roubles into dollars at the higher rate; when the reserves had cashed out, the currency was devalued. The mystery of why a nearly $5 billion loan seemed so ineffective was thus solved: the loan proved extremely effective in enriching Russian elites, which is what it was used for.[90]

Treasury Secretary Robert Rubin found himself in a quandary when he tried to explain this phenomenon to a US Congressional panel the following year. In his testimony, he declared that much of the $4.8 billion 'may have been siphoned off improperly'. When interviewed after the panel hearing, however, he suggested that he had been 'careless' to use the word 'improper': 'there's nothing improper about moving money out of Russia or any other country', he claimed. Rubin's correction, or schizophrenia, is instructive: although the US Treasury was furious with Russian elites for essentially stealing $5 billion, the language of free capital flows offered no phrases of condemnation or censure; even 'improper' may be too harsh a word to describe such extraordinary corruption. Ironically, the Treasury appeared finally to have met its match in Russia, coming across a group of arrivistes and kleptocrats even more unscrupulous than the American cheerleaders of neoliberalism. Faced with the evidence of massive theft, but unable to criticise the free movement of capital, Rubin abdicated from the conversation: 'I can't tell you exactly what happened', he concluded.[91]

After nearly a decade of US 'assistance', Russia now boasts fabulous levels of wealth inequality, crime and political violence, as well as an autocratic governing framework and a moribund economy.[92] The US, meanwhile, insists on the path of 'reform', and warns of dire alternatives – be they communist or nationalist – if the logic of free markets does not prevail. On an official level, at least, the US has therefore claimed that 'reform' has kept undemocratic forces at bay in Russia; and has ignored the possibility that 'reform' may actually encourage the resurgence of nationalism or communism, born from the poverty and failure of US-sponsored market 'freedom'.[93]

WASHINGTON'S CONSENSUS

At the opening of the twenty-first century, US domination of the global economy is extensive and deep-rooted. Emergency measures imposed on poorer countries during the 1980s have matured into an orthodox route of 'reform': the 'Washington Consensus' quickly established itself as the single path of development. The intellectual momentum behind the Consensus was US-generated; in the 1990s, this has been bolstered by a political will on the part of the US government to export the 'reform' model to every region on earth. Bill Clinton's administration has belied any left-leaning instincts and rushed into a fully fledged alliance with super-rich US individuals and institutions; at the heart of the Clinton presidency was Treasury Secretary Robert Rubin, who spent four-and-a-half years at his post working to break down capital controls abroad and to open every foreign market to volatile US investment and speculation.

The Asian financial crisis of 1997/8 did exert a damping effect on the Clinton/Rubin revolution, and seemed to offer ample evidence of the instability of the new arrangement. Capital flowed into and out of Asia at alarming rates, and the actions of stock-market and currency speculators were identified as a major cause of the disaster. Although the US accused some of the Asian countries of corruption, it was hard to distinguish illegal activity from elite greed and self-interest as stunned Americans picked through the wreckage of the Asian 'success stories'. When the crisis spread to other 'emerging markets', such as Russia and Brazil, financial commentators began to talk of the weakness and instability of the new global economy, and the risk of 'contagion effects' which would amplify regional crashes into global depression. Officials from the IMF and World Bank, and even currency speculators like George Soros, called for capital controls or a 'new global architecture' to replace the Washington Consensus.[94]

In 1999, however, this enthusiasm for change largely subsided, and the free-market frenzy began once more. In the light of this turn-around, there are good reasons to believe that the neoliberal agenda will only be derailed by a complete financial breakdown. First, the investors who manage the huge sums of money now channelled into 'emerging markets' and stock market speculation have grown used to the higher returns offered by gambling on Russia, Latin America or even Africa. Wall Street, meanwhile, has enjoyed unprecedented profits from its stewardship of, and occasional participation in, this international casino. The new 'global architecture' would certainly threaten these profits if it sought to limit currency speculation, privatisation, or the whole range of risky new 'financial instruments' which have recently given US speculators more ways to gamble and to win. In the wake of the Asian crisis, as the situation in Thailand, Russia and Brazil spun out of control, the IMF was forced to speak more humbly about the need for new 'reforms'; but the return of speculators and investors soon after these economies had crashed restored much of the confidence (and arrogance) to the Washington-based guardians of the global economy. The creation of even more debt in these struggling countries, and the continuing, systemic weakness of their 'reformed' economies, was less compelling than a new round of speculation in their re-emerging markets.[95]

For now, there is little hope that the United States will change its neoliberal course. The US continues to appoint the (American) head of the World Bank unilaterally, and is angling for a much more active role in the process of selecting the IMF managing director.[96] Wall Street's infiltration of the Democratic Party is extensive; the

Republicans, traditionally sympathetic to business interests, stand ready to take up the reins if Al Gore should fail to succeed Clinton in the 2000 election.[97] Ordinary Americans are not well placed to force change from the grassroots. Many have been persuaded that these larger economic issues are opaque, impenetrable, or the natural preserve of 'experts' like Rubin and Lawrence Summers. Clinton's paean to 'free markets' has linked neoliberalism to some more abstract idea of freedom, which plays well in the US. Labour unions occasionally protest against free trade on protectionist grounds, arguing that US corporate expansion into Mexico or Africa will lead to redundancies at home. Unfortunately, the economic logic of this argument is often diluted by isolationism, and labour leaders are forced into alliances with far-right 'populists' who demonise the IMF and the United Nations in equal measure.[98] Against this shrill protest, Clinton has easily depicted his own course as measured and moderate, as if the only way for Americans to support global development was for them to invest in the Mozambique stock exchange.[99]

Although the picture is still unclear, it may also be true that the zealous US dedication to neoliberalism abroad has, temporarily at least, strengthened the economy at home. Clinton has worked assiduously to funnel increasing sums of money into the US stock market, which has enjoyed an unprecedented upwards sweep for much of his administration. Although the benefits from this bullish trend are not evenly distributed throughout American society, rates of unemployment, inflation and interest have been relatively low, especially during Clinton's second term of office. One factor sustaining the high stock prices has been financial deregulation in the US, which has unleashed a new wave of money (from pensions, mutual funds, and so on) into the financial system. Another factor, however, may be the high degree of instability outside the United States. Foreign investors have returned to the US stock market when 'emerging markets' have disappointed them, suggesting that a widespread global crisis may actually boost the American economy, at least in the short term.[100]

The same dynamic applies to currency trading. Although, in theory, the US dollar is as susceptible to speculative attack as the peso or the rouble, the relative economic strength of the US has largely deterred any challengers. Moreover, recent developments suggest that the dollar will remain strong over coming years. Some countries in Europe have announced their intention to sell part of their gold reserves and hold dollar certificates in their stead, more confident of the dollar's prospects in the medium to long term than of the market price of gold. A genuinely calamitous global crisis, prolonged and extensive, would probably puncture this appearance of strength; but the evidence of 1997/8 suggests a definite stratification in the global economy in the absence of such a nightmare scenario. An elite group of countries will boast relatively stable currencies, and a majority will fall prey to intensive speculation and sporadic collapse. The relentless march of Europe towards a single currency seems prudent in this regard: the euro may be able to establish itself in the top tier (with the dollar), even though the franc or the lira might sink with the peso and the rouble into the lower tier.[101]

What seems certain in all this is that the majority of the world's countries and people will continue to suffer under US-led neoliberal 'reform'. If they choose to embrace 'reform', they can look forward to Russian-style kleptocracy, periodic economic collapse precipitated by rampant speculation, and a reliance on US corporations for products, employment, and even public services. If they decline the offer of 'free-market' development, they have little chance of finding money for their own versions of economic reform, as the US preaches 'trade, not aid' and narrows the definition of acceptable policies to those contained in the African Growth and Opportunity Act. Perhaps developing countries which reject US corporate suitors can take comfort in the fact that the latter will not be gone for long. As one US executive hopefully declared after the 1998 Russian collapse, contemplating the future possibilities for his razor-making company: 'Never forget: there are still 50 million women out there who don't shave their legs.'[102]

In July 1999, to much fanfare, Treasury Secretary Robert Rubin retired from office. Rubin was fêted as the most successful Secretary in history, and moved back to New York.[103] A week later, another Clinton appointment, J. Brian Atwood, also left his post, as administrator of the US Agency for International Development, after six

years of service.[104] While Rubin had masterminded a bonanza for
Wall Street and a booming stock market, Atwood had reluctantly
overseen the devastation of the USAID budget. In his retirement
speech, Atwood lashed out at the Treasury and the Clinton administration for precipitating a 'crisis' in aid and development. 'There's no
money to do anything', he complained, calling the Clinton aid budget
'outrageous' and 'a joke.' Atwood referred more broadly to the
growing inequality between the richest and poorest in the world,
reminding his audience that 10 per cent of the world's population
would soon control 90 per cent of its wealth, and that the 'trade, not
aid' formula had ignored a crucial fact about the poorest countries:
'These nations simply could not afford to buy anything.'[105]

Rubin's departure received much more attention from the US
media than Atwood's, but a few people did note the coincidence of
the two, and the significance of their divergent careers under Clinton.
Jim Hoagland, writing in the *Washington Post*, neatly captured their
entangled fates:

> The rise of Rubin's Treasury, and of US financial markets as unrivaled
> arbiters and sources of power in this administration, and the decline of
> support for developmental aid for poor countries travel along the same arc
> in Washington. The different trajectories of the two men and the two
> worlds they represent trace an important shift in values here.[106]

Although Bill Clinton has continued to spin 'free markets' and 'trade,
not aid' as efforts to 'put a human face on the global economy', our
brief survey in this chapter suggests the opposite: the global economy
is now less human, less forgiving and less stable than it was even a
decade ago, in large part due to the efforts of Clinton and Rubin.
This has already had dire consequences for many of the world's
poorer people, and seems set to continue. Jim Hoagland concluded
his article on the departing public servants with a sketch of the new
mood in the American capital:

> It takes nothing from Rubin's success to say that a large part of his role
> here consisted of providing an elegant rationalization for human acquisi-
> tiveness. He was the man of the Clinton moment. Atwood was an echo
> of a different, increasingly distant Washington era, before the capital be-
> came such a materialist playground and a moral swamp.

Save for a drastic change of course or a catastrophic economic collapse, the evidence we have reviewed suggests a clear pattern for the years to come: the US will shape the global economy in the next century with the same combination of elegant rationalisation, materialist abandon and moral abdication that now enjoys a consensus in Washington.

NOTES

1. Delivered on Capitol Hill, Washington, DC, 19 January 1999.
2. On the importance of the Depression, see Michael D. Bordo, Claudia Goldin and Eugene N. White, eds, *The Defining Moment: The Great Depression and the American Economy in the Twentieth Century* (Chicago: University of Chicago Press, 1998), especially chapters 1, 11 and 12.
3. Daniel Yergin and Joseph Stanislaw begin *The Commanding Heights: The Battle Between Government and Marketplace that is Remaking the Modern World*, second edition (New York: Simon & Schuster, 1999), with the efforts of developed countries to remake the global economy after World War II. For a specific account of the Bretton Woods proceedings and provisions, see Barry Eichengreen, *Globalizing Capital: A History of the International Monetary System* (Princeton: Princeton University Press, 1996), 93–102; the essays in the first section of Orin Kirshner, ed., *The Bretton Woods–GATT System: Retrospect and Prospect after Fifty Years* (Armonk, NY: M.E. Sharpe, 1996); and the essays in part one of Michael D. Bordo and Barry Eichengreen, eds, *A Retrospective on the Bretton Woods System: Lessons for International Monetary Reform* (Chicago: University of Chicago Press, 1993).
4. For an analysis of the predominant US role at Bretton Woods, see Georg Schild, *Bretton Woods and Dumbarton Oaks: American Economic and Political Postwar Planning in the Summer of 1944* (New York: St. Martin's Press, 1995); and Raymond Vernon, 'The US Government at Bretton Woods and After', in Kirshner, ed., *The Bretton Woods–GATT System*, 52–69. Vernon suggests (56) that, by the end of the Conference, 'the US government drew a line in the sand against any provision that imposed significant restraints on its freedom to follow any economic policy it wished to pursue in the future.'
5. On US covert and overt propaganda efforts in Italy, and the CIA's funnelling of funds to right-wing and centrist parties to combat the leftist 'threat', see James Edward Miller, *The United States and Italy, 1940– 1950: The Politics and Diplomacy of Stabilization* (Chapel Hill: University of North Carolina Press, 1986), 248. On the Agency's similar activities in Greece, see Lawrence S. Wittner, *American Intervention in Greece, 1943–*

1949 (New York: Columbia University Press, 1982), 150–51. These propaganda and planning efforts were merely a subset of broader US government attempts to prop up centrist and right-wing parties in both countries.

6. Yergin and Stanislaw install Keynes as the key intellectual influence on the post-war economic system, claiming that in the decades after World War II 'Keynes' theories of government management of the economy appeared unassailable.' *The Commanding Heights*, 14. For the role of Keynes and of the British government at the Bretton Woods conference, see G. John Ikenberry, 'The Political Origins of Bretton Woods', in Bordo and Eichengreen, eds, *A Retrospective on the Bretton Woods System*, 155–82.

7. Barry Eichengreen and Peter B. Kenen suggest that 'the disastrous depression of the 1930s made clear the huge costs of the failure to develop rules and understandings as well as organizational structures to guide the conduct of economic policies.' 'Managing the World Economy under the Bretton Woods System', in P.B. Kenen, ed., *Managing the World Economy: Fifty Years After Bretton Woods* (Washington, DC: Institute for International Economics, 1994), 3–57 at 11. Ikenberry reprints the remarks of American economist and post-war planner Jacob Viner, who suggested that ordinary people had come to see governments as 'obligated' to guide national economies away from potential depression or collapse. 'The Political Origins of Bretton Woods', 163–4.

8. For an account of the context for the GATT deliberations, see Simon Reisman, 'The Birth of a World Trading System: ITO and GATT', in Kirshner, ed., *The Bretton Woods–GATT System*, 82–89. Eichengreen and Kenen sketch the Marshall Aid plans, which were conditional on recipient countries' relaxation of their tariffs and import restrictions, in 'Managing the World Economy Under the Bretton Woods System', 15–18.

9. Fred Block and other economic historians have suggested that the alternative to multilateral, US-led free trade was a kind of 'national capitalism' which would privilege full employment and social policies over a dedication to international free trade. Ikenberry summarises these positions in 'The Political Origins of Bretton Woods', 167–72.

10. Of course, the vast majority of today's nation-states were not represented at Bretton Woods, which took place before the bulk of decolonisation that gave independence to the 'developing world'. The US relationship to development is rather complex, and encompasses support for agro-exporting countries in some cases, and support for industrialisation (especially when led by US investment) in others. In much of Latin America and the Caribbean, at least, the model of import-substitution industrialisation (ISI) was frequently opposed by the US, since it threatened land holdings and commodity exports managed by US companies (as well as excluding many US exports). For an account of the shifting US perspectives on development, see John Brohman, *Popular Development: Rethinking the Theory and Practice of Development*

(Oxford: Blackwell, 1996), especially chapters 1 and 2.

11. Eichengreen, *Globalizing Capital*, 120–35.

12. On the US-sponsored overthrow of Mohammed Mossadegh in Iran, see Mary Ann Heiss, *Empire and Nationhood: The United States, Great Britain, and Iranian Oil, 1950–1954* (New York: Columbia University Press, 1997), especially 135–66. Piero Gleijeses offers an analysis of the extensive contacts between the United Fruit Company (a US corporation) and the US government prior to the Guatemalan coup in *Shattered Hope: The Guatemalan Revolution and the United States, 1944–1954* (Princeton: Princeton University Press, 1991), 361–8. For a discussion of the several CIA-sponsored coups in Latin America, and the cosy relationship between US corporations and the US government, see John H. Coatsworth, *Central America and the United States: The Clients and the Colossus* (New York: Macmillan, 1994); and Lars Schoultz, *Beneath the United States: A History of US Policy Toward Latin America* (Cambridge, MA: Harvard University Press, 1998). Coatsworth, 84–5, puts the case simply: 'For many years the US State Department maintained that the Arbenz regime [overthrown by the CIA in 1954] had fallen under the control of communism and the Soviet Union and that its overthrow was the product of a popular revolt carried out by the Guatemalan people. Neither of these assertions was true.'

13. Eichengreen, *Globalizing Capital*, 109–13; and Robert Solomon, *The International Monetary System, 1945–1981* (New York: Harper & Row, 1982), 9–62.

14. For a sardonic view of the rise of the Eurodollar, see W.P. Hogan and I.F. Pearce, *The Incredible Eurodollar* (London: George Allen & Unwin, 1982). Some economists have argued that the Eurodollar market proved the fallacy of US capital controls, linking the maintenance of such controls in the US with the ballooning of the Eurodollar market in London. For this argument, see Fred L. Block, *The Origins of International Economic Disorder: A Study of United States International Monetary Policy from World War II to the Present* (Berkeley: University of California Press, 1977), 162. This seems to underestimate the extent to which the US tacitly accepted or even encouraged the Eurodollar market.

15. Eichengreen, *Globalizing Capital*, 128–34. See also Maurice Obstfeld and Alan M. Taylor, 'The Great Depression as a Watershed: International Capital Mobility over the Long Run', in Bordo et al., eds, *The Defining Moment*, 353–402 at 391–3. Fred Block suggests that the US might have saved the Bretton Woods system by cutting its military expenditure (and reining in its foreign military adventures), but thinks that this would put the horse before the cart: 'It would be absurd for the United States to abandon its global ambitions simply to live within the rules of an international monetary order that was shaped for the purpose of achieving those ambitions.' *The Origins of International Economic Disorder*, 163.

16. On new financial instruments, and the coincidence of capital mobility and destructive speculation, see Eichengreen, *Globalizing Capital*, 136–

7; Obstfeld and Taylor, 'The Great Depression as a Watershed', 394;
Dilip K. Ghosh and Edgar Oritz, 'The Global Structure of Financial
Markets: An Overview', in Ghosh and Oritz, eds, *The Global Structure
of Financial Markets* (London: Routledge, 1997), 1–14; and John
Williamson, *The Failure of World Monetary Reform, 1971–1974* (New York:
New York University Press, 1977), 45–51.

17. Nicolás Ardito-Barletta, 'Managing Development and Transition', in
Kenen, ed., *Managing the World Economy*, 173–200.

18. Robert Devlin discusses the mismatch of private capital from the developed world and public-interest borrowing by poorer countries in
Debt and Crisis in Latin America: The Supply Side of the Story (Princeton:
Princeton University Press, 1989), 124. For an overview of the shift
from government assistance for developing countries to private lending, see James E. Mahon, Jr., *Mobile Capital and Latin American Development* (University Park: Pennsylvania State University Press, 1996), 29–
57.

19. Many commentators have argued that major banks in the US and Europe
were guilty of 'loan pushing': they aggressively marketed their loans to
developing countries even when they realised that the debtor countries
were likely to run into difficulties with repayment. See William Darity,
Jr., and Bobbie L. Horn, *The Loan Pushers: The Role of Commercial Banks
in the International Debt Crisis* (Cambridge, MA: Ballinger Publishing,
1988). See also Devlin's suggestion in *Debt and Crisis in Latin America*,
77–8, that banks made loans for reasons that were not 'rational', in
economic terms – including the desire to win market share and to
penetrate new markets, and occasional engagement in collusionary or
corrupt practices.

20. For a table of the top ten US banks and their domestic and overseas
profits, see Devlin, *Debt and Crisis in Latin America*, 38. Susan George
launches a stinging attack on the banks in *A Fate Worse Than Debt*
(London: Penguin, 1988), 30–46, noting their inability to conceive of
'development' for poorer countries without maximising their own profits.

21. Steven Solomon, in *The Confidence Game: How Unelected Central Bankers
Are Governing the Changed Global Economy* (New York: Simon & Schuster,
1995), 196, attributes the 'countries don't go broke' line to Walter
Wriston, former chairman of Citicorp. Solomon also identifies a straightforward motive in the loan boom of the 1970s: 'Why did bankers, in
hindsight, lend so much so imprudently? The short answer: profit.'

22. On Mexico's declaration of bankruptcy, and the genesis of the international debt crisis, see Robert Solomon, *Money on the Move: The
Revolution in International Finance Since 1980* (Princeton: Princeton University Press, 1999), 34–40.

23. Robert Solomon suggests that loans from all US banks to merely the
seventeen most indebted countries amounted to more than 150 per
cent of those banks' capital; in the event of a widespread default, combined with a run on the banks from domestic deposit holders, there

was a real possibility that the US banking system would collapse, with dire consequences for the global economy. Ibid., 39–40.

24. For an account of the response of governments and bankers to the first stirrings of the crisis, see Joseph Kraft, *The Mexican Rescue* (New York: Group of Thirty, 1984). The rescheduling and IMF involvement was eased by the banks' original establishment of a lending syndicate in the 1970s; see Devlin, *Debt and Crisis in Latin America*, 32, 93–101, 217–18.

25. For a broad perspective on the effects of 'restructuring' in developing countries, see Michel Chossudovsky, *The Globalization of Poverty: Impacts of IMF and World Bank Reforms* (London: Zed Books, 1997); and Brohman, *Popular Development*, 132–97. A more concise treatment of the management of developing-country debt is offered by Robert Solomon, *Money on the Move*, 39–45.

26. Steven Solomon describes the battle between private banks and the central banks/IMF – the private banks tried to pressure the IMF (and, therefore, developed-country governments) into paying off the developing-country debts; the central banks and the IMF tried to prevent individual private banks from triggering a massive default. *The Confidence Game*, 212–47. The nightmare scenario of global economic collapse following the Mexican crisis is sketched by Darrell Delamaide, *Debt Shock: The Full Story of the World's Credit Crisis* (Garden City, NY: Doubleday, 1984), 6–28.

27. On the inability of developing countries to declare a default, see Kraft, *The Mexican Rescue*, 3–4, and George, *A Fate Worse than Debt*, 67–73.

28. The shift from Keynes to these Chicago School positions is the theme of Yergin and Stanislaw, *The Commanding Heights*; see their treatment of Milton Friedman and his Chicago colleagues, 145–9. I use 'neoliberalism' throughout this book to describe policies which favour free trade (and freedom of capital movement) and which privilege a tight control of the money supply over job-creation, social welfare, etc. It should be noted, however, that the term has been defined in many different ways – and was often used in the 1980s to describe the tax-cutting domestic policies of Margaret Thatcher and Ronald Reagan. See note 30 below for further discussion of the taxonomy of neoliberalism.

29. In an assessment of the new flows of private capital to the developing world, Kunibert Raffer has argued that 'the only "success" of orthodox debt strategies seems to have been shifting some risk onto mutual funds, pension funds and retirement accounts – or onto the public at large.' 'Is the Debt Crisis Largely Over? A Critical Look at the Data of International Financial Institutions', in Richard M. Auty and John Toye, eds, *Challenging the Orthodoxies* (New York: St. Martins Press, 1996), 23–38 at 37. For the general context of new capital flows to developing countries, see Solomon, *Money on the Move*, 113–19.

30. The phrase was coined by John Williamson in a 1990 presentation which also summarised ten policy instruments necessary to Third World development: 'fiscal discipline', a rearrangement of public expenditure,

tax reform, financial liberalisation, competitive exchange rates, trade liberalisation, an openness to foreign investment, privatisation, deregulation, and the preservation of property rights. 'What Washington Means By Policy Reform', in Williamson, ed., *Latin American Adjustment: How Much Has Happened?* (Washington, DC: Institute for International Economics, 1990), 7–38. Williamson has responded pointedly to the charge that this 'Consensus' amounts to a 'neoliberal manifesto', stressing that his ten policy instruments do not mandate minimal taxation or the complete abolition of capital controls. See Williamson, 'Lowest Common Denominator or Neoliberal Manifesto? The Polemics of the Washington Consensus', in Auty and Toye, eds, *Challenging the Orthodoxies*, 13–22. He admits, however, that the Consensus lacks 'many planks, notably those regarding the social dimension'. The Clinton administration, in its assault on capital controls, has moved to shore up the neoliberal credentials of the Consensus.

31. For an upbeat account of US financial deregulation, see Yergin and Stanislaw, *The Commanding Heights*, 331–69. A breathless guide to how to make money in the new global economy is offered by a pair of management consultants from McKinsey and Company: Lowell Bryan and Diana Farrell, *Market Unbound: Unleashing Global Capitalism* (New York: John Wiley and Sons, 1996). At xii, Byran and Farrell excitedly describe the process by which 'the market will force governments, like it or not, to open up their economies'. A more sober review of the new financial instruments and markets is offered by the United Nations Development Programme (UNDP) in its *Human Development Report 1999* (New York: Oxford University Press for UNDP, 1999), 30.

32. Brohman concludes his analysis of the effects of neoliberal 'adjustment' on developing countries with a pessimistic assessment: 'Increasing societal polarization has generated a widespread perception that an elite minority has monopolized the benefits of development under [structural adjustment], while the popular majority has been forced to endure a disproportionate share of the costs.' *Popular Development*, 172.

33. Elizabeth Weiner noted in 1992 that, in Mexico alone, 'at least 42 government scholarship students are returning with Ph.D.s from leading US universities.... Most of them will carry the modernization flag straight into government ministries.' 'The Latin Revolution Has Ivy Roots', *Business Week*, 15 June 1992. See also David R. Francis, 'Improving the World with Academic Advice', *Christian Science Monitor*, 5 June 1992.

34. Clinton's speedy acceptance of the eclipse of 'big government' is celebrated in Yergin and Stanislaw, *The Commanding Heights*, 331–4. These authors make much of the electoral victories of Bill Clinton in the US and Tony Blair in the UK, each supposedly the representative of a 'third way' in politics which transcends the old platforms of right and left. One of the most inadvertently sobering accounts of the 'third way' is by Dick Morris, former Clinton adviser from 1995 to 1996, who helped prepare his boss for the 1996 election by essentially adopting most of

the policies of the right-wing Republican Party opposition: 'If you wander into [the Republican] line of fire, they're going to kill you every time. But they have no other game plan, no other way to win. If you come around behind them or alongside and don't raise taxes, if you're tough on crime and want to reform welfare, use the military effectively, and cut spending, they can't hit you.' Morris doesn't elaborate on the creepy suggestion that a president should 'use the military effectively' to win an election, but the outline here is clear: if you abandon your own policies and adopt those of your opponents, you can beat them – a strategy Morris dubbed 'triangulation'. Dick Morris, *Behind the Oval Office: Getting Reelected Against All Odds*, second edition (Los Angeles: Renaissance Books, 1999), 317–18.

35. The Washington spin on Rubin around the time of his appointment usually stressed the new appointee's 'hardheaded compassion' or his 'social conscience' rather than his estimated $125 million personal fortune. See Beth Belton, 'Wall Streeter with a Heart Defies Stereotype', *USA Today*, 3 March 1993.

36. Nicholas D. Kristoff and David E. Sanger, 'How US Wooed Asia to Let Cash Flow In', *New York Times*, 16 February 1999. In discussing Rubin's wealth, a Treasury aide joked to the reporters that Rubin had a fly-fishing rod that 'probably costs more than your house'.

37. Rubin's personal influence from early 1993 – which even secured him a seat on the National Security Council, the body of advisers which assists the president in foreign-policy decisions – is detailed in James Risen, 'Man to See is Clinton Aide Rubin', *Los Angeles Times*, 10 February 1993. On Rubin's eventual return to New York to head Citigroup, see Joseph Kahn, 'Former Treasury Secretary Joins Leadership Triangle at Citigroup', *New York Times*, 27 October 1999. On the other Wall Street alumni in Clinton's cabinet, and the 'revolving door' which linked the 'New Democrat' White House and Wall Street, see Laura M. Holson, 'White House Externs', *New York Times*, 3 February 1999. Jagdish Bhagwati argued in 1998 that a 'Wall Street–Treasury complex', made up of serving and former public officials with links to high finance, heavily influenced Clinton's policies. This 'complex' was 'unable to look much beyond the interest of Wall Street, which it equates with the good of the world'. 'The Capital Myth', *Foreign Affairs* 77, no. 3 (1998): 7–12. Even presidential aides with high-paying jobs were tempted by the prospect of greater returns from Wall Steet: President Clinton's former adviser Vernon Jordan moved to Wall Street in late 1999, accepting a position with the investment bank Lazard Frères. Jordan, who achieved a degree of notoriety during the Lewinsky sex scandal, had helped the Clinton administration from a position of power and privilege, combining his advisory duties with a law-firm job which paid 'considerably more' than $1 million per year. Stephen Hess of the Brookings Institution speculated on the reasons for his move to investment banking: 'I can only assume that he's going to make more money and have more

fun, not that he hasn't been making a lot of money and having a lot of fun.' Patrick McGeehan, 'A Clinton Advisor to Join Lazard Frères', *New York Times*, 1 December 1999.

38. For a description of Mexico's development in the late 1980s and early 1990s which stresses the nation's economic promise, see Robert Solomon, *The Transformation of the World Economy, 1980–1993* (London: Macmillan, 1994), 187–96. Solomon's book was published just before the peso crisis, and his 1999 *Money on the Move* amended this enthusiasm. Kunibert Raffer notes that Mexico in 1994 was 'enjoying privileged treatment as a debtor and showing excellent debt indicators', which proves the weakness of the IMF and bank assessment methods: 'Is the Debt Crisis Largely Over?', 37. Yergin and Stanislaw offer paeans to Aspe and Salinas amidst details of their US training in *The Commanding Heights*, 257–8.

39. For general accounts of the peso crisis, see Sebastian Edwards and Moisés Naím, eds, *Mexico 1994: Anatomy of an Emerging Market Crash* (Washington, DC: Carnegie Endowment for International Peace, 1997); Sebastian Edwards, *Crisis and Reform in Latin America: From Despair to Hope* (New York: Oxford University Press/World Bank, 1995), 295–302; Stephany Griffith-Jones, *Global Capital Flows: Should They Be Regulated?* (London: Macmillan, 1998), 100–136; and Jeremy Adelman, 'Tequila Hangover: Latin America's Debt Crisis', *Studies in Political Economy* 55 (1998): 5–35 at 22–8. David D. Hale reprints forecasts from various Wall Street banks in 1994, illustrating the general failure of American underwriters and investors to anticipate the crisis: 'The Markets and Mexico: The Supply Side of the Story', in Edwards and Naím, eds, *Mexico 1994*, 201–45.

40. On the *tesobonos*, see Robert Solomon, *Money on the Move*, 122–9.

41. Albert Berry cites this figure from *Forbes* magazine in 'Confronting the Distribution Threat', in A. Berry, ed., *Poverty, Economic Reform and Income Distribution in Latin America* (Boulder, CO: Lynne Rienner, 1998), 9–41 at 39.

42. On the empowerment of Mexican business elites, see Philip Oxhorn, 'Is the Century of Corporatism Over? Neoliberalism and the Rise of Neopluralism', in Philip Oxhorn and Graciela Ducatenzeiler, eds, *What Kind of Democracy? What Kind of Market? Latin America in the Age of Neoliberalism* (University Park: Pennsylvania State University Press, 1998), 227–39; and Alvaro Díaz, 'New Developments in Economic and Social Restructuring in Latin America', in William C. Smith and Roberto Patricio Korzeniewicz, eds, *Politics, Social Change, and Economic Restructuring in Latin America* (Miami: North–South Center Press, 1997), 37–56.

43. On capital flight among domestic elites in the second half of 1994, see Solomon, *Money on the Move*, 123ff; Hale, 'The Markets and Mexico', 215; and Edwards, *Crisis and Reform in Latin America*, 299–300.

44. When interviewed in April 1995, Rubin responded rather circuitously to the suggestion that the Treasury had intervened in Mexico in part to help Wall Street (including his old friends at Goldman Sachs): 'I honestly

have no idea what firms have anything. All I know is, we got involved in Mexico to help deal with an issue that we thought was of critical importance to this country. And I truly do not know what firms have positions.' Paul Starobin and Bruce Stokes, 'No Avoiding Woes of Third World', *National Journal*, 1 April 1995.

45. Bill Clinton, 'State of the Union address', delivered on Capitol Hill, Washington, DC, 24 January 1995.

46. Numerous members of Congress, principally Republicans, argued against using money to bail out Mexico that might be used instead to improve poorer areas of the US, or even to bail out the newly bankrupt districts of Washington, DC and Orange County, California; see the debate in the House of Representatives of the 104th Congress of the United States, 'Foreign Trade Policy Relative to Bailout of Mexico', 19 January 1995. The 'Main Street' remark was made by David Funderbunk, a representative from North Carolina, on the House floor on 1 February 1995.

47. A detailed account of this process, following the reluctance of Congress to agree to loan guarantees, is offered by George Graham et al., 'Mexican Rescue', *Financial Times*, 16 February 1995. Although the other major developed nations issued a press release confirming their support for the bail-out, the *Financial Times* article suggests that they were not consulted over the details of the plan, even though it constituted the largest IMF bail-out in history. 'It was just not acceptable,' said a European official. 'President Clinton goes to the press and says the Fund will do this and that. We are not banana republics.' Of course, the same official would presumably be more sanguine if the economic dictates were levelled at a 'banana republic', a theme to which we will return.

48. On Wall Street's mixed reckoning of the Mexican affair, see Brett Fromson, 'Rescue Package Provokes Disagreement on Wall Street', *Washington Post*, 16 February 1995. The very uneven effects within Mexico are summarised by Christopher Whalen, 'South of the Bailout; The $20 Billion Rescue Plan Won't Help the Mexican People', *Washington Post*, 5 February 1995; and Jorge Castañeda, 'Mexico's Circle of Misery', *Foreign Affairs* 75, no. 4 (1996): 92–105.

49. A recent high-profile example of this free movement of intellectual capital was the appointment of Armínío Fraga, former fund manager for George Soros, as president of the Brazilian central bank. This sparked a hostile debate in the confirmation hearings held before the Brazilian Senate, although Fraga eventually assumed the new position. See Geoff Dyer and Richard Waters, 'Brazil Picks Hedge-Fund Poacher as Economic Gamekeeper', *Financial Times*, 3 February 1999; and Dyer, 'Brazilian Senators Grill New Bank Chief', ibid., 27 February 1999.

50. Yergin and Stanislaw recall Zedillo's thesis in *The Commanding Heights*, 259, arguing that the dissertation was so appealing to the head of the Mexican central bank that he subsequently hired the Ivy League graduate.

51. Quoted in Robert I. Rotberg, 'Post-Clinton Africa: The Wait Begins', *Christian Science Monitor*, 7 April 1998.

52. Gabriel Kolko has argued that US policy towards Africa developed from near-total delegation of the continent to Europe in the 1950s to a much more active programme – consisting of resource exploitation and opposition to radicalism – in the late 1960s and after: see his *Confronting the Third World: United States Foreign Policy, 1945–1980* (New York: Pantheon Books, 1988), 111–16 and 240–47. When Clinton apologised during his African tour for US misdeeds during the Cold War, one US columnist actually attacked the president for his 'dripping contrition', arguing (in reference to South Africa's president) that 'America's moral compromises during the Cold War were at least as justified as Mandela's during his war', and that 'communism caused far more suffering and posed a far greater danger to humanity than apartheid'. Charles Krauthammer, 'In Defense of "Our" Dictators', *Washington Post*, 5 April 1998.

53. For a summary of Africa's predicament, see E. Wayne Nafziger, *The Debt Crisis in Africa* (Baltimore: Johns Hopkins University Press, 1993); and Nikoi Kote-Nikoi, *Beyond the New Orthodoxy: Africa's Debt and Development Crisis in Retrospect* (Aldershot: Avebury, 1996).

54. For overviews of the original HIPC plan, see 'How to Make Aid Work', *Economist*, 26 June 1999; and Michael Holman and Quentin Peel, 'Too Much to Bear', *Financial Times*, 12 June 1999. Holman and Peel relate the difficulties of Mozambique even under the HIPC initiative: 'What should have been a model example of the benefits of a new deal for the poorest of the poor instead stands as a stark illustration of the scheme's inadequacy.'

55. Jubilee 2000 cast an especially wide net in its campaigning, and managed to attract such unlikely advocates as Bono, of the rock band U2. Bono's efforts to win over Harvard economist Robert J. Barro to the cause of debt relief, however, were ultimately fruitless. In a bizarre article, 'My Luncheon with Bono', *Business Week*, 12 July 1999, Barro narrates a meeting with Bono in which the latter's arguments on behalf of debt forgiveness were 'better than I had anticipated' but not persuasive enough for Barro 'to put debt relief on the Top 10 list of growth-promoting policies for poor countries'. In an other-worldly denouement, Barro asked Bono to sign some CDs for his children, and then summed up what had been achieved during this discussion of the fate of the planet's poorest people: 'So, the lunch had clearly succeeded in making me a hero with my kids. What's more important than that?'

56. The campaign for debt relief enjoyed a high profile in the US and especially in Europe: see Diane Coyle, 'Clamour to End the Third World Debt Gets Louder', *Independent*, 14 June 1999. Oxfam criticised the terms of the revised HIPC proposal and the secrecy with which it had been deliberated by developed-country governments: 'The G7 ministries have been negotiating with all the openness of a Masonic lodge.' Michael Holman and Nancy Dunne, 'Debt Relief Plan "Painfully Inadequate"', *Financial Times*, 16 June 1999. Bill Clinton's eventual advocacy in September 1999 of a more substantial debt relief programme owed much

to the efforts of debt-relief campaigners, though was still uncomfortably dependent on Congress and on the acceptance of various neoliberal conditions by debtor countries. See John Burgess, 'Clinton Pledges to Forgive Poor Nations' Debt', *Washington Post*, 30 September 1999; and Eric Schmitt, 'House Passes Compromise Bill', *New York Times*, 6 November 1999. For an account of the ongoing wariness in Africa over the gulf between US rhetoric and intentions, see Norimitsu Onishi, 'US and Africa: Unfulfilled Promises and Skepticism', *New York Times*, 25 October 1999.

57. Martin Wolf, 'The Debt Myths', *Financial Times*, 23 June 1999. Yergin and Stanislaw, *The Commanding Heights*, 385–6, offer a bracing introduction to the prospects for neoliberalism in Africa, even suggesting that the 'private commercial tradition' which would foster privatisation and the retreat of government in Africa 'existed long before the colonial period and, against all odds and in the face of determined opposition, has endured ever since'.

58. Kate Dunn, 'Africa's Dreams Begin to Take Root', *Christian Science Monitor*, 1 April 1998.

59. For a friendly summary of the 1998 plan, see Paul Magnusson and Dean Foust, 'Don't Waste a Huge Opportunity in Africa', *Business Week*, 6 April 1998.

60. 'We must fortify African democracy and peace … by passing the African Trade and Development Act' [the AGOA]. Bill Clinton, 'State of the Union address, 1999'.

61. The text of the 1999 version of the AGOA was entered into the Congressional record as HR 434, and was approved by the House of Representatives on 17 July 1999. Nelson Mandela expressed reservations about the 'national security or foreign policy interests' clause, and suggested that this would make the entire proposal unacceptable to South Africa. Mandela feared that this proviso would be used to pressure South Africa into renouncing allies in Cuba, Libya and elsewhere. See Anne Scales, 'Mandela Lectures Clinton on Peace', *Boston Globe*, 28 March 1998. The problem with the national security construction – as with the AGOA's vague commitment to protect 'worker rights' in Africa, or its discomfiting promise only to take notice of 'gross' human-rights abuses – is that the meaning of these clauses will be decided unilaterally by the US, which seems unlikely to look kindly either on South Africa's independent relations with 'rogue states' or the prospect of union-inspired demands interfering with the operations of US corporations or investors.

62. Witness the flow of money into Africa in mid-1998, as the world's other 'emerging markets' plunged in value. Sheel Kohli, 'Africa Leads Emerging Markets', *South China Morning Post*, 16 August 1998.

63. The AGOA passed the Senate in November 1999. See Eric Schmitt, 'Senate Passes Trade Bills for Caribbean and Africa', *New York Times*, 4 November 1999.

64. On the reduction in aid to Africa, see Kurt Shillinger, 'Carter, Others Say US Has Faltered in Africa', *Boston Globe*, 8 December 1999.

65. Randall Robinson and Ralph Nader, 'A Forced March to Congress' Tune', *Los Angeles Times*, 11 March 1998.

66. As the AGOA was first debated in 1998, Bob Herbert noted in an editorial the oppressive effects of existing IMF adjustment programmes, and lamented the possibility of a broadening of 'austerity' under AGOA-mandated 'liberalisation'; Herbert suggests that many sub-Saharan leaders have only expressed interest in AGOA because they hope that the US 'and its great corporations will alleviate their economic suffering. It's a situation ripe for wholesale exploitation.' 'At What Cost?', *New York Times*, 7 June 1998.

67. Jackson, Jr. is the son of Jesse Jackson, who diverged from his more radical past in Clinton's second term by appearing, alternately, as his president's therapist and confessor. Jackson, Jr., however, has been a fierce critic of the Clinton administration's neoliberal drives. His proposed alternative to AGOA, the Human Rights, Opportunity, Partnership and Empowerment (HOPE) for Africa Act, contained provisions for the protection of labour, the environment and public health. Jackson, an African-American, struck a distinct tone amidst the widespread praise for AGOA in the Congressional debate, introducing the broader historical context of American-African trade: 'Three hundred and eighty years ago our nation's first trade policy landed 19 Africans in Jamestown, Virginia. Since then our nation has struggled with that painful and profound legacy. Undoubtedly, the effects of trade are far reaching and long lasting. In many ways my presence here and that of 33 million other Americans is the result of this nation's first African trade policy.... After centuries of getting it wrong – through slavery, exploitation, as pawns in a Cold War and neglect – it is incumbent upon us to get this new policy right.' *Congressional Record*, 106th Congress, House of Representatives, 16 July 1999, H5715.

68. The Congresswoman was Sheila Jackson-Lee of Texas, who looked hopefully towards Chevron, Mobil, Bank of America, McDonald's and General Electric, among others, for solutions to Africa's HIV catastrophe. Ibid., H5739. According to the UNDP *Human Development Report 1999*, 4, nine countries in Africa face a loss of seventeen years in life expectancy due to HIV/AIDS, 'reversing the gains of recent decades'.

69. For the general context of these events, see Marshall I. Goldman, *Lost Opportunity: Why Economic Reforms in Russia Have Not Worked* (New York: W.W. Norton, 1994); and David Remnick, *Resurrection: The Struggle for a New Russia*, second edition (New York: Vintage, 1998). Kissinger railed against a 'grand bargain' which would transfer responsibility for Russia's probable economic hardship to the US: 'The West should not maneuver itself into imposing conditions that can later be blamed for causing great suffering.' 'No Time For a "Grand Bargain"', *Washington Post*, 9 July 1991.

70. Janine R. Wedel narrates the involvement of the HIID in Russia in *Collision and Collusion: The Strange Case of Western Aid to Eastern Europe, 1989–1998* (New York: St. Martin's Press, 1998), 121–9. The HIID was awarded $57.7 million by the US government from 1992 to 1996.

71. Wedel dubbed the American experts the 'Harvard Boys' in a 1998 article, 'The Harvard Boys Do Russia', *Nation*, 1 June 1998. The soubriquet recalls another gang of 'radical reformers', the so-called 'Chicago Boys' – a group of economists from the University of Chicago, steeped in the ideas of Milton Friedman, who travelled to Chile after the military coup d'état of 1973 to assist General Augusto Pinochet in consolidating his dictatorship.

72. Anders Åslund, one of Sachs's colleagues in the US assistance team to Russia, describes the 'shock therapy' programme in *How Russia Became a Market Economy* (Washington, DC: Brookings Institution, 1995), 174–222; he argues for 'shock' treatment rather than a more gradual approach at 186–7. In his acknowledgements, xi, Anders thanks Sachs for his help, confirming that 'among the Western advisors to the Russian government', Sachs 'has been our undisputed intellectual leader'.

73. Wedel recalls a number of these shock-therapy analogies in *Collision and Collusion*, 21. She also attributes to Ryszard Bugaj, an economist for Poland's Solidarity party, the observation that Sachs's speeches and television appearances in eastern Europe were intended to minister to popular anxieties: 'He talked in such a smooth, confident manner that many responded as if they were hearing a revelation.' Ibid., 48.

74. On the disastrous effects of 'shock therapy', see Goldman, 94–121; and Richard Sakwa, *Russian Politics and Society*, second edition (London: Routledge, 1996), 233–40. On the emergence of the 'Chubais clan', see Wedel, *Collision and Collusion*, 125–6, 129–31.

75. Some commentators have charged that Chubais was involved in subverting the original Supreme Soviet plan to favour a privatisation model more conducive to corruption. For a detailed account of Chubais' battle with the Supreme Soviet, and the obvious inequities in Chubais' plans for speedy privatisation, see Lynn D. Nelson and Irina Y. Kuzes, *Radical Reform in Yeltsin's Russia: Political, Economic and Social Dimensions* (Armonk, NY: M.E. Sharpe, 1995), 133–63; and M. Steven Fish, 'The Roots and Remedies for Russia's Racket Economy', in Stephen S. Cohen, Andrew Schwartz and John Zysman, eds, *The Tunnel at the End of the Light: Privatization, Business Networks, and Economic Transformation in Russia* (Berkeley: Brie/Kreisky Reform Project and University of California, 1998), 86–137.

76. For an account of this affair, see Anatol Lieven, *Chechnya: Tombstone of Russian Power* (New Haven: Yale University Press, 1999), 172–81.

77. Chrystia Freeland, John Thornhill and Andrew Gowers, 'Moscow's Group of Seven', *Financial Times*, 1 November 1996. Andrei Piontkovsky, head of the Moscow Centre for Strategic Studies, contended in 1997 that 'Chubais believes that it is not important how property is distributed,

as long as property owners are created.' Quoted in Lieven, *Chechnya*, 176.

78. Janine Wedel tracks the activities of the 'Chubais Clan' in the midst of this: *Collision and Collusion*, 131–9.

79. Joseph Stiglitz, 'Whither Reform? Ten Years of the Transition', paper delivered at the Annual World Bank Conference on Development Economics, Washington, DC, 28–30 April 1999.

80. Andrei Piontkovsky noted Chubais' hope that the oligarchs would become productive economic citizens after their enrichment: 'After they have had their share of thievery, so the argument goes, they will start to turn their efforts to raising productivity.' Piontkovsky noted, however, that the quick gains of moving money out of the country (especially given insider trading, knowledge of the movements of the Russian central bank, etc.) would also appeal to financial elites with homes throughout the world, and 'a taste of this fabulous means of enrichment.' Lieven, *Chechnya*, 176.

81. For an early expression of the argument against Sachs and his team – that they had not sought the cooperation of Harvard's famous Russian studies scholars, and were preparing to implement 'reform' without proper attention to Russia's particular needs – see Pedro-Pablo Kuczynski, 'What's Needed is Basic Development, Not Harvard Prescriptions', *Washington Post*, 20 October 1991. Sachs eventually came around to the view that 'while Russia's crisis does not challenge the classical economic tenets, successful reforms were not guaranteed'. Reasons for this included 'Russia's sprawling land mass and centuries-old history of authoritarian rule without private property'. Lynnley Browning, 'Russia Ills Shake Faith in Market Cure-Alls', *Boston Globe*, 23 August 1998. (Quotations are Browning's paraphrases from an interview with Sachs.)

82. For a more recent example of this ongoing 'war', see Clinton's speech at the Grand Hyatt Hotel, San Francisco, 26 February 1999: 'We have as much at stake today in Russia overcoming these challenges as we did in checking its expansion during the Cold War. This is not a time for complacency or for self-fulfilling pessimism.'

83. Although George Bush appears to have set less store by Nixon's warning, Clinton regularly solicited Nixon's advice on how to handle Russia. The first section of Monica Crowley's *Nixon in Winter* (New York: Random House, 1998) details Nixon's views on the transition from communism; see 156–8 for a summary of his policy concerns, and his perception of their mixed success in Washington. Dick Morris suggests in his *Behind the Oval Office*, 250, that Clinton remembered Nixon's advice in the run-up to the crucial Russian elections of 1996: 'Russia became to the President's foreign policy what California was to his domestic political strategy: the one place he couldn't afford to lose.'

84. Testimony delivered in Congress by Pete Stavrikis to the House International Relations Committee on 9 June 1999 confirms this fear. Describing US support for Anatoly Chubais, and the allegations that

Chubais had been involved in further corruption surrounding the 1996 Russian presidential election, Stavrikis set Chubais' activities against the broader political context: 'And this is an individual who as one former embassy official said is one of the few reformers that goes for blood. And I believe that. The higher political goal is what he serves. The law is an irritating element that has to be swept aside from time to time. Regrettably, I think his character is such that he retains that even when things get better.'

85. For allegations of formal improprieties in Harvard's involvement, see Wedel, 'The Harvard Boys Do Russia'. See also David L. Marcus, 'US Halts Harvard Contract in Russia', *Boston Globe*, 21 May 1997; David Filipov and David L. Marcus, 'Probe of Russian Work Shocks Harvard Adviser', *Boston Globe*, 25 May 1997; and Victoria Griffith and John Thornhill, 'Harvard Dons to Face Insider Trading Probe', *Financial Times*, 18 January 1999.

86. On the rise of the *nomenklatura*, and the various definitions of the term in circulation, see Sakwa, *Russian Politics and Society*, 158–163; and Bertram Silverman and Murray Yanowitch, *New Rich, New Poor, New Russia: Winners and Losers on the Russian Road to Capitalism* (Armonk, NY: M.E. Sharpe, 1997), 103–27. For accounts of organised crime in post-Soviet Russia, see Stephen Handelman, *Comrade Criminal: Russia's New Mafiya* (New Haven: Yale University Press, 1995); and the essays collected in Phil Williams, ed., *Russian Organized Crime: The New Threat?* (London: Frank Cass, 1997). On the deteriorating levels of health and social welfare, see Nicholas Eberstadt, 'Russia: Too Sick to Matter?', *Policy Review* 95 (1995): 3–24. On poverty, see Stiglitz, 'Whither Reform', 1. The connections between Russia's economic crisis and the 1995–96 offensive in Chechnya are the subject of Anatol Lieven's *Chechnya: Tombstone of Russian Power*. On the psychological basis for the 1999 offensive, see Michael Wines, 'Russia Pines for a New Savior: Victory', *New York Times*, 21 November 1999. On the military brutishness of the attack, see Michael R. Gordon, 'Russia Uses a Sledgehammer in Chechnya War this Time', *New York Times*, 8 December 1999.

87. Martin Wolf, John Thornhill and Stephen Fidler, 'Meltdown', *Financial Times*, 28 August 1998.

88. David E. Sanger, 'IMF Backs $17 Billion For Russia', *New York Times*, 21 July 1998.

89. See Kimberly Blanton, 'Perils of a Fast Buck', *Boston Globe*, 6 September 1998; and Alexei Brayer, 'Futurology and Risk', *Financial Times*, 4 September 1998.

90. See Sharon LaFraniere, 'Russian Banks Served Selves First', *Washington Post*, 30 September 1998; and Martin Wolf et al., 'Meltdown'. The latter quotes from a Credit Suisse First Boston bank report on the August 1998 currency crisis in Russia: 'The current outcome is looking more and more as though the $10 billion saved through the debt restructuring is simply being plundered by the banking system and fleeing the country.'

91. David E. Sanger, 'US Official Questions How Russia Used Loan', *New York Times*, 19 March 1999.

92. The UNDP's *Human Development Report 1999*, 85, estimates that inequality in Russia doubled between 1989 and 1996.

93. The official line from the Clinton administration appears to attribute Russia's ongoing problems to 'the political legacy of communism'. For an articulation of this view, see the speech of Under Secretary of State for Political Affairs, Thomas R. Pickering, at the 1999 annual meeting of the Trilateral Commission, Washington, DC, 15 March 1999. Pete Stavrikis, in his June 1999 testimony to the House Committee on International Relations, suggested that 'the United States and the West did play an important role in arriving at today's sorry state of Russian affairs. This is not simply because of funds misspent, I think. But it's also because of an improper conception of the direction of Russian development.' In her testimony before the same committee, Paula Dobriansky, Washington director of the Council on Foreign Relations, warned that 'many Russians appear to have lost the sense that it is Communism and its legacy as well as the mistakes by its leaders that are to be blamed for Moscow's current predicament. Rather, most Russians seem to equate reform and democracy with their failure and blame the United States for allegedly seeking to inflict misery and humiliation on the Russian people.'

94. This wave of anxiety about unfettered global capital markets appears to have crested in late 1998, and receded markedly by April 1999. For a sense of this alarm, on the part of governments and the IMF, see Louis Uchitelle, 'A Crash Course in Economics: Rethinking What's Driving the Emerging Markets Crisis', *New York Times*, 29 January 1999. The deputies of Michel Camdessus, former IMF Managing Director, made speeches on the subject of a 'new architecture': Alassane D. Ouattara, 'Reforming the International Monetary System', delivered at the Academie de la Paix de la Securité Internationale, Paris, 6 March 1999; and Stanley Fischer, 'Reforming the International Monetary System', delivered as the David Finch Lecture, Melbourne, 9 November 1998. George Soros's call for some form of capital control was made in *The Crisis of Global Capitalism* (New York: Public Affairs, 1998). Note also the pledge of Soros, Paul Volcker and others to form a task force, under the auspices of the Council on Foreign Relations, 'to come up with a new international financial architecture'. 'In Brazil, the IMF Made Things Worse', *Business Week*, 1 February 1999.

95. When Brazil's economic difficulties in early 1999 seemed less severe than many investors had feared, government and IMF officials began to play down talk of capital controls, and to retreat from their earlier, more desperate rhetoric. See David E. Sanger, 'Rubin Proposes Modest Limits on Lending Risk', *New York Times*, 22 April 1999; and Michel Camdessus, 'Governments and Economic Development in a Globalized World', address to the 32nd International General Meeting of the Pacific

Basin Economic Council, Hong Kong, 17 May 1999. On the return of speculators to 'emerging markets', see Wayne Arnold, 'The Casino Effect in Asian Stock Markets', *New York Times*, 22 July 1999. Arnold notes that US investors have been slightly more wary of returning to emerging markets than non-US investors, mainly because of the speculative boom in US domestic stock exchanges.

96. The resignation of Michel Camdessus as IMF managing director in 1999 encouraged US Treasury officials to seek a replacement who would be even more responsive to US interests. (As former Clinton Treasury Secretary Lloyd Bentsen said ruefully of Camdessus, 'Damn right he can be tough. Sometimes you have to lean on him real hard to get things done.') David E. Sanger, 'Longtime IMF Director Resigns in Midterm', *New York Times*, 10 November 1999.

97. On the prospect of almost complete neglect of the international economy in the 2000 US presidential race, see Robert L. Borosage, 'The Global Turning', *Nation*, 19 July 1999. The only obvious challenger to Al Gore for the Democratic presidential nomination was Bill Bradley, who himself raised substantial campaign funding from Wall Street. In a profile of Bradley, David Corn conceded that 'Wall Streeters and financiers — who have generously funded his previous and present campaigns — can back him as an unabashed cheerleader of the global economy.' 'Bill Bradley: Can He Get Into the Game?', *Nation*, 5 July 1999.

98. The current head of the American Federation of Labor–Congress of Industrial Organizations (AFL–CIO) warned of this danger in a 1999 speech. Addressing the substantial US trade deficit, he invoked Pat Buchanan, a famous US right-winger: 'I can tell you one thing. We will either gain greater balance in our trade with China — and with the world — or we will feed a xenophobic populism that may make Pat Buchanan look like Woodrow Wilson.' John J. Sweeney, 'The Global Economy: The Need to Act', address to the Trilateral Commission annual meeting, Washington, DC, 14 March 1999. The leader of the Teamsters union, James P. Hoffa, Jr., noted his 'tremendous amount of respect' for Pat Buchanan during the December 1999 WTO protests in Seattle (see the Afterword for a fuller treatment of the protests). Hoffa conversed with Buchanan on 'Rivera Live', *MSNBC*, 29 November 1999.

99. A rather grim precursor to Clinton's 1998 'trade, not aid' formula came from then-Deputy Treasury Secretary Lawrence Summers in 1997, as Summers reported back to the US media in Washington on a recent trip to Africa: 'What I was struck by was that a new wind is blowing through Africa.... It was there in the recommendation by a major Wall Street firm of the T[reasury]-bills issued by a number of African governments. It was there in the entrepreneurs investing US pension fund money in private African infrastructure.... It was there when I visited Mozambique, by some measures the poorest country in the world, and met the competing Internet providers to that country.' Press Briefing by Larry Summers, The White House, Washington, DC, 17 June 1997.

The UN's 1999 *Human Development Report*, 148, notes that life expectancy in Mozambique is 45 years; that 60 per cent of the population is not literate; and that 70 per cent has no access to health services. Mozambique's stock exchange, meanwhile, opened (after a series of postponements) in October 1999. The *Economist* noted in a generally enthusiastic survey at the end of 1999 that '[n]aturally, the boom has not helped everyone equally. A relatively small middle class, concentrated in Maputo, is doing well ... Mozambicans in the countryside are still depressingly poor, decades of civil war having reduced many to stone-age conditions.' 'Maturing Mozambique', *Economist*, 4 December 1999.

100. On the strength of the US stock market in the context of financial disaster elsewhere in the world, see Louis Uchitelle, 'The Perpetual-Motion Economy', *New York Times*, 21 March 1999. The UNDP's *Human Development Report 1999* notes, 97, that the 'Asian crisis' and its fall-out around the world was 'the worst setback to the global economy since the 1930s'; and yet this coincided with a very strong US economy, apparently unhindered by the Asian difficulties.

101. For a useful comparison between the relatively short-lived problems for the United Kingdom following the run on the pound in 1992, and the much more profound difficulties for Mexico after 1995, see Paul Krugman, 'The Return of Depression Economics', *Foreign Affairs* 78, no. 1 (1999): 56–74. On the move towards a single European currency, and the hope that the euro will be a rival to the dollar, see Solomon, *Money on the Move*, 64. The IMF and the United Kingdom have recently announced plans to sell a large portion of their gold deposits and to hold dollar and euro certificates in their reserves. For perspectives on the future of the dollar and the euro as 'global reserve currencies', see Edward Luce, 'Bonded to a Bright Future', *Financial Times*, 14 June 1999.

102. This 'flash of optimism' from one 'steely-nerved foreign firm' with an interest in Russia is reported in 'Russia's Attempts to Create a Proper Business Culture are Now in Ruins', *Economist*, 24 October 1998. As one management consultant determinedly put it: 'Multinational companies know the demand is still out there.'

103. On Rubin's departure, and the succession of his deputy, Lawrence Summers, see David Wessel, 'Summers Break', *Wall Street Journal*, 13 May 1999.

104. On Atwood, see Philip Shenon, 'Departing Foreign Aid Chief Says Cuts Are Dangerous', *New York Times*, 6 July 1999.

105. George Gedda quotes from Atwood's speech in 'Retiring AID Head Vents Frustration', *Associated Press*, 29 June 1999. Atwood reworked this material for an editorial piece decrying 'Trade, Not Aid', *Christian Science Monitor*, 6 July 1999.

106. Jim Hoagland, 'Glory vs. Obscurity in the Clinton Era', *Washington Post*, 8 July 1999.

CHAPTER 2

THE US AND THE 'INTERNATIONAL COMMUNITY'

You know, no nation in history has had the opportunity and the responsibility we now have to shape a world that is more peaceful, more secure, more free.

William Jefferson Clinton, 1999 State of the Union address[1]

The relationship between the United States and the rest of the world is deeply paradoxical. On the one hand, the US has been the pre-eminent military and economic power since at least World War II, and has developed and defined the capacity to act in its own interest throughout the world. On the other hand, American policymakers have frequently attempted to present their actions as selfless, or dedicated to the good of other nations as surely as the US. This basic tension – between the pursuit of American interests and the presentation of those interests as universal – continues to characterise American foreign policy, and to place strains on the credibility of American intentions as well as on US relations with other countries.

In this chapter, I am going to focus on the diplomatic, legal and political relations between the US and the rest of the world, and particularly on the vexed relationship between the US and various international institutions and agreements. Although the US boasts a formidable rhetorical commitment to universal ideals of peace, justice and human rights, the American record on these issues lags far behind the promises. The gulf between rhetoric and action has been particularly evident under the Clinton administration, which has advanced many policy proposals and commitments that have often been compromised or abandoned when tested by events. Even though Clinton's speeches have pointed towards a new multilateralism and universalism among nations in the twenty-first century, his actions have failed to check American power or to place the interests of the rest of the planet on an equal footing with those of the United States.

In the first section, I want to look at the idea of an 'international community', a group of nations that respect the same laws and acknowledge a common interest. I will argue that the US has a great stake in the idea of this 'community', but has found it hard to abide by its rules and conventions. The difficult American relationship with the United Nations (UN) is a good example of this; recent efforts to lay down international standards on landmines and on international criminal law have also exposed an American antipathy to the rules of a global community. In the second section, I consider the shifting American position on peacekeeping and the responsibilities of the 'international community' to assuage or prevent conflict and suffering around the world. Events in Somalia, Rwanda and Bosnia since 1992 have demonstrated the substantial human cost of American ambivalence towards the rules of an international community: the US is not sufficiently committed to resolve disputes around the world, but is also too attached to its own global reach to allow other nations, or the UN, to become involved in its stead. The result has been a series of messy, equivocal interventions, as well as the kind of international abandonment which allowed the Rwandan killings of 1994 to assume the proportions of a genocide. In conclusion, I use the peacekeeping issue to return to the subject of the US–UN relationship, and to describe both the parlous state of that relationship at the century's end, and its likely consequences for the future.

DEFINING THE 'INTERNATIONAL COMMUNITY'

The United States and the United Nations

Throughout the twentieth century, the nations of the world attempted to maintain an international forum for the resolution of disputes and the articulation of global laws and standards. In the aftermath of World War I, European and American politicians established the League of Nations in the hope that another major war could be averted. The American Congress, however, refused to approve the plan, and the League was forced to operate without American membership and support. During World War II, Franklin Roosevelt laid the foundation for a successor to the League which would feature the US in an integral role. The new United Nations, founded in San Francisco in 1945, would be permanently based in the US and would receive financial and political assistance from the American government.[2]

Although the US was persuaded of the need for the UN, the distribution of power within the international organisation was a contentious topic. If countries' interests were weighed against each other equally, the new UN would adopt a one-nation, one-vote system which would treat the US no differently from any other power. Conversely, if a country's population determined its voting influence, the US would wield more power than the nations of Europe but less than China or Russia. In 1945, the US was not the most populous country but simply the most powerful. The challenge for the founders of the UN was to accommodate this imbalance of power within a voting system which seemed democratic, or at least equitable. They reached an ingenious solution. The UN would be divided into a General Assembly, which would operate a one-country, one-vote system; and a Security Council, consisting of permanent members (with the power to veto proposals) and rotating, temporary members. The General Assembly could thus appear as the democratic forum, whilst the Security Council could preserve the prerogatives of American power.[3]

Given the wave of decolonisation in the 1940s and 1950s, the distance between the Security Council and the General Assembly widened considerably. As the original 50 nations became 120 by the mid-1960s, so American influence in the General Assembly dwindled. The Security Council, meanwhile, had quickly asserted itself as the most powerful arm of the UN. The General Assembly gave smaller countries, especially the newly independent developing countries, the opportunity to state their views on the world stage. Resolutions in the General Assembly, however, were not binding and lacked any means of enforcement. The nations of the world might agree, by a large majority, on a course of action; but the General Assembly did not have the means to carry it through.[4] The Security Council, meanwhile, could authorise the use of force but had first to achieve a consensus among the major powers on the desirability of any operation. The five permanent members of the Council – the United States, Great Britain, France, Russia and China – could each defeat any proposal with a single veto, which heavily curtailed the power and engagement of the Council as a whole.[5]

In the decades following 1945, the veto powers of permanent Security Council members consigned the Council to near irrelevance. As the ideological battle between the US and the USSR hardened into Cold War, each country's efforts to use the UN were threatened by the veto of the other.[6] The post-war hopes for multilateral agreement and a new spirit of cooperation faded fast, replaced by the rejectionist logic of a bipolar world. From the American perspective, talk of an 'international community' was scant indeed: US presidents preferred instead to base their definition of world politics on the tyrannical ambitions of the Soviet Union, seeing the USSR and its satellites as an 'evil empire' ranged against the 'free world' which opposed communist advance. Although the UN continued to function, it was largely sidelined by this grand conflict, and could do little to assert its original mission of promoting the interests of all nations, not simply the most powerful.[7]

As the Soviet Union fell apart in 1989, it appeared that the UN might at last emerge from its long eclipse. The predictable US–USSR antagonism in the Security Council had suddenly disappeared, and the proxy wars waged in developing countries with American or Russian guidance seemed likely to subside.[8] Rhetorically, at least, American presidents promised a new era of internationalism. George Bush led the US to war with Saddam Hussein under UN auspices in 1991, declaring in a victory speech that the multilateral effort against Iraq heralded the coming of a 'new world order'.[9] Bill Clinton, as he campaigned to succeed Bush in 1992, went even further in his vision of that new order, suggesting that the UN be strengthened, and given its own unit of troops to respond quickly to conflicts across the globe.[10] With the nomination of Egyptian politician Boutros Boutros-Ghali as the new secretary-general in 1991, with a mandate for reform, the UN seemed set for a period of renewed significance in international affairs.[11]

Two major difficulties disrupted this picture. First, the US retained its tremendous power and influence even with the end of the Cold War; in fact, US predominance has increased in the absence of the Soviet counterweight. Although this has made it easier for the Security Council to mandate action, the risk of conflating US interests with the global interest has increased commensurately. The UN has also become more dependent on the good faith of US leaders and their promises of an internationalist American foreign policy. The US has been able to exert economic influence over Russia and China in the 1990s to win their acquiescence in UN operations which enjoy US support; however, there is no obvious balance to this influence since no other country has the political or economic power to force American acquiescence in UN activities which don't obviously advantage the American government. As we will see, this has left the UN at the mercy of US politicians, and sometimes even the American domestic political scene.[12]

The second difficulty proceeds from the first. If the US has often used the UN to advance its own interests, the American government has marginalised the efforts of other countries to organise effectively without US support. The US is happy to see a strong UN if that multilateral effort is directed towards familiar targets of American opprobrium: UN sanctions against Muammar Gaddafi or a UN task force against Saddam Hussein have proved perfectly acceptable to US policymakers. The idea of UN action in more ambiguous areas, however, has confounded and often angered the US: the abortive peacekeeping efforts in Rwanda and Bosnia, and the UN efforts to establish an International Criminal Court, have raised a fundamental question: is the US prepared to allow the UN to develop and succeed without US approval? Recent events suggest that the answer is no.[13]

Boutros Boutros-Ghali's term as UN secretary-general coincided with this moment of post–Cold War realignment, and Boutros-Ghali's fate is a useful index to the eventual US understanding of the UN. At the beginning of his term, Boutros-Ghali was persuaded of the need to keep the US at the heart of the UN. In a memoir of his experience at the UN, Boutros-Ghali recalled his frank admission to an American official just before taking office: 'Without American support, the United Nations would be paralyzed.'[14] As he assumed his responsibilities, however, Boutros-Ghali realised that his desire to toe an American line was compromised by the bullying and occasional contempt that the US manifested towards the UN. In the first place, the American government, and especially Congress, demanded substantial changes in the structure of the UN and in its funding arrangements. Although Clinton's 1992 campaign promises implied a bolder role for the organisation, the new American President quickly made clear his preference for a slimmed-down UN bureaucracy. The US Congress, meanwhile, set out to reduce the level of US contributions to the UN, upsetting those poorer countries which felt that the richest nation in the world should shoulder a commensurate burden of the UN's expenses.[15]

The questions of reform and funding were further complicated by the embarrassing failure of the US to pay its dues to the UN. Throughout Bill Clinton's presidency, the US slipped further into arrears, making minimal stopgap payments to maintain its seat in the General Assembly. By 1999, the American debt stood at more than $1.6 billion, and the UN was in the grip of a serious financial crisis.[16] Although Clinton had pledged to remedy this in his occasional visits to the UN headquarters in New York City, he seemed content to accept the stigma of American indebtedness (perhaps distracted by his many other embarrassments) and reluctant to pressure Congress into a settlement.[17] In fact, some Congressional representatives even proposed backdating their claims for a reduction in US contributions, unilaterally reducing the monies outstanding to the UN. This prompted one dissenting (and lonely) US Senator to ask: 'If someone was your debtor, would you let them lay out conditions of repayment of monies they owed? What would you think if your debtor unilaterally demanded a change in the rate of assessments as a condition for past, due, and future payments?'[18]

Boutros-Ghali might reasonably wonder how the US view of the UN had changed so rapidly, from the lofty heights of Clinton's campaign rhetoric to a messy, unresolved battle over funding. Part of the answer lies in the frosty American response to Boutros-Ghali's efforts to strengthen and expand UN peacekeeping operations, a subject we will explore in more detail later in this chapter. On a fundamental level, however, the US remains ambivalent towards the idea of the UN. Policymakers are happy to bend the UN to their purposes, but reluctant to strengthen it lest it stand freely without

US support. The UN continues to be a powerful weapon in the US arsenal, against Saddam Hussein for example, but lacks the agency and autonomy to act independently in situations where the US is less interested. The recent funding crisis thus serves to remind the UN of its reliance (political and financial) on its largest contributor. At the grassroots level, this American ambivalence sustains those Congressional representatives who are reluctant to give American money to any kind of international organisation. Without a firm lead from President Clinton, Senators like Jesse Helms and Rod Grams have peddled their own brand of isolationism and pride in the moral authority of unilaterial US actions overseas. As Grams reminded a Senate committee on UN reform, 'I mean, the UN might have some problems with us, but we definitely have some problems with the UN.' By the end of the century, these 'problems' threatened not only the future of American-led multilateralism but the survival of the UN.[19]

'Slaying the monster': international law and American objections

As we have seen, the United Nations Security Council and General Assembly each has its own disadvantages in the resolution of disputes and the maintenance of international law. The General Assembly can pass resolutions in favour of an outcome or a wronged party, but can do little to intervene in a situation. The Security Council, meanwhile, can be hijacked by the interests of any one of its five permanent members, or derailed by their apathy. These weaknesses in the UN system have prompted countries to seek new mechanisms for the establishment and policing of international standards, and have given impetus to efforts to reform international law. In general, this effort to codify international standards presents a particular challenge to the US, since international law seeks to equalise the differences between nations and submit each of them to the same framework. The irony of recent US policy, then, has been the apparent willingness of President Clinton to support or even initiate changes in international law – only to dissent from final agreements when their practical implications for American foreign relations become clear. Clinton has been particularly attentive to the publicity and benefits which accrue from leading the international community; unfortunately, however, he has been embarrassed by the extent to which other countries have made good on their internationalist rhetoric, leaving the US behind.

To illustrate the difficult relationship between the US and this reinvigorated concept of international law, I want to offer two examples from Bill Clinton's presidency: the debate over a ban on landmines, and the creation of an International Criminal Court to prosecute human-rights abuses. In each case, the pattern was the same: Clinton expressed initial enthusiasm for the idea; subsequently viewed the speed and progress of negotiations with alarm; and finally refused to allow the United States to sign the agreement reached by virtually every other country. In this final stage, with the US isolated and even attempting to scuttle the accords reached by the rest of the world, we can see that the United States is as ready to defy the international community as any of the 'rogue states' it usually lambasts for doing so.

When Bill Clinton rose to address the United Nations General Assembly in September 1994, he was particularly excited by a new initiative which might spread from the US to all the members of the UN:

> And today, I am proposing a first step toward the eventual elimination of a less-visible, but still deadly threat: the world's 85 million anti-personnel land mines – one for every 50 people on the face of the earth.... Ridding the world of those often hidden weapons will help to save the lives of tens of thousands of men and women and innocent children in the years to come.[20]

Revelling in the applause for his proposal, Clinton could hardly have realised how speedily and sharply it would backfire. The facts of the case were straightforward: around 25,000 people each year were killed by landmines, and many more were horribly injured. Advocacy groups in the US and elsewhere had been pushing for a ban on their production and use, arguing that landmines were unusually cruel weapons which predominantly injured civilians, often years after they had been planted. Campaigners hoped that landmines might be consigned – along with mustard gas and exploding bullets – to that blacklist of armaments outlawed under international law. Clinton, looking to carry out a 'sacred mission' and 'to build a new world for our children', was happy to lead the charge.[21]

It is hard to assess how seriously Clinton had embraced the cause in 1994, since the international response to his proposal quickly wrong-footed the US government and ruined the president's original plan. In the first instance, Clinton hardly placed the issue on a fast track: the US submitted the landmine issue to the UN Conference on Disarmament, a body described glumly by the *Washington Post* as 'ponderous' and regarded by many countries as unlikely to achieve a ban.[22] As American officials began the slow process of convening the Conference, a group of states led by Canada broke away to start separate negotiations on a comprehensive agreement. By the summer of 1997, nearly one hundred countries had gravitated towards the Canadian position; but the US persisted in its own course. Finally, in August of that year, American negotiators joined the Canadian deliberations, hoping (even at this advanced stage) to push the talks towards US priorities and concerns.[23]

The other reason to doubt Clinton's 1994 commitment became clear at this time, as the various American objections to the draft treaty (to be signed in Ottawa, Canada) were made public. Although the US Department of Defense appeared nervous about the timetable for the phasing out of mines – even though the Ottawa treaty would allow nine years for this – the principal American objections concerned the Korean peninsula, and the need for US forces there to deploy anti-personnel mines to protect larger anti-tank mines.[24] The Korean exception was straightforward, if unconvincing. American military officials argued that the standoff between forces of North and South Korea could only be guaranteed by the extensive use of landmines, bluntly arguing that 37,000 US troops stationed in South Korea would be threatened by a universal landmine ban. As some experts pointed out, however, this was a disingenuous position for the US military to adopt. The overwhelming US advantage in military technology on the Korean peninsula hardly depended on these landmines, and the threat of American air power and even nuclear weapons made the Pentagon's arguments for landmines seem superfluous.[25]

The other American objection to the treaty concerned the anti-personnel mines which accompany anti-tank mines. The larger anti-tank weapons were exempted from the Ottawa treaty; but the US had designed its anti-tank mines to include a cluster of anti-personnel mines, a booby-trap to deter any soldiers from reaching the larger mines and trying to defuse them. The anti-tank mines are dropped from helicopters or planes, and the anti-personnel mines fan out around them, forming a network of explosive tripwires. If a soldier clips the wire, the mine sends a grenade flying towards his or her chest; this grenade subsequently explodes in lethal fragments.[26] Although these mines are labelled 'smart', meaning that they have a limited lifetime and are designed to self-destruct, the consequences of their failure to operate correctly (or of their self-destruction around any living thing) are just as dire as any 'dumb' mine. As such, anti-landmine campaigners, along with other governments committed to the Canadian negotiation track, were unimpressed with the US excuse for not signing. Even Tom Daschle, leader of Clinton's Democratic Party in the US Senate, criticised the president: 'It's pretty hard to justify going slow on something as heinous as this.'[27]

Sensing an imminent public-relations disaster, Clinton tried to mask the basic American refusal to sign the treaty. One arm of this strategy consisted of a semantic battle, waged by various Pentagon 'experts'. In September 1997, presidential spokesperson Michael McCurry introduced the White House press corps to Robert Bell, a National Security Council defence consultant, who tried to persuade a wary media that the anti-personnel mines which clustered around American anti-tank mines were not really anti-personnel mines at all:

> These explosive devices that protect our anti-tank mines are not anti-personnel landmines. They are not being banned ... because they are not anti-personnel landmines. These things are explosive devices just like the explosive devices that protect our allies' anti-tank mines. They are built into this munition. It's sealed at the factory. It's an integral unit.[28]

Bell's Pentagon handlers had given him a whole range of synonyms, clustered around the forbidden 'anti-personnel mine' and intended to ward off the curious reporters: the mines were 'anti-handling devices', 'little kinds of explosive devices', or just 'munitions'. At least one commentator made his way through this tangle of evasive language, asking drolly: 'When is an anti-personnel landmine no longer an anti-personnel landmine? When the President of the United States says so.'[29]

The other element of Clinton's rearguard action consisted of a promise to bring the US into compliance with the Ottawa treaty eventually: the president pledged to end the use of mines outside of the Korean peninsula in 2003, and to remove them from Korea as well by 2006. For various reasons, this promise sounded hollow. Clinton would leave office in January 2001, and he made no proposal for legislation which would guarantee the pledge after his retirement.[30] Still more worryingly, the commitment was premissed on the ability of the Pentagon to devise an (unspecified) 'alternative' to anti-personnel landmines which would confirm their obsolescence.[31] Not only had Clinton caved in to the military in 1997, he had tied the future of any landmine ban to the Pentagon's priorities and perspective. The first fruits of this trusteeship became evident in February 1999, as the Pentagon requested $50 million from Congress for a new landmine system. This new weapon was not an alternative to anti-personnel landmines, but a more efficient and deadly combination of anti-tank and anti-personnel mines. James Schear, the embarrassed Clinton administration official pushed out to announce the new mine to the press, admitted that 'it does not technically meet Ottawa standards', before announcing (with no apparent irony) that 'this system is a more humanitarian alternative to the existing suite of systems that we now have'. There was no shortage of observers to question the 'humanitarian' credentials of the new mine, and to marvel at the surrealism of relying on the Pentagon to come up with an alternative to landmines. Stephen Goose of Human Rights Watch wryly noted 'the very odd situation where the Pentagon is saying we are going to get to a ban on anti-personnel mines by producing a new anti-personnel mine system'.[32]

Bill Clinton visited Canada in November 1997, two weeks before the signing of the Ottawa treaty, and faced stiff questioning from the press about his failure to approve the agreement. As if reminding himself of how badly things had gone since 1994, he retorted that 'I was the first world leader at the United Nations to call for a total ban on landmine production and development.'[33] Three years later, the US had been left behind by the rest of the world, languishing in the company of Russia, China, Libya and other countries the US was wont to decry.[34] On one level, Clinton's failure was indicative of the reluctance of the US to uphold genuine international standards which might clip its wings, even in negligible ways. In practical terms, however, the American rejection of the treaty made it almost impossible for campaigners and national signatories to put pressure on Russia, China and other nations involved in the manufacture and distribution of mines. Clinton was correct to draw media attention to US de-mining operations throughout the world, and a ban on the export of US-made mines; but his neglect of the treaty standards created the space in which other nations could continue to make mines and sell them overseas.[35] By 1999, as the treaty went into effect, the US had little to offer save for a tentative promise to sign in 2006, itself conditional on a Pentagon which was busy designing new mines.[36] The anti-landmine agreement, hailed by the United Nations secretary-general Kofi Annan as 'an historic victory for the weak and vulnerable of our world', had succeeded not because of American actions, but in spite of them.[37]

The other major initiative in international law during the Clinton administration was the proposed International Criminal Court (ICC), a new United Nations body that would investigate and prosecute human-rights violations across national boundaries. Again, Clinton and his aides were caught off guard by the proposal. The US had given its support to international war-crimes tribunals following the genocide in Rwanda and ethnic cleansing in Bosnia, and was pleased with the progress of these ad hoc bodies. The Security Council had voted separately for the creation of each, and legal experts (as well as many concerned nations) wondered whether a formal, standing international court might be given responsibility for all such cases. This would obviate the need for a lengthy process of consultation and Security Council deliberation before action might be taken against war criminals, and might even deter such crimes from taking place.[38]

The Clinton administration appears to have been wrong-footed in the process of creating such a court, perhaps because US officials did not fully consider the pitfalls ahead.[39] In simple terms, the question of an ICC could be put in two very different ways. Following the Bosnian and Rwandan examples, one might argue for an institution which could implement international law under the guidance (and with the approval) of the Security Council. This would give each of the five major powers the opportunity to veto an investigation, and probably confine the court's activities to those 'rogue states' and weaker countries with little influence on the international stage. This would also avoid the embarrassing (and even hazardous) spectacle of an investigation by the court into, say, Boris Yeltsin's war in Chechnya, or Bill Clinton's prolonged assault on Iraq. The permanent members of the Security Council could work together to ensure that their own foreign adventures were largely beyond the reach of international law, and immune from the threat of prosecution.

The other model for an international court would be much more radical, circumventing the control of the Security Council and establishing independent means for the universal policing of international law. Judges from many different countries would staff the court, and consider cases brought by an independent prosecutor acting within the guidelines of existing laws such as the Hague Regulations and the Geneva Convention. The implied multilateralism of this proposal would be truly unprecedented: the stranglehold of the Security Council would finally be broken, and signatories would submit their citizens to a binding, consistent legal process. This would obviously present the greatest challenge to the Security Council's permanent members; and especially to the US, which has intervened overseas more often than any other country, but which has leaned on its power, influence and permanent member status to defend its actions.

The Clinton administration favoured the first version of the court: when the president told the UN General Assembly in 1997 that 'we should establish a permanent international court to prosecute the most serious violations of humanitarian law', the examples of Rwanda and Bosnia were firmly in his mind.[40] As with the landmine negotiations, however, the rest of the world could not be relied on to share Clinton's limited vision of the prospective court. The international debate quickly ran away from the US, as nations rushed to approve more radical plans for a sovereign, independent court.[41] To the alarm of American officials, the 'international community' had taken another one of their ideas seriously, and a more sweeping vision of the ICC was agreed upon at a conference in Rome in July 1998. David Scheffer, the chief American representative to the Rome conference, had argued in 1996 for the advantages of the court: 'In a civilized world's box of foreign policy tools, this will be a shiny new hammer to swing in the years ahead.' In the summer of 1998, however, Scheffer stood alone in opposition to this 'shiny new hammer', as virtually every other country signed the treaty which would create an ICC. Recalling Scheffer's metaphor and adding one of his own, former Bush administration official John Bolton mocked Scheffer's plight in testimony before a Congressional committee as the treaty was being signed: 'I think what happened is the administration took the genie out of the bottle and the genie took the hammer and broke their nose.' The US had been unable to argue for its much more limited version of the ICC, and was now isolated along with Iran, Iraq, Libya, China, Yemen and Israel in opposition to the Rome proposals.[42]

The debate over the court in the US was basically conducted between two camps. On the one hand, the supporters of the court argued that there was virtually no chance it would ever pass judgement on American citizens. Apart from the obvious threat of incurring the wrath of the US, ICC enquiries into the actions of Americans could also be curtailed by a US investigation of a possible crime, or overturned by a majority decision of the UN Security Council. These safeguards against prosecution had actually been added to the Rome treaty at the request of the US, in the (forlorn) hope that they might persuade the American delegation to sign. Arguing for the treaty on the grounds of this safety net, Michael Scharf, an American professor of international law, told Congress that

> The United States bullied its way into getting the US stamp on almost every single provision in the International Criminal Court statute. It really is a US statute with just a couple of exceptions, a couple of things that we did not get.[43]

Scharf and others urged Clinton and Congress to see the ICC as a 'US statute', and to disregard their fears that the agreement might substantially curtail American foreign policy. It is worth noting that this argument in favour of the ICC was not based on the idea that the US would submit its own citizens and conduct to the ICC's · scrutiny, but the likelihood that, in practice, Americans would be immune from its jurisdiction.[44]

The opposing camp was not persuaded by this line, and argued that the mere possibility of the US being investigated by the ICC should deter the United States from signing the agreement. Senator Rod Grams put the case bluntly: 'The US will not cede its sovereignty to an institution which claims to have the power to override the United States legal system and to pass judgement on our foreign policy actions.' Grams and others used the example of American soldiers on peacekeeping missions to suggest what was at stake: supposing honest and well-meaning US military personnel were involved in a 'friendly fire' incident, or an episode of 'collateral damage' (i.e. civilian casualties) when serving overseas?[45] The ICC, its American opponents argued, would submit these honest Americans to an alien and unpredictable jurisdiction. Lurking behind the sympathetic picture of the US military-as-victim was a darker fear: what if the ICC should indict US commanders, or even American politicians, for an invasion or the bombing of another country? John Bolton warned Congress that the court 'could well have a chilling effect on top decision-makers', suddenly held accountable for their actions beyond the shores of the United States.[46]

The most obvious observation on this internal American debate over the International Criminal Court is that neither the supporters nor the opponents of the ICC wanted to see US citizens subjected to international investigations or prosecution. This in itself is revealing of a myopia within the US policymaking establishment, most notably on the part of its more liberal members, who praised the idea of the court without following through its logic. The ICC's opponents, at least, were alive to the dangers of submitting the US to a genuinely equitable and multilateral international law. Jesse Helms, chair of the powerful Senate Foreign Relations Committee, promoted not isolationism but America's right to invade or bomb wherever it pleased as he put into words what the Clinton administration was too nervous to express:

> So, what this court proposes to do is this. It will sit in judgement of the national security policy of the United States. Now just imagine what would have happened if this court had been in place during the US invasion of Panama or the US invasion of Grenada or the United States' bombing of Tripoli. In none of these cases did the United States seek permission from the United Nations to defend our interest. So long as there is breath in me, the United States will never – and I repeat, never, never – allow its national security decisions to be judged by any international criminal court.[47]

Helms was right to suggest that the ICC posed this kind of danger; his colleague, Rod Grams, pointed out that the UN World Court, a kind of toothless predecessor to the ICC, had ordered the US to desist in its covert war against Nicaragua in 1984 and 1986, an injunction which the American government (headed by Ronald Reagan) swiftly dismissed.[48] Unless the US was proposing a major change in its foreign policy, it made little sense to sign on to a much stronger World Court, which might not only criticise US foreign policy but which might indict the secretary of defense or the secretary of state on their travels abroad.[49]

On 17 July 1998, the court was approved by an overwhelming majority of nations, leaving the US uncomfortably exposed alongside those countries it typically derided as 'rogue states'. Although 120 nations agreed to submit themselves to the most powerful and comprehensive international legal regime in human history, the United States remained on the sidelines. This tells us something important about the true state of the American relationship with the 'international community' – instead of leading the drive towards a single standard of humanitarian law, the US sought to exempt itself and to preserve its right to conduct and judge its own foreign policy, away from the standards agreed to by everyone else.[50]

This picture would be grim enough if the United States was simply left out of the treaty, unwilling to abide by its provisions. In fact, the imperatives of US policy, and the desire of American policy-makers to preserve their immunity, has pushed the US into confrontation with the ICC treaty itself. The Rome provisions allowed for the prosecution not only of the nationals of those countries which signed the treaty, but of anyone who commits a crime within the territory of a signatory. The Clinton administration feared that US citizens might still come under ICC jurisdiction if they were charged with a crime committed overseas, an anxiety made acute by the huge number of countries that had signed the founding agreement. Michael Scharf told a worried Foreign Relations Committee that:

> We are not alone in the world, and what other countries do does make a difference, contrary to what some people might wish or hope. The other countries in the world made it clear early on that there was going to be an international criminal court. There will be such a court and the US will have to deal with it.[51]

Current proposals for 'dealing with it' are ominous. Although Scharf's preferred method would involve diluting those provisions which might threaten US citizens, hardened opponents of the ICC in the US have adopted a more aggressive line. William Cohen, Clinton's secretary of defense, was painfully direct in his dealings with the German government over the Rome treaty: US troops would be withdrawn from NATO operations in Europe unless some kind of ICC exemption was granted to American forces.[52] The US was ready to put its substantial military power into the assault on the ICC, forcing other countries to dilute the Rome treaty or to give up their various security arrangements with the United States, some of which had been in place for decades. Senator Joseph Biden did not mince words in backing Cohen's threat: 'In my experience, spanning more than two decades on this committee, nothing gets the attention of our friends like discussing the status of forces agreements we have with them.'[53]

After the treaty signing, then, it was clear that the ICC was not only unwelcome to the US, but incompatible with the continued pursuit of US foreign policy. To the secretary-general of the UN, the ICC was 'a gift of hope to future generations, and a giant step forward in the march towards universal human rights and the rule of law.'[54] To Jesse Helms, however, the court was a 'monster – and it is our responsibility to slay it before it grows to devour us'.[55] Once more, the US stood outside the boundaries and rules agreed by virtually every other nation, even trying – through threats and coercion – to destroy the 'monster' of a genuinely multilateral commitment to global justice.

The examples of the anti-landmine campaign and the International Criminal Court demonstrate that the US has serious reservations about binding international laws, and is particularly reluctant to forgo the safety net of its Security Council veto in the reckoning of its international actions. What is surprising, perhaps, is the extent to which other countries have abandoned similar concerns over sovereignty and self-interest, and contributed fully to the creation of new international standards which are at least promising and perhaps profound in their implications for the future. American efforts to violate, undermine or destroy these standards are therefore of particular concern, and augur very badly for the century ahead of us. An international community without the United States will struggle to uphold human rights and the rule of law; an international community at odds with the US will find the task impossible.

'SAVING EVERY CHILD':
THE US AND INTERNATIONAL PEACEKEEPING

Although the US has always expressed a rhetorical commitment to the maintenance of peace and human rights throughout the world, the demise of the Soviet Union in 1991 appeared to clear the way for a much more active American foreign policy. After decades of proxy wars with the USSR, the US could now intervene, without Cold War distractions, to promote humanitarian values or political stability throughout the world. The logical instrument of this intervention was the United Nations, which might stand as a kind of guarantor of American actions and motives. In 1991, one of Boutros Boutros-Ghali's first tasks as secretary-general was to map out a plan for multilateral peacekeeping operations – which culminated in a report entitled *An Agenda for Peace*. Boutros-Ghali suggested that the UN develop its own capability to respond quickly and decisively to conflicts, even establishing a rapid-reaction force (made up of soldiers from the various member nations) to combat instability before it became uncontrollable. At the heart of these plans lay the idealistic hope that conflicts in the 1990s and beyond would be deterred or contained by the will of the international community. Since the world had been relieved of the burden of superpower rivalry, the UN might now be able to resolve disputes and defend the innocent on a consistent and equitable basis.[56]

Given its unrivalled power, the US would inevitably determine the fate of these ideals; the initial signs, moreover, were promising. In 1992, an American election year, Boutros-Ghali's plan appeared to enjoy the favour of both major political parties. George Bush had benefited from the UN's sanction of the US-led war with Iraq in 1991, and his personal success in that conflict had made him more sympathetic to the idea of (selective) multilateral action. Bush's presidential challenger, Bill Clinton, was even more supportive. Surrounded by advisers who spoke enthusiastically of the UN and the possibilities for a more settled international outlook, Clinton's campaign for the presidency stressed the benefits of a new US–UN partnership. When Clinton won the election, Boutros-Ghali's vision of a strengthened UN seemed closer to reality.[57] It would not be long, however, before Clinton's commitments were put to the test.

'Assertive multilateralism': intervention in Somalia, 1992–1993

After his defeat in the 1992 election, George Bush initiated a final foreign-policy action which came to haunt his successor. The collapse of government in Somalia in 1991 had unleashed fierce fighting between various groups of Somalis, and the resulting instability had brought the country to the brink of mass starvation. President Bush, exercising his powers for the last time, proposed a massive US relief force which would enter the country and secure the distribution of food and humanitarian relief. Presenting his offer to the UN, Bush obtained Security Council approval for a unified task force (UNITAF), comprising around 30,000 US Marines, to combat the impending famine. UNITAF reached Somalia on 9 December 1992, and immediately made headway with the delivery of food and medical supplies. The leaders of the various warring factions in Somalia were driven into the shadows by such an impressive show of strength, and many Somalis who had been threatened by starvation were saved.[58]

Bush left office in January 1993, bequeathing the enormous UN/US operation in Somalia to the new Clinton administration. Clinton's own calls for a more humanitarian and multilateral foreign policy appeared to have been answered even by his predecessor, and the Clinton team quickly set out to define their approach to international peacekeeping and humanitarian actions. Although Clinton's secretary of state, Warren Christopher, was responsible for the execution of foreign policy, the intellectual drive behind the administration's new ideas came from Anthony Lake, Clinton's national security adviser, and Madeleine Albright, the new US ambassador to the UN. Albright frequently used the phrase 'assertive multilateralism' to describe new American thinking on foreign affairs. The US would not stand idle as conflicts raged around the world, nor would the American government resort unilaterally to its military and political power if the UN might act instead. In the summer of 1993, Albright and Lake drafted Presidential Review Directive 13 (PRD-13), a policy proposal which pledged American troops to UN operations, a first step towards the implementation of 'assertive multilateralism'. The new president was apparently eager to consolidate his ideas and to make good on his promises to the UN.[59]

The US/UN mission in Somalia, however, would quickly unravel these policy strands, exposing an American reluctance and apathy which had always been lurking behind the new Clinton rhetoric. When George Bush initially dispatched troops to Somalia, Boutros Boutros-Ghali had made it clear that long-term stability would only be guaranteed by engagement with Somalia's political scene, or by a concerted effort to disarm the various Somali factions.[60] Despite the overwhelming American force, however, Bush was adamant in his refusal to use the US military to confiscate the caches of arms stored by the warring factions. Since the US had supplied many of these weapons to the former Somali regime in the 1980s, the American government was well placed to understand the dangers they posed to humanitarian and political stability; however, neither Bush nor Clinton showed an interest in using the substantial American military presence to create a climate for meaningful political engagement.[61]

This raised the question of what American troops were doing in Somalia in the first place. Bush had limited the involvement of the US task force to a six-month tour of duty, and Clinton had continued Bush's policy of minimising any US strategy of peace enforcement. When the bulk of US troops left Somalia in May 1993, therefore, the fate of the UN mission (now renamed UNOSOM) was seriously in doubt.[62] The Somali factions retained all of their weapons, and the dwindling number of US troops (complemented by UN soldiers and personnel) would find it harder to maintain the humanitarian effort, still less to preserve social stability. The American intervention had saved many Somalis from the immediate threat of famine, but had done very little to underpin the political development of the country. The US military, even in this UN-sanctioned mission, had always been under American command, and had not heeded the UN calls for a major push towards disarmament.[63]

The other option for an American force was to pursue political negotiations with the various factional leaders, and to try to achieve through diplomacy and mediation what the US was not prepared to seek through military force. However, the new UN force proved no more willing to engage in this task than its predecessor; and since American troops still comprised the bulk of the offensive force in Somalia, the UN was poorly positioned to demand a change in American policy. As UNITAF gave way to UNOSOM in the summer of 1993, Boutros-Ghali effectively acknowledged that the US would control the destiny of Somalia by appointing an American admiral, Jonathan Howe, to head the UNOSOM mission. Despite the UN mandate, and Boutros-Ghali's own views on the need for disarmament, the effort in Somalia was now divided into two elements which were either ineffective or unresponsive to the UN: an overwhelmingly American military force, in which US troops answered to their own chain of command and formulated their own strategy, and a broader UN operation, entirely dependent on US forces and, in any case, directed by an American admiral. Given the later efforts of American politicians to present Somalia as a UN-led situation, it is worth noting that operational control and strategic planning rested wholly in the hands of US personnel.[64]

Faced with a choice between disarmament and political engagement in Somalia, the American government and commanders on the ground opted for a disastrous mixture of the two. Instead of disarming all the various factions, or engaging their leaders in dialogue, American officials in Washington (and commanders on the ground) became fixated on Mohammed Farrah Aideed, head of the Habir Gedir subclan. Aideed was certainly no friend of the UN, and had been accused of the murder of twenty-four Pakistani peacekeepers after a UNOSOM raid in June.[65] However, the decision to direct US military action against Aideed alone had the dangerous consequences of involving UNOSOM as a party to the conflict, implicitly allied with Aideed's rivals, and of destroying the efforts to negotiate a peaceful accord between the Somali factions.[66] Although the Pakistani deaths aroused little media interest in the US, the Clinton administration and the American Congress took note of the escalation in the UNOSOM mission, and received cogent warnings that this escalation would end in disaster. Frank Crigler, the former American ambassador to Somalia, testified in July 1993 before a House of Representatives committee that, after the initial humanitarian success of the US operation, 'we are turning triumph into tragedy, applying brute military force to a situation that calls for quiet diplomacy, patient mediation, steadiness and understanding.'[67]

If such remarks had minimal impact on Washington, they had no effect whatsoever in Mogadishu, the Somali capital, where UN forces waged an increasingly nasty battle to track down and apprehend Aideed, now routinely described as a 'warlord' by the US government. Even if one had recognised that goal as desirable, however, it was hard to see how the reduced US troop numbers in UNOSOM could achieve it. Caught between a desire to engage in Somalia and an eagerness to bring the troops home, the Clinton administration had dramatically reduced its contingent in May, and then instructed a small military force to carry out a much more aggressive role. Frank Crigler noted in July that the new policy 'has cast US combat troops in the ugly role of airborne bullies whose aim is to force peace on the Somalis at gunpoint'. The common understandings of peacekeeping (monitoring an existing agreement) and peacemaking (encouraging the conditions for stability and a political agreement) seemed alien to this new situation. The United States had declared war on Aideed, even bringing into Somalia a small unit of crack commando troops to ensure his arrest or elimination.[68]

The American public could be forgiven, during the summer and autumn of 1993, for thinking that the US military was keeping the peace in Somalia; but, in fact, the reconfiguration (and militarisation) of the UNOSOM mission was hardening suspicions between Americans and the Somali people they had come to help. Armed raids on downtown buildings, the scaling back of humanitarian efforts, and the remorseless drone of low-flying helicopters helped many Somalis to redefine the US/UN effort as an invasion rather than a relief operation.[69] Meanwhile, American soldiers had come to describe Mogadishu as 'Dodge City', as Indian country filled with 'Skinnies' and 'Sammies'. The overwhelmingly white company of US Rangers which undertook the bulk of offensive operations seemed especially ill-suited for the subtleties of a peacekeeping mission, disastrously inclined to see the Somalia intervention in black-and-white terms.[70]

The 'war on Aideed' came to a bloody end on 3 October 1993, as

US Rangers and Delta Force commandos became pinned down in a firefight in central Mogadishu after yet another raid on Aideed's followers. The soldiers came up against concerted resistance not only from Aideed's lieutenants, but from women and even children, who, in some cases, returned the American fire. US forces had been largely insulated from the full impact of deteriorating relations with Mogadishu's residents, buzzing over the city in their helicopters and keeping out of serious trouble. On 3 October, American soldiers confronted the true extent of local anger, even hatred at the mutation of the UNOSOM mission. Before the battle was done, eighteen Americans died on the streets of the city; hundreds, perhaps more than a thousand Somalis were killed by the retreating American forces. The Somali situation had come full circle, with the 'peacekeepers' now engaged in an indiscriminate shooting match with the Somali population. By any account, the US mission in Somalia had failed.[71]

The working out of this failure was to have a profound effect on the course of US foreign policy. The American public was understandably shocked to learn of the deaths of American soldiers on a UN mission to keep the peace in a distant country: urgent questions – What were they doing there? How could this happen? – were directed at a Clinton administration which was already particularly sensitive to the ebb and flow of public approval.[72] The underlying causes of the disaster were readily identifiable: the massive reduction in the size of the US force in May 1993; the simultaneous American move to offensive operations against Aideed; the initial neglect of disarmament efforts, and the later disregard for political progress in negotiations among the faction leaders.

A simple admission of these facts by the American government was complicated, however, by the knowledge that they might embarrass the administration. Madeleine Albright had heralded this new era of US–UN relations, and was personally identified with the 'assertive multilateralism' that had brought the US to Somalia; American politicians and military chiefs, meanwhile, had ensured a tight American control over UNOSOM, and would be particularly vulnerable to charges of mismanagement or poor planning. In the days after the raid, high-level Clinton officials admitted that the United States had made mistakes. Warren Christopher, secretary of state, conceded in an interview that 'we focused very heavily on the military track and we lost focus on the political track'.[73] Given time to consider how best to spin the failed mission to an angry American public, however, the same officials soon began to shift the blame to the UN. Although the US had led the efforts against Aideed, and had escalated American military engagement, Bill Clinton began to imply that the UN was responsible for this fatal policy error. In speeches and interviews, Clinton thundered that in future operations US troops would be 'under American command', as if that had not been the case in Somalia; and suggested that American forces remaining in Mogadishu would rediscover their humanitarian mission in spite of the UN vendetta against Aideed.[74]

Somewhere behind these immediate events was PRD-13, still under consideration by Clinton and his advisers but now influenced by the debacle in Somalia. As Clinton prepared to bring home the remaining US forces by March 1994, leaving the UN to deal with the continuing wreckage of civil society in Somalia, Christopher, Albright and Lake revamped PRD-13 in accordance with recent events. Although the American participation in UNOSOM offered an excellent example of how not to run a peacekeeping operation, Clinton's team drew the lesson from Somalia that the US should not undertake peacekeeping in the first place. Somalia was interpreted not as a model of a flawed intervention, but as the justification for a new international apathy from the US government. This was to have dire consequences in 1994, when the American contraction of 'Somalia syndrome' contributed to the success of genocidal murder in Rwanda.[75]

'A new realism': genocide in Rwanda, 1994

The Clinton administration's original announcement of PRD-13 in early 1993 had attracted attention from Congress and the US media, and Washington buzzed with anticipation of the finished policy directive even as the administration's deliberations stretched into 1994. After Somalia, moreover, observers were still more interested to learn the fate of Albright's 'assertive multilateralism', and to see whether the events of October 1993 would affect the hopeful rhetoric of earlier policy statements. On 5 May 1994, the finished version of

PRD-13, the newly renamed Presidential Decision Directive 25 (PDD-25), was finally unveiled. Anthony Lake briefed the press on the lengthy process of deliberation that had led to the new policy, and set up the context of international political instability alongside America's humanitarian impulse:

> When I wake up every morning and look at the headlines and stories and the images on television of these conflicts, I want to work to end every conflict. I want to work to save every child out there. And I know the president does, and I know the American people do.

With Somalia firmly in view, however, Lake invoked 'the reality that we cannot often solve other people's problems: we can never build their nations for them'. PDD-25, therefore, was an American effort to ask 'hard questions' about peacekeeping, and to make 'hard choices about where and when the international community can get involved'.[76]

What this amounted to was not only a shift in American policy – the end of 'assertive multilateralism', for one thing – but a serious undermining of the more flexible and responsive UN envisaged by Boutros Boutros-Ghali and, back in 1992, by Clinton himself. According to the arrangements for funding UN peacekeeping operations, the US was assessed around 30 per cent of the total cost. PDD-25 suggested that the US would seek to deter UN missions which were too expensive, asking 'hard questions' and, presumably, forcing the UN to give hard answers to various calls for assistance from the victims of civil conflict and humanitarian disaster.[77] Clinton's initial commitment to multilateralism had two elements: the US would seek its own foreign-policy goals through the UN framework, and would contribute its share to UN humanitarian and peacekeeping missions even beyond the narrow confines of American self-interest. PDD-25 substantially altered this emphasis. Anthony Lake reasserted the US right to act unilaterally on the international stage in the pursuit of its own interests, even as he doubted the viability of collective action and peacekeeping efforts.[78] The earlier proposals for a UN standby military force were rejected outright, and Madeleine Albright's relationship with Boutros Boutros-Ghali deteriorated markedly. The problem was not just the new US reluctance to participate in UN operations, but the active efforts of Albright and the Clinton administration to prevent the UN from intervention in areas outside a US sphere of interest. Noting Boutros-Ghali's scepticism at the shift in American policy, Albright offered a frank assessment of the balance of power between the US and UN: 'He cannot veto US policy. That is ridiculous.'[79]

Naturally, the US retained the right and the inclination to veto UN initiatives, and Clinton administration officials soon had an opportunity to demonstrate what Albright called 'a new realism' in peacekeeping deployment.[80] As the text of PDD-25 was finalised in April 1994, conflict broke out in the central African nation of Rwanda.[81] A plane carrying the Rwandan president was shot down over Kigali, Rwanda's capital, on 6 April and triggered massive violence.[82] The Rwandan population was divided along ethnic lines into Hutus (who made up the majority of the population) and Tutsis, and a vocal (and extremist) Hutu leadership had spent the early months of 1994 laying the ground for widespread murder of Tutsis. UN forces based in Rwanda, who had been monitoring an earlier political agreement, were aware of the Hutu plans and sent messages to the head of UN peacekeeping in New York and to the permanent members of the Security Council conveying their alarm at developments. These messages were dispatched well before the plane crash and the subsequent killing spree. The commander of the UN Assistance Mission in Rwanda (UNAMIR), Romeo Dallaire, sought permission to confiscate caches of arms, and requested reinforcement of his 2,700 peacekeeping troops. Although the request unquestionably reached the UN and the US, no response was forthcoming; and Dallaire's small contingent was left alone to deal with the spiralling murder in April.[83]

Once the genocide had begun, Dallaire's forces, along with international aid agencies and other observers, were able quickly to clarify the nature of the fighting in Rwanda. Although an army of Tutsis (the Rwandan Patriotic Front, or RPF) did begin to fight government (Hutu) troops after 6 April, the vast majority of the killing was taking place in areas under Hutu control, where there was no fighting whatsoever. Hutu extremists had swiftly murdered Hutu moderates in the wake of the plane crash, eager to consolidate their own power and to close off any route of reconciliation; advocates of 'Hutu Power' then incited gangs of Hutus to undertake the mass slaughter of Tutsis.

These killings took place away from the armed skirmishes between the RPF and Hutu government forces, and were usually accomplished in sickeningly low-tech fashion: Tutsis were killed with small arms fire or, more typically, were hacked to death with machetes.[84]

Even after taking stock of the scale of the killing, the UNAMIR forces were convinced that they could stop the genocide with only modest reinforcement – Romeo Dallaire pledged to restore order with only 5,000 troops, cutting off the Hutu Power radio network and disarming the machete-wielding gangs.[85] The UN Security Council, however, was inclined to withdraw UNAMIR altogether. The murder of ten Belgian troops on the first day of the massacre had confirmed Belgium in its desire to withdraw, and no other country was willing or able to take its place. Boutros Boutros-Ghali pleaded with Security Council members to offer the necessary reinforcement, and finally managed to keep at least a token force of 500 men in Rwanda, over the objections of the US.[86] These 500 UN troops managed to protect around 30,000 Tutsis at various locations around the Rwandan capital, Kigali – a figure which suggests both the effectiveness of those peacekeepers that remained, and the many more lives that would have been saved had the international community been willing to reinforce UNAMIR and to stop the genocide.[87]

From an American perspective, of course, there was little at stake in Rwanda. According to PDD-25, the relevance of a crisis to US interests, and the likely cost of a peacekeeping operation, had to be considered carefully before any 'hard choices' were made. The only American motive for intervention in Rwanda would be humanitarian, the desire (as Anthony Lake had put it) to 'save every child'. The Somalia experience, however, had largely evaporated the reservoir of American goodwill, and Clinton officials did their best to parry media calls for a US relief effort.[88] As early as 11 April, the State Department had deferred the issue to the UN; by the end of April, when UNAMIR forces had confirmed the dimensions and the direction of the genocide beyond any doubt, State Department officials tried to blur the picture by pointing to 'violence which is going on among different groups and factions'.[89] Although the UN forces had warned of the mass slaughter of Tutsis in advance, and now stood witness to the one-sidedness of the killings, American spokespeople still denied the crucial facts: 'It's not one simple perpetrator against another', one State Department official told a curious press corps.[90]

Although the US correctly perceived that it had little interest in Rwanda, it had still to evade its responsibilities in international law to put down an episode of mass slaughter. According to the 1948 Convention Against Genocide, to which the US is a signatory, contracting parties 'confirm that genocide is a crime under international law which they undertake to prevent and to punish'.[91] This simple clause should have forced the US (and every other signatory) to intervene in Rwanda even if its immediate interests were not affected. Instead, the Clinton administration pursued a two-track strategy to downplay the need for American involvement.[92] First, administration officials displayed great reluctance to use the word 'genocide', often employing elaborate euphemisms for the mass killing to avoid any responsibility in international law for failing 'to prevent' these crimes.[93] Second, Clinton officials tried to dilute the 1948 Convention by suggesting that it merely enabled an international response in cases of genocide, and did not compel any signatory to act.[94] If the first strategy betrayed the immediate victims in Rwanda, the second implied a more profound disregard for those threatened by the ultimate crime in international law. It seemed that the Clinton administration was so committed to PDD-25, and its new policy of retreating from peacekeeping responsibilities, that it was content to allow even genocide to take place without an American response. As Madeleine Albright proudly declared to a House of Representatives committee on 17 May, as the killings continued in Rwanda: 'We cannot be made to go along with any mission that is not in our interests.'[95]

Albright, who had seemed previously to be the administration's biggest supporter of UN operations, acted as Clinton's chief 'realist' on the subject of Rwanda. As Boutros-Ghali and UNAMIR prodded the Security Council into some form of response, Albright threatened to veto proposals for reinforcing the UNAMIR troops on the grounds that the UN mission was too vague and open-ended.[96] For two weeks in May, Albright effectively delayed the UN plan for 5,500 new troops to be dispatched immediately; on 17 May, she argued that 'sending a UN force into the maelstrom of Rwanda without a sound plan of operations would be folly', and killed the proposal for a major strengthening of Dallaire's forces.[97] Employing the language of PDD-25, inflected with the sentimentalism of Clinton himself, Albright patiently explained the situation to a sceptical interviewer:

> Well, the issue here, Margaret, is everybody wants to help in Rwanda. It's a horrendous situation. We know that hundreds of thousands of people have been killed or displaced, and there is a massive desire to do something. However, we felt that it was very important to act responsibly and not make hollow promises. It didn't do anybody any good to talk about sending in a force for which there were no answers yet as to what the force would do, what we call 'concept of operations'.

Albright delivered this line even though UNAMIR forces had had a 'concept of operations' since January, and had repeated their willingness to stop the genocide in April. In the US, Albright's hesitation was not universally well received, and many commentators questioned her effort to avoid any engagement in Rwanda. Even fellow Democrats were appalled; interviewed on the same television news programme as Albright, Congressman Donald Payne angrily rejected her justification for inaction: 'You would think we were some third-rate country that was confused about what to do. I am shocked and disappointed at the statement I just heard.'[98]

The persistent American efforts to evade any responsibility in Rwanda confirmed the demise of multilateralism, as well as a collapse in the fortunes of the UN. Boutros Boutros-Ghali, when presented with further US delays at the end of May, finally lost patience and denounced the Rwandan effort as 'a scandal':

> All of us are responsible for this failure. It is a genocide which has been committed. More than 200,000 have been killed, and ... the international community is still discussing what ought to be done.[99]

As May turned to June, a pledge by the Organisation for African Unity to provide troops for a Rwanda mission was delayed by the reluctance of the US to make available armoured vehicles for these troops. In spite of its debts to the UN, the American govenment had decided to charge for the rental of these vehicles, further postponing the arrival of a force which might contain the killings.[100] Only in July was the UNAMIR presence in Rwanda substantially strengthened. In the one hundred days of US-led inaction, at least 500,000 people had been shot or hacked to death.[101]

The genocide in Rwanda exposed the fatal consequences of the new American peacekeeping policy, and confirmed the gulf between the avowed responsibilities of the international community and the willingness of nations to make good on their commitments. The Clinton administration had announced in 1993 its support for 'assertive multilateralism'; a year later, after the mistakes in Somalia and killings in Rwanda, this policy had been abandoned. Reluctant to give up its central role in world affairs but unwilling to commit troops and money for UN operations, the US atrophied the cause of peacekeeping just as the situation in Rwanda required a flexible and dynamic response. Although the killings of early April might still have taken place, prompt reinforcement of the UNAMIR force would surely have saved thousands, perhaps hundreds of thousands of lives. Instead, American officials did everything in their power to avoid committing American soldiers to the effort, and stymied attempts to send any kind of force on the grounds that the US might have to pay for part of it. While this enabled Madeleine Albright to boast to Congress of a 'new realism' in American foreign policy, it represented a nadir in US commitments to human rights and the rule of law. The US led the international community away from recognising genocide in Rwanda, averting its gaze until the killings had run their course.[102]

THE US AND THE UN:
THE END OF MULTILATERALISM

Unsurprisingly, the new American shift away from multilateralism put great strain on the US–UN relationship and forced UN officials to re-evaluate their earlier optimism about the Clinton administration. The growth of UN peacekeeping operations in 1992 and 1993 had taken place with US approval; by 1994, as PDD-25 was unveiled, the US had decided to change course. In Congressional testimony of March 1995, Madeleine Albright elaborated on the new US–UN relationship:

Because we have a veto, we can block any peace operation that is not consistent with our interests. Because we believe UN peacekeeping grew

too fast in 1992 and 1993, we have adopted rigorous guidelines for decid-
ing when a new operation should begin. As a result, there are fewer UN
peacekeepers today than in almost two years.[103]

The original goal of the Clinton administration had been reversed:
instead of additional UN operations and more peacekeepers, Albright
was hailing a reduction in the numbers as a success for the US. From
the perspective of other countries, and especially the UN, this American retreat was troubling and problematic. Albright was publicly committing the US to veto any UN operations 'not consistent with our
interests', a phrase that seemed clearly to indicate the rejection of
multilateralism and humanitarian principles, which would motivate
many peacekeeping missions. If the US was no longer interested in
multilateralism, how could the UN function as anything other than
an instrument of American foreign policy?

This question haunted high-level UN officials, and especially
Boutros Boutros-Ghali, after 1994. Boutros-Ghali's ambitious programme to reform the UN, and to re-establish its relevance, had
been built on the very commitments which Clinton and Albright
had now rescinded. As a result, the UN's relationship with the US
entered a tailspin. This became particularly evident in the response of
the international community to the break-up of the former Yugoslavia. As with Somalia, the American response to the crisis was
initially complicated by the transition from George Bush's presidency
to the Clinton administration. Clinton had campaigned against Bush
in 1992 on a platform of greater assertiveness in foreign affairs, and
had committed the US to supporting UN efforts to broker peace in
Bosnia. By early 1993, however, the intensity of the fighting and
Clinton's reluctance to commit ground troops had complicated US–
UN relations. Bosnian Serb attacks on Sarajevo and other towns put
pressure on Clinton to do something to alleviate the situation; the
new administration's fear of American casualties kept this impulse in
check, however. European nations had dispatched thousands of troops
to Bosnia to serve under UN command, but the US remained aloof
from this effort. Understandably, this created serious tensions over
the direction of the UN's operation in Bosnia.[104]

For most of its first two years in office, the Clinton administration showed little interest in solving the Bosnian problem. Moreover,
the limited engagement of the US hampered the multilateral attempts

to ameliorate the situation. Clinton rejected the first major peace plan, brokered by former American secretary of state Cyrus Vance in February 1993, but finally backed an entirely American negotiation track in its drafting of a similar agreement two-and-a-half years (and tens of thousands of lives) later.[105] Meanwhile, the American response to Serb military threats was to promise NATO air strikes rather than the deployment of American ground forces. The eagerness of the US to employ air power became a major source of disagreement between the Clinton administration and the UN, since the UN was responsible for the safety of those ground troops which served under its authority. For Clinton, air strikes were a relatively safe and cheap way of looking tough on Bosnia; for the UN troops deployed on the ground, these air attacks represented a physical danger and increased the likelihood that they would be taken hostage by better-armed Serbs.[106]

The troubles of the UN forces in Bosnia offered an example of what it would take to accomplish a 'peace enforcement' mission: the 20,000 or so UN troops were hard-pressed to maintain humanitarian relief to the suffering, and tried to concentrate the threatened civilian population in several large towns which were designated UN 'safe havens'. By 1995, however, these 'havens' were coming under concerted attack from advancing Bosnian Serbs. A larger international force would have found the task easier, but would have required more troop contributions and more funding from UN member states; the US, the richest and most heavily armed nation in the world, was ready to commit neither.[107] Only in the summer of 1995, after the disastrous collapse of one of the 'safe havens', Srebrenica, did the American policy become untenable. It was obvious that the UN forces lacked the numbers or the weapons to do an effective job, and that only the US was in a position to turn the situation around; and so the Clinton administration had to choose between simply abandoning Bosnia or making a firm commitment. This was the environment in which the UN troops were withdrawn, NATO air strikes were carried out, and the US pledged ground troops to enforce a political agreement.[108]

Once again in Bosnia, the UN was maligned for its role, especially after the humiliating (and bloody) fall of Srebrenica to the Bosnian Serbs. The American media had already castigated Boutros-Ghali for his weakness in failing to support US calls for air strikes, even though the UN had primary concern for the safety of its forces on the ground.[109] In the autumn of 1995, as if to punish Boutros-Ghali and his colleagues, the US excluded the UN from the diplomatic process and began to broker peace talks entirely on its own authority. This seemed to confirm the sense of UN officials that they had been duped by the US all along. Boutros Boutros-Ghali wrote in his memoirs that 'the UN had been used to "internationalize" the United States' and NATO's desire to avoid the war in Bosnia.' In Boutros-Ghali's view, the weak UN troops had been forced to create a peace while the better-armed and more numerous NATO troops eventually assumed a less hazardous peacekeeping role:

> By pushing the UN to the fore yet depriving it of the tools it needed and using it as a scapegoat, the United States and the West bought time, but at an unwarranted cost. The harm done to the mangled and nearly bankrupt United Nations would not be easily reversed, nor would the damage done to key principles of international behavior: no acquisition of territory by force; no genocide; and guarantees of integrity and existence of UN member states.

For Boutros-Ghali, the Bosnian war had claimed two main victims: 'the people of this unfortunate land, and the United Nations, charged with failing to find a solution to the catastrophe'.[110]

The UN emerged from the Bosnian war with a crippling budget deficit of more than $3 billion; the US, meanwhile, enjoyed a diplomatic triumph as it shepherded the various Balkan parties towards an agreement.[111] In Bosnia, a renewed Croatian military offensive had scaled back the territorial gains of the Serbs, and the UN negotiators effectively backed these offensives with a view towards an eventual settlement. The presidents of Bosnia-Herzegovina, Croatia and Serbia were flown to the US to hammer out the peace deal, pressured by American negotiators to stay on American soil until an agreement was signed. Although these negotiations, conducted at an air-force base in Dayton, Ohio, were co-chaired by the European Union and Russia, there was little doubt that they proceeded on an overwhelmingly American agenda. Confirming that the US sought no outside interference in the peacemaking process, the leader of the US team at Dayton, Richard Holbrooke, agreed with Madeleine Albright that a UN presence in the talks 'would further complicate them'; and so the UN representative was excluded.[112]

The result of these talks, the Dayton Agreement, was a precarious pledge to preserve the integrity of Bosnia even as the country was divided into a Serb and a Muslim–Croat sector. Under the Vance–Owen plan of 1993, which the US had opposed, the Serbs had been given 43 per cent of Bosnian territory, scattered in small regions within a single, unified state; the Dayton plan gave 49 per cent of the territory to Serbs, and concentrated these holdings in one bloc, contiguous with Serbia. Given the tenuous nature of the Muslim–Croat 'Federation' within Bosnia, the US-brokered plan appeared to have laid the ground for the eventual partition of the new country between Serbia and Croatia, an ambition of Serb and Croat leaders since the war's first days. That this outcome could be considered a success, even a diplomatic triumph, says much about the discrediting of the UN and the American domination of the Dayton proceedings. The speed of the conference attracted the attention (and admiration) of the assembled media, whilst the agonisingly slow US reaction to the crisis since 1991 had fallen from view.[113]

Two further consequences of the Bosnian example are worth noting. First, the US affirmed its right not only to act unilaterally but also to assume control over the direction of an international peace process. In arguing for air strikes against the Bosnian Serbs, and then managing the Dayton agreement, the US appeared to be pressing for a greater role in international affairs. In reality, the US had been forced into this position by the weight of public opinion and the grim defeat of the overstretched UN forces inside Bosnia. Behind the tough talking of Holbrooke and Albright lay very little political or military will to defend the rights and values of international law, which may explain why the eventual Dayton agreement threatened to compromise the territorial integrity of Bosnia-Herzegovina. It was obvious, however, that an agreement could not be reached without US approval, even though American officials had tried to keep out of the war for three years. That the Dayton agreement was brokered by the US in spite of American apathy prompted much pride in the US at the 'indispensable' American role in world affairs; few people commented on the flip side of this truism, that the international community had become too weak to assert itself without major American involvement.[114]

The second consequence of the Bosnian crisis was that the US effectively declared war on the UN, and particularly on its secretary-general. By late 1994, Boutros-Ghali's candour in condemning the international community over Rwanda had already prompted some American commentators to question his chances of a second term as secretary-general, a privilege extended to each of his predecessors in the job.[115] His reluctance to sanction US air strikes against Bosnian Serbs in 1995, given the danger of such strikes to UN personnel on the ground, enraged American government officials who were used to getting their own way with the UN bureaucracy. Unsurprisingly, Boutros-Ghali's strong and independent view of the UN had won him many supporters outside of the US; but an American veto would end his chances of re-election to a second term when the issue came before the Security Council in November 1996. The US desire to be rid of Boutros Boutros-Ghali translated into a bizarre campaign to remove him from the running, with American tactics ranging from flattery (Boutros-Ghali would retire with the title 'Secretary-General Emeritus', promised Madeleine Albright and her unlikely messenger to Boutros-Ghali, Barbara Walters) to threats (nations eager to vote for re-election were asked if they would rather have Boutros-Ghali or Clinton as their friend). As the US became more explicit in its suggestions that it would withdraw from the UN if Boutros-Ghali was reappointed, it was apparent that the overwhelming international support for the secretary-general would weigh less than the American view. On 18 November 1996, the Security Council voted 14 to 1 for the appointment of Boutros-Ghali to a second term. The single US veto meant that the vote would not carry, and a round of behind-the-scenes arguments followed, in which the US offered a list of alternative candidates that it would be prepared to accept. Although the international community was united in its condemnation of US tactics, the American veto could not be revoked by any measure of international disapproval. After three weeks of US obstinacy, then, the other nations reversed their decision for Boutros-Ghali, and approved the US-favoured candidate, Kofi Annan.[116]

If Boutros-Ghali's removal gave some indication of the drift of the US–UN relationship, the appointment of his successor was also

not without significance. Kofi Annan had been in charge of UN
peacekeeping operations under Boutros-Ghali, but appeared much
more sympathetic to the US view of limited engagement than to his
boss's vision. Moreover, he had given UN approval for NATO air
strikes in Bosnia in the summer of 1995, endearing himself to those
American officials who had grown frustrated with Boutros-Ghali's
obstinacy. Annan had been, in the words of Richard Holbrooke, 'the
UN official in whom we had the greatest confidence', a fact that
suggested to other UN employees that loyalty to the US might bring
grand rewards. By forcing the other Security Council members to
choose Annan, the Clinton administration effectively domesticated
one of the most important international posts; in December 1996, in
the wake of Clinton's re-election to the presidency, the *New York
Times* even described Annan as 'another key appointment' for
Clinton's second term, as if the UN were a division of the US
government.[117]

Meanwhile, Madeleine Albright's campaign to oust Boutros-Ghali
was also rewarded. In spite of her volte-face on 'assertive multilateralism' in 1994, the tragic US policies toward Somalia and Rwanda, and
the disastrous fate of the UN's peacekeeping mission in Bosnia,
Albright was named secretary of state just as Boutros-Ghali was dismissed. The impression that Clinton favoured those who could overcome or bypass the UN was confirmed by the July 1999 appointment
of Richard Holbrooke, the impresario of Dayton, to Albright's old
job as American ambassador to the UN. Albright had led the charge
against the UN after Somalia; Holbrooke helped Albright to exclude
the UN from any role in the Bosnian peace negotiations. Each had
contributed to the US rejection of multilateralism and collective
responsibility under the Clinton administration, and each was rewarded for their services with promotion to higher office.

In his account of the Dayton negotiations, Richard Holbrooke recalled the American decision to remove Boutros-Ghali with sadness,
but without regret:

> Although the American campaign against Boutros-Ghali, in which all our
> key allies opposed us, was long and difficult – especially for Albright, who
> bore heavy and unjust criticism for her role – the decision was correct,
> and may well have saved America's role in the United Nations.[118]

Holbrooke did not go on to explain what he meant by this, an unfortunate omission since the question of America's role in the UN seems as vexed as ever. Although Kofi Annan initially enjoyed better relations with the Clinton administration than Boutros-Ghali, the US arrears in UN contributions actually worsened during Clinton's second term. Moreover, Annan himself committed some of the same mistakes as his predecessor, pursuing his own line on some issues and suggesting that all military actions throughout the world should be based on UN authority. This did not endear him to the Clinton administration or to the American Congress, and more than $1.6 billion dollars in American debt to the UN had amassed by the century's end. It would be hard to overstate the extent of US hostility to the UN, especially on the part of those lawmakers in Congress who are responsible for the appropriation and delivery of the American contribution to the UN's administrative and peacekeeping funds. Even the unexpected budget surplus in the US in the late 1990s was diverted from payment of outstanding American debts to the United Nations; the House of Representatives and the Senate voted to approve nearly $800 billion in tax cuts in 1999, even though the settlement of the UN debt would represent only a fraction of this sum.[119] The eventual decision of the US Congress in November 1999 to pay around $1 billion in dues to the UN, across four years and in return for a reduction in the US assessment of UN upkeep, merely confirmed the diminished stature of the United Nations in the US Congress: American legislators voted to settle part of their debt mainly to avoid the loss of the US vote in the General Assembly, and combined their gesture with an effort permanently to lower the American contributions to the UN. With the UN desperate for further funds, struggling to maintain its many operations around the world, its most powerful member continued to withdraw its support.

The consequences of the funding crisis are grave. In addition to cutting back on peacekeeping missions and slashing its administrative staff, the UN has been forced to limit funds to projects in other areas – health, education, development – which can scarcely afford any reduction.[120] If the US continues to default on its debts, the UN will have either to declare itself bankrupt or to turn to other sources for funding. In September 1997, media magnate Ted Turner, owner of CNN, offered a $1 billion donation to the UN which may set a precedent for future funding. Although Turner's money was a gift, UN agencies have been courted by corporations which see a 'partnership' with the UN as good for business. In December 1999, the *New York Times* noted that companies had once given money or products for use in developing countries on a philanthropic basis; now, however, 'the new trend is for companies to use UN collaboration as a market tool'. The UN's original aims may therefore be subverted under these new financial constraints, with the private sector eager to supply some of the funds which the US continues to withhold, in return for favourable treatment from the UN or access to this globally recognised 'brand'.[121]

To some extent, the UN has reached this lamentable state through the apathy and mismanagement of the Clinton administration. It would be a mistake, however, to overlook the fundamental difficulties which underpin the relationship between the US and the UN. The UN has found it nearly impossible to function without American support; the US, on the other hand, is well able to pursue its objectives without UN approval. Madeleine Albright told a Congressional committee in March 1995 that the UN was no more than an additional resource in the American arsenal:

> UN peacekeeping adds to our capabilities, without subtracting. It offers us a choice between unilateral action and standing aside while conflicts fester. It allows us to influence events without assuming the full burden of costs and risks. And it lends the weight of law and world opinion to causes and principles we support.[122]

For all the usefulness of the UN, it remains a peripheral concern for American policymakers, who are used to acting unilaterally whenever they see fit. Albright's language here is grimly appropriate: the UN has no means of 'subtracting' an American commitment to pay its dues, nor can it force the US to uphold international law or to intervene where human rights are threatened. The US, meanwhile, can choose not only to cooperate with the UN, but to delegate responsibility for those international disasters and conflicts which hold little interest for an American audience. Thus the UN offers the US not only 'a choice between unilateral action and standing aside', but a way of doing each and maintaining a posture of international engagement – as in the Gulf War of 1991, or Madeleine Albright's stalling of a Rwandan relief mission in 1994. Albright correctly argued that the cost of selective American engagement, and of regular US apathy towards human-rights violations and humanitarian catastrophes, was relatively cheap for the United States. Predictably, the 'full burden' of this self-interested policy is carried by those – in Bosnia, Somalia, Rwanda and elsewhere – least able to bear it.

NOTES

1. Delivered on Capitol Hill, Washington, DC, 19 January 1999.
2. On the founding of the League of Nations, see Gary B. Ostrower, *The League of Nations from 1919 to 1929* (Garden City Park, NY: Avery, 1996), and F.S. Northedge, *The League of Nations: Its Life and Times, 1920–1946* (New York: Holmes & Meier, 1986). General accounts of the American role in the creation of the United Nations are offered by Robert C. Hilderbrand, *Dumbarton Oaks: The Origins of the United Nations and the Search for Postwar Security* (Chapel Hill: University of North Carolina Press, 1990); and Townsend Hoopes and Douglas Brinkley, *FDR and the Creation of the UN* (New Haven: Yale University Press, 1997).
3. Roosevelt appears to have been a strong advocate of veto power from the earliest stages of planning the UN, which was built around a conception of the 'Big Four' (the US, Britain, China and the USSR; France would soon be added to this elite club) acting in concert: Hilderbrand, *Dumbarton Oaks*, 32–6. The hardening of the veto power in the American conception of the UN is discussed by Hoopes and Brinkley, *FDR and the Creation of the UN,* 116–17. For a comparison of the relatively weak but democratic General Assembly and the much stronger but autocratic Security Council, see Geoff Simons, *The United Nations: A Chronology of Conflict* (London: Macmillan, 1994), 56–60.
4. Stanley Meisler observes that the US exerted a strong influence over the General Assembly until the mid-1960s, but then effectively ceded control to a bloc of developing nations and essentially bypassed or ignored the Assembly. *United Nations: The First Fifty Years* (New York: Atlantic Monthly Press, 1995), 295–7. Simons, 58, confirms that 'there is no sense in which the General Assembly is a world parliament,' and notes that the US 'became increasingly hostile' to the Assembly with the growth of an 'Afro-Asian bloc'.
5. On the inequitable distribution of power in the Security Council, and the regrettable effects of the veto, see Sydney D. Bailey and Sam Daws, *The Procedure of the UN Security Council*, third edition (Oxford: Clarendon Press, 1998), 227–39, 386–90.
6. On the deterioration of relations between the US and the USSR, and

the subsequent effect of the Cold War on the workings of the UN, see
Simons, *The United Nations*, 81–105. The US achieved some early
successes in subverting the UN mechanism to its own foreign-policy
purposes, most notably in Korea where the UN offered its sanction to
an overwhelmingly American invasion force (after the USSR had
absented itself from a Security Council meeting authorising the Korean
operation); see Bruce Cumings, *The Origins of the Korean War: The Roaring
of the Cataract, 1947–1950* (Princeton: Princeton University Press, 1990),
634–7.

7. For an account of the early freezing of relations between the US and
   USSR in the context of the UN, see Meisler, *United Nations*, 23–6;
   Meisler points to George Kennan's famous 'long telegram' of February
   1946, dispatched from the US embassy in Moscow, as a founding document of Cold War hostility: according to Kennan, the USSR had insisted
   that 'our traditional way of life be destroyed' and 'the international
   authority of our state be broken' as a prerequisite for the maintenance
   of 'Soviet power'. The 'evil empire' figure was employed most extensively
   and explicitly by Ronald Reagan in the 1980s, although it merely
   clarified polar understandings of the Cold War which had predominated
   since Kennan's first warning.

8. On the development of 'New Thinking' towards the UN from the
   USSR in the late 1980s, see Linda Melvern, *The Ultimate Crime: Who
   Betrayed the UN and Why* (London: Allison & Busby, 1995), 283–7.

9. Bush employed this phrase in his victory address to the US Congress
   on Capitol Hill, Washington, DC, 29 January 1991: the UN-sanctioned
   operation against Saddam promised a new order 'based on respect for
   the individual and for the rule of law, a new world order that can lead
   to the lasting peace we all seek'.

10. For an analysis of the proposals to give the UN a standby military
    force, and the influence of this debate on the 1992 US presidential
    election, see John M. Goshko, 'Idea of a Potent UN Army Receives a
    Mixed Response', *Washington Post*, 29 October 1992. Clinton had pledged
    to 'explore the possibility of creating a standby, voluntary UN rapid
    deployment force to deter aggression against small states'.

11. Although Boutros-Ghali was generally presented at the time of his
    nomination as a force for change in the UN system, the US seems to
    have reacted coolly to his candidature because it feared that he would
    not be assertive or radical enough in office. This is especially ironic
    given the outright US opposition to Boutros-Ghali's re-election in 1996,
    on the grounds that the secretary-general had been much too assertive
    and radical. See Meisler, *United Nations*, 278–9.

12. Meisler's conclusion, 330–33, summarises the UN dependence on the
    US, and the corrosion of the UN's credibility under the attack of US
    domestic political opponents. Geoff Simons, *The United Nations*, 163, is
    more explicit: 'The end of the Communist threat quickly induced
    American policymakers to speculate on how the United Nations could

be further exploited to US advantage.' Rosemary Righter has argued in
Utopia Lost: The United Nations and World Order (New York: Twentieth
Century Fund Press, 1995), 121–4, that the relative power of the US
and 'the West' might have the opposite effect of encouraging the strongest
powers to seek solutions to their problems outside the UN – Righter
suggests that Bush's 'new world order' was imagined as an alliance
between great powers rather than as the apotheosis of the UN. This
analysis seems persuasive given the cavalier disregard for the UN in
right-leaning policymaking circles in the US.

13. Meisler, *United Nations*, 332, puts the case bluntly: 'When the United
States reined itself in to play an ineffectual role at the UN, the UN
became ineffectual.' Meisler depicts this US posture of non-engagement
as a kind of benign neglect; the examples of Rwanda and Bosnia, which
we will explore in this chapter, suggest a more deliberate and hard-
nosed effort to stymie international peacekeeping operations for reasons
of American apathy and a desire to avoid incurring the costs of a UN
operation in personnel and, especially, money.

14. Boutros Boutros-Ghali, *Unvanquished: A US–UN Saga* (New York:
Random House, 1999), 12.

15. For an overview of UN funding issues, see Ronald I. Spiers, 'Reforming
the United Nations', in Roger A. Coate, ed., *US Policy and the Future
of the United Nations* (New York: Twentieth Century Fund Press, 1994),
19–40 at 35–8; and Ruben P. Mendez, 'Paying for Peace and Development', *Foreign Policy* 100 (1995): 19–31. An extreme perspective on
'fraud and inadequate financial controls at the United Nations' is offered
by Stefan Halper, 'Systemic Corruption at the United Nations', in Ted
Galen Carpenter, ed., *Delusions of Grandeur: The United Nations and
Global Intervention* (Washington, DC: Cato Institute, 1997), 127–36.
Richard Sklar, the Clinton administration's 'Representative for UN
Management and Reform', told Congress in 1997 that other member
countries 'deeply resent the US position and attitude' on a reworking
of the scale for national contributions: 'They see the richest nation in
the world demanding a discount from an assessment rate that they believe
should be predicated on, quote – the words I hear night and day –
capacity to pay, i.e. gross national income.' Testimony before the Subcommittee on International Operations, Senate Committee on Foreign
Relations, 105th Congress, 1st session, 6 November 1997.

16. Although Congress had agreed to settle part of the US debt in April
1998, the addition of a rider to the funding bill which would effectively
prevent federally funded organisations from working to facilitate birth
control and abortion in other countries led President Clinton to veto
the proposal. It is unclear whether this pro-life rider was intended to
produce a presidential veto, or merely reflected the low priority given
by the Congress to the settlement of American debts. For contrasting
perspectives, see Ambassador Peter Burleigh, 'Remarks at the New York
Foreign Press Center', press release of the US Mission to the UN, 18

September 1998; and Jesse Helms, 'A Day to Pay Old Debts', *New York Times*, 21 September 1998. A repeat of this situation took place in the summer of 1999: see Philip Shenon, 'Senate Backs UN Payment, But More Hurdles Remain', *New York Times*, 23 June 1999. Stefan Halper praised Congress for holding the UN to ransom in this way, arguing that 'no avenue other than the threat to withhold payment is available to force the UN bureaucracy and the hallucinogenic salon that passes for the General Assembly to reexamine their practices': 'Systemic Corruption', 129. Unfortunately for Halper, the 'Third World domination' of that 'hallucinogenic salon' seemed set to continue given the prospect of the mandatory exclusion of the US from General Assembly voting for its serial and prolonged failures to pay its dues: see Paul Lewis, 'UN Warns US on Payments', *New York Times*, 23 March 1999. It is not clear how the UN will respond to the US offer in late 1999 to pay off part of its debt, and to write off the rest.

17. Clinton's handling of the UN funding issue is a particularly good example of the gulf between rhetoric and action that would characterise many of his policy initiatives as president. Although Clinton consistently promised the UN that he would resolve the funding difficulties and persuade Congress to settle the American dues, the US was the largest debtor to the UN throughout his presidency. Understandably, UN personnel were exasperated by the American failure to pay, particularly given the many unkept promises to do so. One official indicated the depth of Clinton's dereliction by comparing him unfavourably to Ronald Reagan: 'At least with Reagan we knew where we stood and the United States more or less paid its bills on time. But Clinton has made so many unfulfilled promises, then he stabs us in the back and tells us that he feels our pain.' Judith Miller, 'As US Relations with UN Languish, is Clinton or Congress to Blame?', *New York Times*, 5 August 1999.

18. The comments were made by Senator Paul S. Sarbanes before the Subcommittee on International Operations, 6 November 1997.

19. Remarks of Senator Rod Grams before the Subcommittee on International Operations.

20. Remarks by President Clinton at 49th Session of the UN General Assembly, New York, 26 September 1994.

21. For an overview of the landmines issue, see *Landmines: A Deadly Legacy* (New York: Human Rights Watch, 1993); and Shawn Roberts and Jody Williams, *After the Guns Fall Silent: The Enduring Legacy of Landmines* (Washington, DC: Vietnam Veterans of America Association, 1995).

22. Dana Priest and Charles Truehart, 'US Makes One Last Pitch on Mine Treaty', *Washington Post*, 16 September 1997.

23. Raymond Bonner, 'US Seeks Compromise to Save Treaty Banning Land Mines', *New York Times*, 17 September 1997.

24. Steven Lee Myers, 'Clinton Says Ban on Mines Would Put US Troops At Risk', *New York Times*, 18 September 1997.

25. The Korean exception failed to convince many independent analysts

and even some famous US military personnel, including H. Norman Schwarzkopf, commander of US/UN forces in the Gulf War: Norman Kempster, 'Pentagon Prevails on Land Mines But Takes Heavy Fire', *Los Angeles Times*, 19 September 1997. For a specific rebuttal of the Korean exemption to the treaty's terms, see Michael O'Hanlon, 'US and Landmine Ban', *Christian Science Monitor*, 4 June 1998. Even Bill Clinton's former adviser George Stephanopoulos decried the US failure to sign as 'a surrender to the military': 'The President is Wrong', *Newsweek*, 22 September 1997. Since his election in 1992, Clinton had been vulnerable to attacks on his alleged 'draft-dodging' in Vietnam, and his relationship with the Pentagon began with the fiasco of his policy contortions on the subject of gays in the military. The decision to give in to Pentagon advice on the landmines issue may well be rooted in this anxiety over his own credibility to make military decisions. Note the euphoria in the Pentagon over Clinton's 'courageous' action: Dana Priest, 'Mine Decision Boosts Clinton–Military Relations', *Washington Post*, 21 September 1997.

26. For a brief history of the US development of these 'aerial mines', and an account of their devastating effects, see Eric Prokosch, *The Technology of Killing: A Military and Political History of Antipersonnel Weapons* (London: Zed Books, 1995), 107–14.

27. Allan Thompson, 'Canada's Land Mine Plea Gets US "No"', *Toronto Star*, 18 September 1997.

28. White House Briefing, Washington, DC, 17 September 1997.

29. Dana Priest, 'Clinton Directive on Mines: New Form, Old Function', *Washington Post*, 24 September 1997.

30. The *New York Times* described Clinton's pledge as 'symbolic', given his impending retirement from office. Steven Lee Myers, 'Clinton Agrees to Land-Mine Ban, But Not Yet', *New York Times*, 22 May 1998. See also Julian Beltrame, 'US Derided for its Latest Initiative', *Montreal Gazette*, 1 November 1997.

31. Clinton announced that the US would sign the treaty in 2006 only 'if the Pentagon is successful'. Anthony DePalma, 'As US Looks On, 120 Nations Sign Treaty Banning Land Mines', *New York Times*, 4 December 1997.

32. Mark Fritz, 'Pentagon Seeks Funds for New Type of Land Mine', *Los Angeles Times*, 20 February 1999.

33. Peter Baker, 'A Dispute Between Neighbors', *Washington Post*, 24 November 1997.

34. George Stephanopoulos emphasised Clinton's insalubrious allies in his opposition to the treaty: 'So it's Clinton, Castro, Kaddafi and Helms against the world.' 'The President is Wrong'.

35. For perspectives on the likely dilution of the treaty's effects given the US refusal to sign, see Norman Kempster and Craig Turner, 'Clinton Says US Won't Join Treaty to Ban Land Mines', *Los Angeles Times*, 18 September 1997; and James Carroll, 'The People vs. Land Mines', *Boston*

Globe, 9 December 1997. At the signing ceremony in Ottawa, Senator Patrick J. Leahy announced that 'by not signing, we weaken the treaty; we give others an excuse not to sign, and thereby we become part of the problem.' Craig Turner, '125 Countries Line Up to Sign Land-Mine Ban', *Los Angeles Times*, 4 December 1997.

36. For a sense of the Pentagon's priorities, we might note the announcement in 1999 that the Defense Department's Advanced Research Projects Agency (DARPA) was investing not only in mines but in mine-detecting wasps, each one to be equipped with 'an electronic backpack and a helmet' and instructed to clear mine-fields. According to DARPA, the wasps 'are highly trainable and respond well to positive reinforcement and rewards'. Jeff Nesmith, 'Uncle Sam's Unlikely Allies', *Atlanta Journal and Constitution*, 1 August 1999.

37. For Annan's remark, see Turner, '125 Countries'.

38. For a brief argument in favour of a permanent court over the temporary tribunals, see Ruth Wedgwood, 'The Case for a Permanent War Crimes Court', *Christian Science Monitor*, 16 August 1995.

39. As with the ban on landmines, the speed with which other countries tackled the issue of the ICC may have discombobulated the US. American support for a court was directed towards a slow process of UN committee meetings before the drafting of proposals; Canada led a fast-track negotiations process, much to the annoyance of Clinton administration officials. See the editorial 'Time for a Global Criminal Court', *New York Times*, 21 November 1994.

40. Remarks by the president to the 52nd Session of the United Nations General Assembly, New York, 22 September 1997.

41. On the contrast between the enthusiasm of many countries and the alarm of the US at the broader conception of the ICC, see John M. Goshko, 'UN Moving Toward Creation of Criminal Court', *Washington Post*, 21 April 1996.

42. Scheffer's original remark was recalled by John Bolton at a special meeting of the Subcommittee on International Operations, Senate Committee on Foreign Relations, 105th Congress, 2nd session, 23 July 1998. The meeting was entitled 'Is a UN International Criminal Court in the US National Interest?' and timed to coincide with the completion of the Rome negotiations which finalised the ICC treaty. On the US refusal to sign, see the testimony of Scheffer delivered before this committee; and, for the State Department view, James P. Rubin, State Department daily press briefing, 20 July 1998. Rubin feared that the Rome treaty would create a court that would hear 'complaints from well-meaning individuals in organizations that will want the court to address every wrong in the world. This will turn the court into a human rights ombudsman', a prospect which the US was keen to avert. A useful critique of US fears was offered by Thomas W. Lippman, 'America Avoids the Stand: Why the US Objects to an International Criminal Court', *Washington Post*, 26 July 1998.

43. Testimony of Michael P. Scharf, Subcommittee on International Operations, 23 July 1998.

44. A good example of such a 'supporter' of the ICC is Ruth Wedgwood, Professor of Law at Yale Law School, who argued that the American team in Rome lost 'an historic opportunity to shape the court in America's image', but that the US might still sign up in the future, providing the court behaves itself in the meantime: 'The court's future will hinge ... on the enunciation of prosecutorial priorities. The ICC was set up to address the horrors of contemporary civil wars, not cut down America's preeminence in the post-Cold War world.' 'Fiddling in Rome: America and the International Criminal Court', *Foreign Affairs* 77, no. 6 (1998): 20–24. Wedgwood's rather direct injunctions are an odd inversion of the usual relationship between courts and individuals; and the tenuous nature of her 'support' was heightened by her accompanying boast that 'The US military role in international security will not be altered by the evangelism of an international court, and the ICC would be foolish to try.' With friends like these...

45. Remarks of Rod Grams et al., Subcommittee on International Operations, 23 July 1998.

46. Testimony of John Bolton, Subcommittee on International Operations. Bolton was specific in his warning: 'Our main concern should be for the President, the cabinet officers on the National Security Council, and other senior leaders responsible for our defense and foreign policy. They are the real potential targets of the ICC's politically unaccountable prosecutor and that is the real problem of universal jurisdiction.'

47. Statement of Jesse Helms, Subcommittee on International Operations. Of course, Helms's view of the Court's dangers is similar to that of Ruth Wedgwood, putatively at the other end of the US political spectrum; the main difference between them is that Helms has less faith that the ICC will behave itself, or (in Wedgwood-speak) 'enunciate' the correct 'prosecutorial priorities'.

48. See John Vinocur, 'World Court Acts to Overrule US in Nicaragua Case', *New York Times*, 27 November 1984; and Paul Lewis, 'World Court Supports Nicaragua After US Rejected Judges' Role', *New York Times*, 28 June 1986.

49. However fantastic this possibility might have seemed, the pulse rate of many State and Defense Department officials and alumni must have quickened at the news of General Augusto Pinochet's arrest in the UK in October 1998. For a sense of the fears, see Mary McGrory, 'Pinochet Ricochet', *Washington Post*, 15 August 1999. The US citizen often described as most vulnerable to a similar indictment is Henry Kissinger, one of the chief architects of the American destabilisation programme in Chile which brought Pinochet to power in 1973. One Amnesty International official told McGrory that the claim that Kissinger was in danger of prosecution (which led to an American reluctance to engage with the ICC) had been repeated so often in the US in 1999 that

human-rights workers had taken to calling it the '"Poor Henry" argument.'

50. We should also note the hypocrisy of US statements on its putative leadership of the international community, given its dissent on issues like the ICC. Note Bill Clinton's 'apology' to Rwanda in March 1998, in which the president promised 'to remedy the consequences of genocide', in part through support of the ICC. Remarks by Bill Clinton to genocide survivors, Kigali Airport, Rwanda, 25 March 1998.

51. Scharf, 'Testimony'.

52. See John Hooper, 'US Troops Will Quit, Allies are Warned', *Guardian*, 15 July 1998.

53. Remarks of Senator Joseph Biden, Subcommittee on International Operations, 23 July 1998. Biden suggested that if the US made such a threat, 'we may very well get [the ICC supporters] to focus on aspects of the treaty I suspect they have not really fully focused on.'

54. Statement by Kofi Annan at the signing ceremony of the ICC, Rome, 18 July 1998.

55. Jesse Helms, 'We Must Slay This Monster', *Financial Times*, 31 July 1998.

56. Boutros-Boutros Ghali, *An Agenda For Peace* (New York: United Nations, 1992). On the proposal to create a permanent UN response force, see 25.

57. See supra note 10.

58. A number of accounts of the UN/US intervention in Somalia have been published in the US. General accounts are offered by John L. Hirsch and Robert B. Oakley, *Somalia and Operation Restore Hope: Reflections on Peacemaking and Peacekeeping* (Washington, DC: United States Institute of Peace Press, 1995); Terence Lyons and Ahmed I. Samatar, *Somalia: State Collapse, Multilateral Intervention, and Strategies for Political Reconstruction* (Washington, DC: The Brookings Institution, 1995); and Mohamed Sahnoun, *Somalia: The Missed Opportunities* (Washington, DC: United States Institute of Peace Press, 1994). Oakley and Sahnoun each has his own axe to grind: Oakley was responsible for the original UNITAF mission, and was sent by the US to broker its withdrawal from Somalia in October 1993; Sahnoun, the original head of UN negotiations in Somalia before the UNITAF mission, fell out with Boutros-Ghali over his close relationship with Somali faction leaders and the putative entanglement of UN relief operations with Somali organised crime. A variety of views are collected in Walter Clarke and Jeffery Herbst, eds, *Learning from Somalia: The Lessons of Armed Humanitarian Intervention* (Boulder, CO: Westview Press, 1997). Perhaps the most compelling account of the UN/US effort, which locates the 1992/3 events in a broader context of international intervention in Somalia, is Michael Maren's *The Road to Hell: The Ravaging Effects of Foreign Aid and International Charity* (New York: The Free Press, 1997), especially 203–56.

59. For an early idea of the Clinton administration's drift towards 'assertive

multilateralism', see the confirmation hearing of Madeleine K. Albright as US Ambassador to the United Nations, Senate Committee on Foreign Relations, 103rd Congress, 1st session, 21 January 1993. On PRD-13, see R. Jeffrey Smith and Julia Preston, 'United States Plans Wider Role in UN Peace Keeping', *Washington Post*, 18 June 1993. Albright's testimony before the International Security Subcommittee of the House Foreign Relations Committee, 103rd Congress, 1st Session, 24 June 1993, offers a useful clarification of 'assertive mulitlateralism', and includes an ominous exchange between Albright and a Congressman who wondered if the new policy was oxymoronic. In 1993 and especially 1994, the original phrase seems to have mutated in US political discussion into 'aggressive mulilateralism', perhaps reflecting the increasingly violent US operation in Somalia. Since the Clinton administration had mothballed the concept by the autumn of 1993, the malapropism was allowed to stand in the media and even in Congressional debates.

60. On Boutros-Ghali's push for disarmament, see John Drysdale, 'Foreign Military Intervention in Somalia: The Root Cause of the Shift from UN Peacekeeping to Peacemaking and its Consequences', in Clarke and Herbst, eds, *Learning from Somalia*, 118–34 at 128–9; Hirsch and Oakley, *Somalia and Operation Restore Hope*, 102–6; and Boutros-Ghali's *Unvanquished*, 59–60, 99–102.

61. On the 'undulating' and 'erratic' US approach to disarmament, see Jonathan Stevenson, *Losing Mogadishu: Testing US Policy in Somalia* (Annapolis, MD: Naval Institute Press, 1995). On US support for the Somali dictator, Mohammed Siad Barre, in the 1970s and 1980s, see Maren, *The Road to Hell*, 14, 33, 36–37.

62. It should be noted that the restriction of the US mission was an initiative of the Pentagon as much as the Clinton administration; the US military's Central Command (CENTCOM) was involved in the planning of the mission from its earliest stages, and exercised control over the direction of operations in Mogadishu throughout 1993. See Hirsch and Oakley, *Somalia and Operation Restore Hope*, 40–47; and Stevenson, *Losing Mogadishu*, 50–53. The new UN mission in May 1993 was actually referred to as UNOSOM II, in deference to the UN operation which preceded the US intervention of December 1992.

63. Estimates of the numbers of Somalis saved from the immediate threat of famine vary wildly, from hundreds of thousands (in many US estimates) to a fraction of that number. Maren, *The Road to Hell*, 213–15, explores the tangled methodology of calculating such statistics (and the inevitable contamination of the process by political imperatives), and himself favours a much lower estimate of around 10,000 lives saved after December 1992. Virtually all commentators note that the handover from UNITAF to UNOSOM II was extremely problematic. For contrasting views, see Hirsch and Oakley, *Somalia and Operation Restore Hope*, 106–14; and Boutros-Ghali, *Unvanquished*, 92–4.

64. UNOSOM II comprised around 18,000 personnel at the time of the

handover from UNITAF, but the 4,000 US troops were easily the best equipped and most powerful element in the mission; they also took orders independently from the US government and the military's CENTCOM, and were obviously the most familiar and immediate resource in the mind of the UNOSOM II commander, Admiral Jonathan Howe. Howe himself was appointed under duress by Boutros-Ghali, at the insistence of the US State Department. On UNOSOM II's composition, see Hirsch and Oakley, *Somalia and Operation Restore Hope*, 111–12. On Howe's appointment at American urging, see Maren, *The Road to Hell*, 228; and Boutros-Ghali, *Unvanquished*, 92. Boutros-Ghali writes that he was personally instructed to appoint Howe by Anthony Lake.

65. The details of the Pakistani operation are still unclear. Maren, *The Road to Hell*, 222–6, offers the most complete investigation, and is scornful of the hasty UN enquiry which levelled blame directly at Aideed. See also Hirsch and Oakley, *Somalia and Operation Restore Hope*, 117–19.

66. Although Boutros-Ghali stood by Howe throughout UNOSOM's operation, the admiral's earlier role in the US invasion of Panama in 1990 (Howe was involved in the efforts to capture Manuel Noriega, Panama's embattled leader and former US client) might have given some indication of how he would respond to a 'warlord' like Mohammed Aideed. See Maren, *The Road to Hell*, 227.

67. T. Frank Crigler, testimony before the Subcommittee on Africa, House Committee on Foreign Affairs, 103rd Congress, 1st session, 29 July 1993. Crigler went on to describe the mutation of 'Operation Restore Hope' (UNITAF) into 'Operation Inflict Punishment' as 'a throwback to gunboat imperialism'.

68. On the escalating violence of the US mission, see Drysdale, 'Foreign Military Intervention in Somalia', 132–3; and Hirsch and Oakley, *Somalia and Operation Restore Hope*, 119–127. Stevenson, *Losing Mogadishu*, 91–2, narrates the arrival of US Rangers and Delta Force Commandos, after Howe's request for an elite force to capture Aideed received 'civilian Washington's rubber-stamp'. The military appears to have been a little more cautious, but then to have sent more troops when its initial contingent proved ineffective. The CIA also appears to have been on hand to provide 'intelligence' which confirmed the importance of apprehending Aideed – as well as specific tip-offs for elite US commando operations, which ended, in one notorious case, with the mistaken arrest of eight employees of the UN Development Program.

69. Relations were bad enough between the US forces and the rest of the UN operation; the limited mandate of UNOSOM, the reluctance of US commanders to make relief work a priority for their soldiers, and the near-absolute ban on fraternising between the UN forces and ordinary Somalis led to fear and suspicion on both sides. See the testimony of Major F. Andy Messing, Jr., before the House Armed Services Committee, 103rd Congress, 1st session, 21 October 1993; see also

Stevenson, *Losing Mogadishu*, 56–65, who offers a detailed and scathing account of the breakdown (or non-existence) of trust between US personnel and Somalis.

70. Lieutenant General Robert Johnson admitted in testimony to the House Armed Services Committee, 21 October 1993, that US forces had referred to Mogadishu as 'Dodge City'; Mark Bowden notes the racial epithets used to describe Somalis in *Black Hawk Down: A Story of Modern War* (New York: Atlantic Monthly Press, 1999), 8–9, and observes that the US Rangers company was 'nearly all white'. Bowden also believes that US military personnel longed to end the phony war of the summer of 1993 and engage in 'a genuine balls-out firefight'. Racism, implicit and explicit, was not limited to the soldiers in the field: Defense Department spokesperson Kathleen DeLaski clumsily described the encirclement of US forces by 'a swarm of Somalis' in a Pentagon press briefing, Washington, DC, 5 October 1993.

71. The most complete account of the battle is Bowden's *Black Hawk Down*, which is packed with details of the fighting but much less interested in the context of American involvement in Somalia. Estimates of Somali casualties are complicated by the absence of any government in Somalia, the hasty departure of US forces, and the indiscriminate nature of the fighting.

72. Note Clinton's harried initial response to the Mogadishu battle, anticipating the questions of his audience: 'Why are we still [in Somalia]? How did a humanitarian mission turn violent?' Statement by Bill Clinton on Somalia, White House, Washington, DC, 7 October 1993.

73. Warren Christopher's remark was broadcast on 'Nightline', *ABC News*, 7 October 1993.

74. For Clinton's argument that the UN had forced the US into playing 'police officer' and waging 'a highly personalized battle' in Somalia, see the presidential press conference, The White House, Washington, DC, 14 October 1993. Madeleine Albright offered the most concise abdication of US responsibility for the UNOSOM disaster in her testimony before the Senate Armed Services Committee, 103rd Congress, 2nd session, 12 May 1994. Of course, these attacks on the UN, and the general strategy of suggesting that the UN had expanded an operation which the US sought to limit, were extremely effective, ministering to a need felt by the US military to explain its own disastrous actions and the need of the US media to explain the transition from Somalis cheering the arrival of the US Marines to Somalis cheering the desecration of American corpses. In the face of this damage-limitation operation, commentators could say nothing except the one unutterable fact that it wasn't true. For a succinct rejection of the official US line, albeit after the fact, see Walter Clarke and Jeffrey Herbst, 'Somalia and the Future of Humanitarian Intervention', in Clarke and Herbst, eds, *Learning from Somalia*, 239–53 at 241: '[I]t is simply not true that the UN greatly broadened the mission that the United States had decided to limit. In

fact, all the major Security Council resolutions on Somalia ... were written by the United States, mainly in the Pentagon, and handed to the UN as a fait accompli.'

75. For an early articulation of 'Somalia syndrome', see Daniel Williams, 'Joining the Pantheon of American Missteps', *Washington Post*, 26 March 1994.

76. Press briefing by Anthony Lake and General Wesley Clark, The White House, 5 May 1994. A summary of the contents of PDD-25 was provided in a briefing released by the Bureau of International Organizational Affairs, Department of State, 22 February 1996.

77. See ibid. for details of the US efforts to 'reduce the US share of peace-keeping costs'.

78. US interests were the lodestar of Lake's presentation to the press on 5 May 1994: 'We'll choose between unilateral and collective approaches, between the UN or other coalitions depending on what works best and what best serves American interests.'

79. Boutros-Ghali later described PDD-25 as dealing a 'deadly blow to cooperative multilateral action to maintain peace and security'. The secretary-general was particularly incensed by the wrecking efforts of Albright: 'It was one thing for the United States to place conditions for its own participation in UN peacekeeping.... It was something else entirely for the United States to attempt to impose its conditions on other countries. Yet that is what Madeleine Albright did.' *Unvanquished*, 134–5. Albright's dismissal of a Boutos-Ghali 'veto' on US/UN policy is quoted in Jacob Heilbrun, 'Albright's Mission', *New Republic*, 22/29 August 1994.

80. For Albright's declaration of 'a new realism' in the US/UN relationship, see her interview with Margaret Warner, 'Macneil/Lehrer NewsHour', *PBS*, 19 May 1994. See also Stanley Meisler, 'Crisis in Central Africa', *Los Angeles Times*, 23 May 1994.

81. For general accounts of the Rwandan genocide, see Gérard Prunier, *The Rwanda Crisis, 1959–1994: History of a Genocide* (London: Hurst, 1995); Philip Gourevitch, *We wish to inform you that tomorrow we will be killed with our families: Stories from Rwanda* (New York: Farrar, Straus & Giroux, 1998); and Alison Des Forges's massive and impressively documented *Leave None to Tell the Story: Genocide in Rwanda* (New York: Human Rights Watch, 1999).

82. The identity of President Habyarimana's assassins has still not been determined. For an account of the plane crash, and the theories of its provenance, see Prunier, *The Rwanda Crisis*, 213–29; and Des Forges, *Leave None to Tell the Story*, 181–5.

83. On Dallaire's initial warnings of genocide, and the failure of Kofi Annan's peacekeeping office to respond, see Gourevitch, 103–7; and, for an extensive and detailed account, Des Forges, *Leave None to Tell the Story*, 141–79. The obvious mistakes made by UN personnel, as opposed to the reluctance of UN member states to take action, were effectively

covered up by Kofi Annan (in his new role as secretary-general) as he refused to allow UN employees to testify before a Belgian investigation into the genocide in 1997; see Alan Zarembo, 'Toward a True History', *Newsweek*, 17 November 1997. Annan finally allowed a UN investigation to take place in 1999, although some commentators feared that it would amount to little more than a whitewash of the peacekeeping division under Annan's direction. See Joe Lauria, 'Probe Begins of UN Response to Rwanda', *Boston Globe*, 19 June 1999; and Peter Worthington, 'Don't Expect Miracles from Rwanda Probe', *Toronto Sun*, 22 April 1999. Although Gourevitch and especially Des Forges are clear about the massive UN failure in Rwanda (the genocide of April was planned and staged under the noses of the UN troops based in the capital), the question of UN culpability is inevitably entangled with the reluctance of the international community (and, especially, the US) to agree to any reinforcement of UNAMIR. See Des Forges, *Leave None to Tell the Story*, 172–4.

84. On the perpetrators and methods of the genocide, see Prunier, *The Rwanda Crisis*, 237–50; Gourevitch, *We wish to inform you...*, 114 ff.; and Des Forges, *Leave None to Tell the Story*, 205–16, 222–62.

85. On Dallaire's commitment to put down the genocide with modest reinforcements of UNAMIR, see Gourevitch, *We wish to inform you...*, 150; Des Forges, *Leave None to Tell the Story*, 598, 606–9; and Boutros-Ghali, *Unvanquished*, 135, 139. Julia V. Taft, president of the American Council for Voluntary International Action, told a joint House/Senate Subcommittee on African Affairs (104th Congress, 1st session, 5 April 1995) that Dallaire had been 'telling Senators, the Secretary-General and anyone who would listen that if he could just get about 5,000 to 8,000 troops, he could stop the genocide.' Some observers (both at the time and in subsequent enquiries) suggested that an even smaller force, albeit with a more assertive posture, could have prevented the killings in the first few days of the genocide.

86. On the US suggestion of 7 April that UNAMIR be withdrawn entirely, see Des Forges, 603–4. The United Kingdom may have provided support for the US position.

87. For this estimate of the number of Rwandans saved by UNAMIR, see Des Forges, *Leave None to Tell the Story*, 24. For a slightly lower estimate, see the testimony of Jeff Drumtra of the US Committee for Refugees before the Subcommitee on African Affairs, Senate Foreign Relations Committee, 103rd Congress, 2nd session, 26 July 1994.

88. On the specific influence of 'Somalia syndrome' on US thinking over Rwanda, see Arthur Jay Klinghoffer, *The International Dimension of Genocide in Rwanda* (London: Macmillan, 1998), 95–9. Klinghoffer notes that 'Somalia syndrome' was merely the latest version of 'Vietnam syndrome', which had cast its shadow over US policymaking since the early 1970s. On the influence of Somalia on the UN effort in Rwanda even before the genocide, see Des Forges, *Leave None to Tell the Story*,

132; and the PBS interview with Iqbal Riza, assistant to Kofi Annan in the UN Peacekeeping Operations department (reproduced on the Web at www.pbs.org/wgbh/pages/frontline/shows/evil/interviews/riza.html). The eventual UN report into the disastrous international response to the genocide largely avoided ascribing responsibility to particular countries (preferring to place the blame on the anonymous-sounding 'member states' as a whole); however, it did make explicit reference to PDD-25 and 'the shadow of Somalia'. Ingvar Carlsson, Han Sung-Joo and Rufus M. Jupolati, 'Report of the Independent Inquiry into the Actions of the United Nations during the 1994 Genocide in Rwanda', United Nations, 15 December 1999.

89. See the remarks of spokesperson Michael McCurry, State Department daily press briefing, 11 April 1994.

90. Christine Shelly, State Department daily press briefing, 28 April 1994. In an effort to dispel any sympathy from the media for the victims of the genocide, Shelly claimed to have 'pretty solid information that there are savage acts being undertaken by a variety of different parties over there.'

91. On the Convention's influence on the international response to Rwanda, see Des Forges, *Leave None to Tell the Story*, 639, 644.

92. For an overview, see Klinghoffer, *The International Dimension*, 99–100.

93. Christine Shelly was the unfortunate State Department spokesperson charged with the job of finessing 'genocide': see Gourevitch, *We wish to inform you...*, 152–3, for an account of her efforts; and the State Department daily press briefings of 28 April, 10 June and especially 16 June 1994 for examples of Shelly at work. The doggedness with which some reporters questioned her on the terminology (Shelly referred to 'acts of genocide' rather than 'genocide', and then became irritated when asked to clarify the difference) gives some indication of how generally accepted the facts of the genocide had become to those with even cursory knowledge of the situation, except the US government. Shelly gave an indication on 10 June of the reason for American reluctance, noting that US 'lawyers' had been alerted to the use of 'genocide' since 'there are obligations which arise in connection with the term'. This implied that the State Department was at least aware of its commitments under the Convention Against Genocide.

94. On 28 April 1994, Shelly told reporters that, under the Genocide Convention, 'there is not an absolute requirement if a determination on genocide is made to intervene directly in the particular crisis under international law.' Shelly dodged the question altogether when it was asked directly on 10 June. Jeff Drumtra, in his 26 July 1994 Senate testimony, addressed the 'massive failure' of the US to acknowledge the genocide: 'US officials compounded their egregious error by issuing dubious interpretations of the Genocide Convention that, if allowed to stand, may leave it permanently eviscerated as a component of international law.' On the State Department's policy of forbidding its

spokespeople to recognise the genocide, see Douglas Jehl, 'Officials Told to Avoid Calling Rwanda Killings "Genocide"', *New York Times*, 10 June 1994.

95. Madeleine Albright, testimony before the International Security, International Organizations and Human Rights Subcommittee, House Foreign Relations Committee, 103rd Congress, 2nd session, 17 May 1994.

96. On Albright's stonewalling, see Stanley Meisler, 'Albright Defends Rwanda Troop Delay', *Los Angeles Times*, 18 May 1994; Meisler, 'Crisis in Central Africa'; Paul Lewis, 'US Opposes Plan for UN Force in Rwanda', *New York Times*, 12 May 1994; Boutros-Ghali, *Unvanquished*, 135–6; and Gourevitch, *We wish to inform you...*, 150–51. Gourevitch is particularly incensed by Albright's actions: 'Her name is rarely associated with Rwanda, but ducking and pressuring others to duck, as the death toll leapt from thousands to tens of thousands to hundreds of thousands, was the absolute low point in her career as a stateswoman.'

97. Albright's 'maelstrom' remark was made in her testimony before the International Security Subcommittee, 17 May 1994. On the US efforts to atrophy an international response to the crisis, see Des Forges, *Leave None to Tell the Story*, 644–6; and Klinghoffer, *The International Dimension*, 50–55.

98. 'Macneil/Lehrer NewsHour', *PBS*, 19 May 1994.

99. Boutros Boutros-Ghali, remarks to reporters, UN Headquarters, New York, 26 May 1994.

100. See Gourevitch, *We wish to inform you...*, 151; Des Forges, *Leave None to Tell the Story*, 646; and the State Department daily press briefing by Christine Shelly, 16 June 1994.

101. The original (1994) UN estimate of numbers killed in the genocide was 800,000; this is adopted by Gourevitch, and supported by Prunier (261–5), who reached a similar figure from his own calculations. Des Forges, however, believes that 500,000 deaths may be a more accurate estimate. *Leave None to Tell the Story*, 15–16. The unreliability of population surveys before the genocide is a strong complicating factor in calculating the toll. Although the exact figure is important, the uncertainty should not distract us from the fact and the horror of the genocide.

102. The American response to the 1999 UN Carlsson inquiry into the international failure in Rwanda hardly suggests that the US has learned lessons from the experience. Briefing the media on the publication of his report, Ingvar Carlsson noted that the US had provided little help to the inquiry, either in terms of documents relating to American policy, or access to key policymakers who had made the decisions concerning US non-intervention and stonewalling at the UN. The United States also failed to initiate its own inquiry into its actions, despite the efforts of other countries involved in the Rwanda events (Belgium, Canada and France) to investigate what had happened. Barbara Crossette, 'Inquiry

Faults US Inaction in '94 Rwanda Genocide', *New York Times*, 17 December 1999.

103. Madeleine Albright, testimony before the Foreign Operations Subcommittee of the House Appropriations Committee, 104th Congress, 1st session, 15 March 1995.

104. For general accounts of the Balkan conflict, see Misha Glenny, *The Fall of Yugoslavia: The Third Balkan War*, third edition (New York: Penguin, 1996); and Laura Silber and Allan Little, *Yugoslavia: Death of a Nation*, revised edition (New York: Penguin, 1997). On the response of other nations to the conflict, see James Gow, *Triumph of the Lack of Will: International Diplomacy and the Yugoslav War* (London: Hurst & Co., 1997); and the essays collected in Richard H. Ullman, ed., *The World and Yugoslavia's Wars* (New York: Council on Foreign Relations, 1996). For a detailed account of the American perspective on intervention, see Wayne Bert, *The Reluctant Superpower: United States' Policy in Bosnia, 1991–95* (London: Macmillan, 1997)

105. Vance's proposal was brokered with the European Union mediator David Owen, and proposed the creation of ten regions within a single Bosnia-Herzegovina, each one (with the exception of Sarajevo) ethnically homogeneous. The Vance–Owen plan allotted more territory to the Bosnian Muslims than the 1995 Dayton Agreement and, unlike Dayton, did not lay the ground for a simple partition of the country. For an account of the plan and its ultimate rejection by the US, see Silber and Little, *Yugoslavia*, 276–90; and Glenny, *The Fall of Yugoslavia*, 224–32. Glenny, 224, describes the plan as 'an exceptionally good document which has been roundly abused by politicians and media throughout the world and particularly inside the former Yugoslavia and the United States'. Silber and Little note that the US rejection of Vance–Owen coincided with the Clinton adminstration's effective abandonment of the Bosnian issue, and peddling of the line that the Balkan conflict was intractable, driven by 'ancient hatreds'.

106. Clinton's advocacy of 'lift and strike' (air strikes accompanying the lifting of the arms embargo on the region, and the consequent arming of the Bosnian army) is discussed by Bert, *The Reluctant Superpower*, 175–9. Boutros Boutros-Ghali outlines the threat of 'lift and strike' to UN forces on the ground in Bosnia in *Unvanquished*, 68–71. James Gow, *Triumph of the Lack of Will*, 213, suggests that the US rejection of the Vance–Owen plan was based in part on an American 'determination to avoid deploying ground forces'; the resulting notion that air strikes alone could bring peace to Bosnia was thus an unpleasant blend of moralism and realpolitik: 'the impulse of moral indignation to act was in conflict with an overriding desire to protect an all-important domestic agenda from the damaging intrusion of foreign policy entanglements.'

107. The UN Security Council created the 'safe areas' policy on 16 April 1993, but the member states were unwilling to commit more than 7,000 additional troops to police the 'havens' (as opposed to the 34,000

requested by Boutros-Ghali). Silber and Little, *Yugoslavia*, 274–5, detail the contradictions which produced the 'safe areas' resolution, and note that the Security Council 'saddled itself with a responsibility it was not prepared to honor'.

108. On the fall of Srebrenica, see Jan Willem Honig and Norbert Both, *Srebrenica: Record of a War Crime* (London: Penguin, 1996); and David Rohde, *Endgame: The Betrayal and Fall of Srebrenica* (New York: Farrar, Straus & Giroux, 1997). On the influence of this disaster on US policy, see Silber and Little, *Yugoslavia*, 351–2; Gow, *Triumph of the Lack of Will*, 274–5; and, for an insider's view, Richard Holbrooke, *To End a War*, revised edition (New York: Random House, 1999), 68–72. It is worth noting that, alongside its simple embarrassment at the fall of Srebrenica, the Clinton administration realised that the failure of the 'safe areas' policy would probably lead to a withdrawal of UN troops from Bosnia, which would oblige the US to send ground troops (possibly in huge numbers) to oversee the retreat. The prospect of some kind of meaningful US military involvement was therefore not simply an option for Clinton after Srebrenica, but a certainty.

109. See Tom Prost et al., 'Blues for the Blue Helmets', *Newsweek*, 7 February 1997, which suggested bluntly that the UN operation in Bosnia, and especially the UNPROFOR (UN Protection Force) troops on the ground, were an expensive way for the US to avoid deploying troops. 'UNPROFOR can't end the war in Bosnia. But it still serves a useful purpose – as a whipping boy for the West.'

110. Boutros-Ghali, *Unvanquished*, 247–8.

111. On the Dayton talks, see Holbrooke, *To End a War*, 231–312; Boutros-Ghali recounts the $3.24 billion UN deficit in *Unvanquished*, 249.

112. Holbrooke, *To End a War*, 201; Silber and Little, *Yugoslavia*, 364–81.

113. For assessments of Dayton, see Glenny, *The Fall of Yugoslavia*, 290–93; Silber and Little, *Yugoslavia*, 386–90; Holbrooke, *To End a War*, 362–6. Glenny observes that, in spite of Holbrooke's protestations, 'most commentators' agree that Dayton 'amount[s] to the partition of Bosnia'. Silber and Little note that Bosnia-Herzegovina's fate was 'the most tragic' of all the Balkan countries: 'From the Vance–Owen plan to the Dayton summit, despite the intervention of Washington, each successive peace plan gave the Muslims less territory than that which preceded it.'

114. Madeleine Albright had taken to calling the US the 'indispensable nation' by the end of 1996, most notably in the January 1997 Senate hearing on her nomination as secretary of state. We will return to this perspective on the US in Chapter 4.

115. For an early indication of the shift in American attitudes towards Boutros-Ghali, see Richard Dowden, 'Too Blunt for His Own Good', *Independent* (London), 31 October 1994.

116. On the US campaign to oust Boutros-Ghali, which pitted Madeleine Albright against virtually every other nation represented at the UN, see Thomas W. Lippman and John M. Goshko, 'Albright Led Challenge to

UN Chief', *Washington Post*, 7 January 1997. The extraordinary efforts
to replace the secretary-general were widely and critically reported in
the US; an editorial in the *Boston Globe* ('The Misuse of US Power', 26
January 1997) lamented the 'disgraceful campaign on the part of the
Clinton administration to get rid of' Boutros-Ghali. For the victim's
perspective, see *Unvanquished*, 267–335.

117. For Holbrooke's enthusiasm towards Annan, see *To End a War*, 200–202.
On Annan's 'key appointment', see 'Cast of Characters is Set for Clinton's Second-Term', *New York Times*, 15 December 1996.

118. Holbrooke, *To End a War*, 202.

119. For a snapshot of the moribund relationship between the US and the
UN in 1999, see Judith Miller, 'As US Relations With UN Languish,
is Clinton or Congress to Blame?', *New York Times*, 5 August 1999. On
the massive tax-cut proposals, see John Aloysius Farrell and Aaron Zitner,
'Awash in Spending Ideas, Parties Put Their Faith in the Numbers',
Boston Globe, 6 August 1999. Of course, none of these 'spending ideas'
involved settling the US debt to the UN. On the eventual deal to settle
some of the US debt to the UN, see Jeffrey Bartholet and Debra
Rosenberg, 'Victory or Sellout?', *Newsweek*, 29 November 1999. The
Economist noted that the US 'concession' to pay off only a part of its
debt, and to insist on a reduction in its future contributions and a series
of other demands, marked a low point in the history of US–UN relations: 'If there was ever any doubt about how little the United Nations
expects from the United States, this week probably ended the argument. The deal that has been hashed out by Congress and the White
House ... has been hailed as a victory for the world's foremost international organisation. That the world's richest country still owes the
UN some $600m, and that the deal includes the sort of constraints no
national government would ever dream of accepting, have barely reg-
istered as footnotes.' 'Don't Ask for More, Mr. Annan', *Economist*, 20
November 1999.

120. For an example of the funding squeeze within the UN Development
Program, see Judith Miller, 'UN Poverty Agency Vying with Aid Offices
for Cash', *New York Times*, 11 July 1999; and Miller, 'Outgoing UN
Development Chief Berates US', *New York Times*, 1 May 1999.

121. On Turner's gift (which was actually used to establish the 'UN Foundation', an independent organisation which considers applications from
the UN for funding), see David Rohde, 'Ted Turner Plans a $1 Billion
Gift for UN Agencies', *New York Times*, 19 September 1997. Kofi Annan
pledged in his 1998 *Report of the Secretary General on the Work of the
Organization* (New York: United Nations, 1998), paragraph 10, to 'establish a mutually beneficial dialogue with the international business
community' – 'business,' suggested Annan, might be happy to help the
UN if the UN can 'lay the stable foundations that the expansion of its
own opportunities requires'. For the suspicion that such corporate gifts
would put 'this public institution far too much under the sway of a

private institution', see Colin Woodard, 'Turner's $1 Billion Gift Starts Giving', *Christian Science Monitor*, 7 July 1999. See also Claudia H. Deutsch, 'Unlikely Allies Join with the United Nations', *New York Times*, 10 December 1999.

122. Madeleine Albright, testimony before the Subcommittee on Foreign Operations, Senate Committee on Appropriations, 8 March 1995.

CHAPTER 3

THE US AND MILITARY POWER

As we work for peace, we must also meet threats to our nation's security
– including increased dangers from outlaw nations and terrorism. We
will defend our security wherever we are threatened.

William Jefferson Clinton, 1999 State of the Union address[1]

The United States has the most powerful and well-equipped military
in the world, and intervenes abroad more often than any other
country. Although Soviet armed forces rivalled the US during the
Cold War, the collapse of the USSR left the American military with
an enormous advantage over every other nation. By the early 1990s,
commentators in the US and elsewhere routinely referred to the US
as the world's last remaining superpower, a designation which recognised the ability of the US to project its military power decisively
around the globe.[2]

In this chapter, I want to explore the changing conception of the
US military in the 1990s, and to outline the ways in which American policymakers have consolidated US military power following the
demise of the USSR. I also want to locate the US military in the
wider context of American business interests and the international
arms trade, and finally to consider the recent deployment of American
forces in Iraq, Kosovo and elsewhere. In the first section, I'm going
to look at the debate within the US over the size of the military
which followed the end of the Cold War, and the efforts of American
politicians and the Pentagon to devise new threats which might justify
continued military spending. I'm also going to consider American
approaches to military alliances, and particularly the consolidation
and expansion of NATO. In the second section, I will examine
more closely the politics of defence spending, including the relationship between American businesses and the Pentagon, the persistent

pursuit of high-tech weaponry and arms sales, and the many ways in which the Pentagon has dodged public scrutiny to pursue its own priorities. In the third section, I'm going to focus on the actual use of US military forces in Iraq in the 1990s, and in Kosovo in 1999. Although the American military has produced myriad documents predicting the kinds of wars the US will face in the post–Cold War world, neither the persistent US war with Iraq, nor the bombing campaign in Kosovo and Yugoslavia, suggests that the reality of military conflict will bear out the Pentagon's predictions. Developing this theme, I want to consider the increasingly aggressive US posture towards 'terrorism', including the attacks on Sudan and Afghanistan in 1998. With these examples in mind, I will return in conclusion to American rhetoric on the use of military force, and reckon this against recent evidence of the effects of American military power.

STRATEGY

The elusive 'peace dividend'

Between 1945 and 1985, the rationale for a large and heavily armed US military was simple: American forces were a bulwark against the Soviet Union, which might easily sweep through Europe or elsewhere if the US and its allies dropped their guard. Given the enormous stocks of nuclear weapons held by the US and the USSR by the early 1960s, this argument for enormous spending on conventional forces was hardly self-evident; but the proximity of Russian forces, and the rhetorical firestorm between the sides, ensured that most American commentators supported a large and well-equipped military over the decades of the Cold War. In the late 1980s, however, this argument crumbled with the collapse of Soviet rule in Europe and the eventual disintegration of the USSR itself. The economic crisis facing the new Russian nation contributed to a more relaxed American view of the familiar enemy, and the gradual depletion of the once-mighty Soviet military eased the old tensions between the rival superpowers. Even former hawks in the US began to speak of a 'peace dividend', and of the rewards that would follow the inevitable cuts in military spending which would surely accompany this safer international climate: the US could afford to spend more on education or on health, and might improve its citizens' quality of life since it had no longer to divert so many resources to their defence.[3]

Against this optimistic backdrop, however, many powerful players in the US were extremely nervous at the prospect of a 'peace dividend', largely because the money or power bound up in any 'dividend' would be redistributed from them to others. The most obviously reluctant party was the military itself, which was alarmed by the rhetoric surrounding the outbreak of peace in the late 1980s and early 1990s. As hopeful commentators floated the idea of massive cuts in defence spending to an eager public, Pentagon chiefs who had served their country for decades found themselves in the firing line. If the military was to retain a semblance of its former might, the Department of Defense and the most influential military leaders in the US would have to declare war on optimism, to discover new threats to replace the increasingly implausible Russian challenge. Although the odds seemed against the Pentagon, the advocates of a strong military were in the fortunate position of advising or even constituting the various committees and consultative bodies which would consider the future of American defence spending. While the military obviously had a strong interest in preserving the status quo, the Pentagon's top brass and leading planners were largely responsible for reviewing the nation's military requirements – this inevitably encouraged more pessimistic and cautious assessments of the international environment, which would in turn lead to minimal reductions in the strength of US forces and American defence expenditure.[4]

The Pentagon was well placed to defend its own interests against the advocates of a 'peace dividend', but might have struggled to make its case without the support of a crucial ally: the US business community. At first glance, the idea of redirecting defence funds to domestic spending priorities (including investment in infrastructure, education, health, etc.) might seem irresistible to American companies. Many of the largest and most prestigious US corporations, however, were major suppliers to the Pentagon: defence contracts funnelled hundreds of millions of dollars each year to companies like Boeing, General Electric, AT&T and General Motors. These contracts were prized by many firms, since the Pentagon was a perfect customer: it spent huge sums of money, often spread steadily over the course of years or even decades, and it paid its bills in full and on time. Some of the largest defence contractors, like Boeing and Lockheed, were dependent on military orders to sustain their non-military operations: without the billions of dollars in Pentagon cash, Boeing could hardly hope to keep ahead in research and development, and to ensure that its commercial products remained truly competitive in the global market. New technologies – in aerospace design, computers and electronics – were essentially subsidised by the Pentagon, before private corporations eventually reaped a profit in converting these technologies to commercial use. If the American government was now to withdraw its funding following the demise of the Cold War, these subsidies – and the vital support they gave to corporate profits – would disappear.[5]

Unsurprisingly, then, defence contractors (including companies whose primary business lay outside of the sphere of military hardware) rallied behind the military's efforts to keep defence spending high. One of the most potent arguments against a reduced military budget concerned the redundancies which would follow major defence cuts: the biggest Pentagon suppliers made it clear to the public (and to members of Congress) that large-scale job losses would attend any major cut in spending, an argument which dovetailed with the Pentagon's dire warnings of the effects of military base closures. As optimists in the media and Congress painted a happy picture of increased national spending on education and the like, defence contractors and the military mobilised local communities to protest against the job losses which would surely follow the closure of a particular aircraft plant or army base. Those Americans employed in these facilities, along with many others who depended on revenues from the bases and factories to support their own businesses, saw little prospect of a 'peace dividend' and joined the ranks of those searching the skies for a new threat to national security.[6]

The final opponent of post-Cold War optimism was the US government itself, which had failed to predict the collapse of the USSR and which found itself in a position of unprecedented global supremacy in the early 1990s. Although the demise of the Soviet Union suggested a historic opportunity for a new multilateralism, the apparent 'victory' of the US in the Cold War also established the

reality of American predominance in world affairs. Alongside the
prospect of widespread disarmament and international reconciliation,
then, was a singular possibility for the US to ensure its own power
and supremacy. Put differently, the disappearance of the USSR
suggested a choice between two possible visions of the future: a global
arrangement based on multilateralism, disarmament and a resurgent
UN, or an international configuration dominated by a single superpower. Since the Soviet collapse had effectively left the US in this
second position, American policymakers would have actually had to
renounce US dominance and dismantle the American military had
to bring about a more multilateral world order; unsurprisingly, they
chose instead to preserve and even to make permanent the US
advantage.[7]

Although George Bush began the process of reviewing the size and
make-up of the military, the most complete and radical overhaul of
US forces was expected from the new, Democratic administration of
Bill Clinton. By the time of Clinton's inauguration in January 1993,
however, the post-Cold War environment had already shifted somewhat from the optimism of 1989. The US-led war with Saddam
Hussein in the first months of 1991 had given the American military
its first major outing since Vietnam, and the success of US forces had
strengthened the military's credibility and its case for substantially
preserving the defence budget. Although we will look at the Gulf
War in more detail in the third section of this chapter, it is worth
noting here that the conflict was integral to the Pentagon's domestic
battle with the advocates of a 'peace dividend'. Not only was Saddam
Hussein enshrined as the perfect example of the post-Soviet 'threat'
to world peace, but the method used to defeat him – overwhelming
military power – was established as the proper way in which the US
should assert its armed forces. The chairman of the Joint Chiefs of
Staff, General Colin Powell, espoused the view that the US should
only enter military situations with clear goals and ample resources
(personnel and equipment) to get the job done quickly and decisively. This approach to military actions, which became known as the
'Powell Doctrine', quickly became an orthodoxy in Washington and
informed the ongoing debate over defence spending.[8]

Les Aspin, Bill Clinton's secretary of defense, finally announced the results of the US government's spending assessments in September 1993. The 'Bottom-Up Review' (BUR) was the culmination of extensive consultation within the Pentagon, Congress and the various armed services, and constituted the most complete US assessment of the post-Cold War environment and the likelihood of any peace dividend. To the surprise of many observers, the cuts in spending and in the military's size were relatively modest. The Pentagon and the defence industry had resigned themselves to a reduction in military expenditure and force strength from their Cold War peak, but they had succeeded in averting the most dire predictions of a settled international climate and a commensurately reduced US military. Moreover, the Clinton administration had accepted the military's basic strategic assessments without argument. At the heart of these assessments was the Pentagon's demand that the US maintain sufficient forces to wage two 'Major Theater Wars' (MTWs) simultaneously, and without allies. The US, according to the BUR, should always be ready to fight two conflicts on the scale of the Gulf War at once, and without the assistance of any of the nations (NATO allies and others) that had contributed to the coalition against Iraq. Although there has been no sign of another MTW since 1991 (with the possible exception of Kosovo), this policy of readiness for two conflicts simultaneously was reaffirmed in the next major defence review in 1997, and formed the basis of Bill Clinton's vision for a twenty-first century American foreign policy, the minimum requirement for US military spending and force levels.[9]

As we have seen, the modest changes of the BUR reflect the desire of the Pentagon, many US companies and many defence-industry-dependent local communities to keep the status quo intact even after the eclipse of the Soviet Union. The power of this coalition is evident, moreover, from the skill with which they sold the BUR and its successors to an American public that had cheered the demise of communism. The BUR, and the requirement to maintain forces sufficient to fight two major wars at once, were hardly self-evident to many Americans. In the first place, the huge US conventional and nuclear arsenal was an effective check to any regional power which might challenge a neighbour or US ally; the same weapons which had deterred the USSR and its massive conventional forces for forty years might also contain the much smaller armies of North Korea, Iraq or Iran. Second, the US plans for waging two MTWs simultaneously ignored the likelihood that traditional US allies – such as the UK – would quickly side with the US against any potential adversary. The disregard for such allies in the minds of US planners seems the more bizarre when we consider the substantial sale (or donation) of high-tech US weaponry to American allies throughout the world – the Gulf states and Israel have developed extensive military power with US assistance, making the prospect of a unilateral American war effort in the Middle East seem highly unlikely; the same is true for South Korea, frequently mentioned by Pentagon planners as a vulnerable nation in need of US assistance. If the sophisticated US airplanes, missiles and computers supplied to these nations count for nothing in the US defence reviews, why does the United States make them available in the first place?[10]

The final premiss on which the BUR was made to rest is more fundamental: the notion that, in the aftermath of the Soviet Union, the greatest threat to global stability comes from a number of 'outlaw nations' or 'rogue states', which have noted the end of superpower rivalry and stand ready to exploit international complacency and threaten the new pillars of global order. With Saddam Hussein as their chief of operations, these 'rogue states' and leaders were characterised by Les Aspin and Colin Powell as 'demons and dangers', distinctly echoing the old American rhetoric of the Soviet 'evil empire', but refracting the threat through the developing world. Forced to find a threat to justify a continued posture of overwhelming military predominance, US policymakers had, within two years of the fall of the Berlin Wall, created a new international menace which required vigilance and American military deterrence.[11]

Rogue states, failed states

When Saddam Hussein invaded Kuwait in August 1990, he inadvertently provided the Pentagon planners with exactly what they had been looking for since Gorbachev had taken over the USSR: a new enemy against which the US could rail and a security threat which might justify the maintenance of Cold War military spending. Before and during the US-led war with Iraq in January and February of

1991, President Bush and his military staff frequently alluded to the severity of Saddam's mischief: he was a threat to world order, a proponent of totalitarianism, or even a new Hitler. Although some of this rhetoric was surely intended to persuade a wary American public to accept a distant war, the demonisation of Saddam marked a shift towards a new vision of world politics: the simple conflict between US and USSR had given way, in the speeches of US policy-makers, to a more complex world of law-abiding nations – the 'international community' – and lawless, anarchic 'rogue states', hell-bent on challenging the peace and security of the former.[12]

At first glance, the roster of 'rogues' seemed rather anticlimactic – the Pentagon identified Iraq, Iran, Syria, Libya, Sudan, Cuba and North Korea as 'outlaw' nations, but the relatively marginal status of most of these in world affairs hardly suggested a threat to global security comparable to the Soviet challenge. The Bush and Clinton administrations, therefore, set about a multi-level strategy of impugning and inflating the 'rogues'. In the first place, the leaders of these countries were frequently portrayed not only as undemocratic (a charge with some validity, but one which might as easily be leveled at many US allies) but as fanatical or crazy. In the case of Iraq and Libya, the strategy was simply accomplished by questioning the sanity of Saddam Hussein or Muammar Gaddafi; in the case of Iran, the spectre of 'Islamic fundamentalism' was invoked to stress the rejectionism and impenetrability of the Iranian leaders and people. Having established the irrational and erratic mindset of the 'rogues', US officials played up their efforts to acquire nuclear, chemical and biological weapons (weapons of mass destruction, or WMDs), as well as the missiles and delivery systems necessary to use them against their law-abiding, legitimate neighbours. Just as fears of a 'missile gap' with the USSR had fuelled US military spending in the 1960s, so talk of the 'nuclear outlaws' persuaded US congressional representatives in the 1990s to fund a huge American army, many new weapons programmes, and an array of 'anti-missile missiles' which might defend the world from the rogue 'threat'.[13]

The apparent acceptance of the rogue threat by the American public suggests that this demonisation strategy has been successful; moreover, the evidence from Iraq and North Korea in particular suggests that these countries have, indeed, made strides towards the acquisition of WMDs. It should be noted, however, that this hardly distinguishes the 'rogues' from other nations – such as India, Pakistan and Israel – which have developed an independent nuclear arsenal, or from countries like the US which retain huge stockpiles of WMDs. The principal distinction between 'rogues' and full members of the international community has less to do with some essential evil or malfeasance which would separate, say, Egypt and Iran, and more to do with the economic, cultural or political reluctance of the 'rogue' states to acquiesce in the US vision of a global family of nations. By this logic, states such as Turkey, Indonesia, Saudi Arabia and Egypt – all of which have been accused of serious human-rights violations against their own people, and none of which enjoys a genuinely democratic government – can be allies of the US, and members of the international community; while nations such as Cuba and Libya are decried as outlaws.[14]

The effect of this US taxonomy has been to lump together countries which have very little in common save for the distaste with which they are regarded by Washington; and to provide a rationale for constant and substantial American military readiness, given the alleged propensity of the 'rogues' to attack at any time.[15] Although the US effort to magnify the danger posed by the 'rogues' has suffered a few setbacks in the 1990s – the election of a more moderate government in Iran; the willingness of Gaddafi to give up Libyan suspects to be tried in connection with the Lockerbie bombing; peace feelers from North Korea – the State Department is committed to the idea of the 'outlaw' nation, and to tracing the implications of this threat for US foreign policy.[16] In an article in *Foreign Affairs* in November 1998, Madeleine Albright offered 'four basic categories of countries' which made up the post-Cold War world:

> Full members of the international system; those in transition, seeking to participate more fully; those too weak, poor, or mired in conflict to participate in a meaningful way; and those that reject the very rules and precepts upon which the system is based.

As we saw in the last chapter, Presidential Decision Directive 25 marked the end of the Clinton administration's interest in 'failed states'; Albright's creation of a separate category for these countries completed

the American abdication, at least in terms of peacekeeping commitments. Her characterisation of the 'rogues', meanwhile, captured the
dogmatism and posturing of the US position: the rejectionist states
are firm in their opposition to the international community, violating
'global norms' and presenting a threat which must be repelled.[17]

We have already seen the effects of this US perspective on military
planning and defence spending; its consequences for the 'rogues' are
less certain. The relentless American effort to isolate, demonise and
contain 'rogue states' has certainly subjected the civilian populations
in these countries to substantial hardship. In many cases, it has
hardened autocratic regimes, creating a common enemy (the US)
and distracting ordinary people from the iniquities of their own
leadership. It has also contributed to a widespread suspicion in these
countries of American power and intentions, and to the view that
the only means of challenging American coercion are military force
or, more plausibly, terrorism. In this way, the US 'rogue doctrine' is
ultimately self-fulfilling – the threat alleged in the first instance will
surely be produced given prolonged exposure to economic hardship,
sanctions, or American bombing. Although the consequences of this
will be dire, for the civilians of the 'rogue states' and for the victims
of terrorism in Western states, the danger of the 'rogues' will finally
be real, and the US defence budget will once more be justified.

Military alliances and NATO expansion

The various reviews of US defence spending have been premissed
on the idea that the US will fight its overseas battles without any
foreign assistance. As we have seen, this argument has been used to
sustain a military budget at near-Cold War levels; but, in reality, the
US has made use of allies and coalitions in the planning and execution
of recent military operations. In the Gulf War, the US assembled a
coalition of fifteen nations in its conflict with Saddam Hussein.[18]
Although the superior technology of the US, and the American
insistence on a US command structure, restricted the military contribution of these allies, their participation in Operation Desert Storm
bestowed the priceless appearance of multilateralism on what was
essentially an American fight. The US need to claim a multilateral
motive in its foreign wars suggests that this kind of ad hoc alliance

will appeal to American policymakers in the future, even if the military contribution of any 'allies' is a token one.[19]

The largest and most enduring Western coalition during the Cold War was the North Atlantic Treaty Organisation (NATO), a collective security agreement signed in 1949 by ten European nations as well as Canada and the US. During four decades of impasse with the USSR, NATO served as an effective division between eastern and western Europe, paralleling the line of the Iron Curtain. Although NATO forces did not exchange a single shot with the Warsaw Pact armies, the sheer fact of the huge Western military build-up effectively kept the status quo. In 1989, as the Warsaw Pact collapsed, it seemed as if NATO's reason for being had also disintegrated. Given the rapid decay in Russian force strength and the withdrawal of the Soviet army, it seemed there was no longer an enemy for NATO to confront. However, the US argued strongly for the perpetuation of the Alliance, and even suggested the expansion of NATO into eastern Europe. In 1994, the US Congress passed a bill authorising President Clinton to invite Poland, Hungary and the Czech Republic to join NATO; in 1999, these countries were formally admitted to the Alliance.[20]

Given the continuing decline of Russia's military in the 1990s, we might justifiably wonder why the US has placed a premium on NATO's survival, let alone its expansion. There are several explanations for this. Most obviously, the US is keen to preserve NATO since the Alliance constitutes a strong political bond between the US and Europe. With the rapid consolidation of the EU in the 1990s, the possibility of a strengthened and more independent European foreign policy has increased; NATO, which is heavily slanted towards US command, can serve as an American counterweight to this process. Beyond the existing EU boundaries, the US has used the prospect of NATO membership to entice the former Warsaw Pact countries into an American sphere of influence. The language of the 1994 NATO Expansion Bill in the US Congress required eastern European NATO aspirants to 'maintain their progress towards establishing free-market economies', a powerful bulwark against a resurgence of communism or socialism in the nascent democracies of Poland, the Czech Republic and Hungary.[21]

The fear of alternative economic development, or of those Madeleine Albright has described as 'communist backsliders', is a powerful force behind NATO expansion.[22] Although some policy-makers in the Clinton administration have talked of the promise of a democratic, free-market Russia as a future ally of the US, others have been more sceptical, and have looked to the past in defining Russia as a future threat to European security. Such distinguished State Department alumni as Henry Kissinger have echoed this view, playing up Russia's 'four hundred years' as an 'imperialist country' and suggesting that, as in the Cold War days, the correct US policy is to stare down and contain the Russian menace.[23] The practical consequence of this mindset has been to reassert the old Cold War divide in Europe, but merely to move the boundary a few hundred miles to the east. Instead of engaging Russia in NATO, or abandoning the old alliance and devising a new one for the changed circumstances of the present, the US has effectively declared the continuation of the old standoff, unnerving ordinary Russians and providing inflammatory rhetoric for Russia's resurgent nationalists.[24]

The most sketchy but discomfiting development in NATO's recent renaissance has been the tentative American suggestion that the Alliance shift towards endorsing an offensive rather than a defensive posture, and respond to 'threats' outside Europe. Although NATO was conceived as a defensive league, a collective security agreement which would deter Russian invasion, the reconfiguration of NATO's mission in the 1990s has licensed NATO forces to strike first against potential 'threats' or sources of instability. The limited NATO air-strikes in Bosnia in 1994/5 offered a glimpse of this new policy; the bombing campaign against Yugoslavia in 1999 was its first significant application.[25] Given that the NATO charter allows for first use of nuclear weapons by NATO in any conflict, the shift to an offensive stance is alarming; the more so if we consider Madeleine Albright's December 1998 suggestion that 'tomorrow's NATO' must be prepared to act 'beyond NATO's immediate borders'. Albright's vision pushed the European collective security pact towards an offensive force targeting the new US enemies outside North America and Europe; a NATO with a global reach, reserving the right to make first use of weapons of mass destruction against the leaders and people of the world's 'rogue states'.[26]

The initial European reaction to a global NATO was lukewarm at best, but the prospect of a much-expanded sphere of NATO

operations is a real one.[27] Western Europe vacillates between assertions of its independence and acquiescence in US–led foreign–policy
initiatives and conflicts – the spectre of Bosnia, and the EU's failure
to resolve that crisis, still lingers over the various foreign ministries
and makes deference to the US seem easy and attractive. Eastern
Europe, meanwhile, has a still greater interest in toeing the American
line, hungrily eyeing the possibility of economic and military assistance. Given the strictness of qualifying criteria for the European
Union, membership of NATO can seem to such countries a consolation prize, a badge of identification with the West to substitute for
the full political and economic integration of the EU. This has cast a
shadow over the efforts of EU countries to create common defence
institutions and a single policy on the use of force. As long as NATO
is more solicitous of the eastern European nations, it seems unlikely
that Europe as a whole will achieve much distance from American
perspectives and priorities in foreign policy.[28]

Looking to the future, the redivision of the European continent
along NATO's expanded borders, and the American desire to globalise
its offensive capabilities, do not inspire confidence in the security of
Europe or the rest of the world. The opponents of NATO expansion
in the US pointed out the dangers of isolating Russia at a time
when the more placid security environment should license dialogue
and inclusion – to no avail, as NATO's advocates (and the Cold War
Russophobes) trumpeted the expanded Alliance.[29] Meanwhile, the
prospect of NATO mobilising against Iraq or Korea has been floated
by the US, eager to bolster its 'rogue doctrine' with the appearance
of multilateralism.[30] Once again, the US has chosen to define its
purpose and interest in foreign policy away from the UN, preferring
a heavily skewed military coalition for the resolution of international
problems. The Russian 'threat', then, is not only military but
diplomatic – as Henry Kissinger observed in testimony to a 1997
Congressional committee on NATO expansion:

> You asked me, one of you asked me, what is the Russian strategy? The
> Russian strategy cannot be to build NATO. It is against their whole
> tradition. So they have every interest to water down NATO into some
> vague multilateral UN-type talk shop.

Kissinger's candour is instructive: NATO expansion is not only a way of containing Russia militarily, but of containing many countries diplomatically which might otherwise object to US foreign-policy imperatives. An expanded NATO gives the appearance of multi-lateralism to US goals, but without the nagging dissent of a 'UN-type talk shop'.[31]

The US has thus emerged from the Cold War with a largely intact military force, a dubious taxonomy of nations (including the fearsome 'rogue states'), and an aggressive assertion of its own right to act unilaterally. This has already led to tensions with North Korea, Iraq, Sudan and Cuba, and has contributed to a global environment in which the UN is largely marginalised as a truly multilateral influence. Even with the existing roster of 'rogues', the new American defence strategy is extremely provocative and risky; if China or Russia slips from 'transitional' to 'rogue' status in the years ahead, the prospects for sober and reasoned resolution of disputes with the US will be bleak indeed.

TECHNOLOGY

In addition to the strategic rationale for a strong military, we have already seen a powerful economic argument in favour of extensive defence spending. In virtually every nation, the connections between military priorities and the commercial imperatives of defence corporations are venerable and insistent; with the end of the Cold War, and the consolidation of various international industries, however, American military suppliers have attained an unprecedented control over the market. In this section, we will look in more detail at the impact of commercial factors on defence spending, and consider some of the more high-profile Pentagon technologies of the past few years in this context. We can then see more clearly the ways in which these economic factors exert their influence over debates on national security and regional stability, even those debates which seem at first glance to be free from commercial considerations.

Military corporations and a corporate military

In 1999, Bill Clinton pointed to declining levels of defence spending in the previous fifteen years, and argued for a major increase in the military budget to pay for weapons upgrading and modernisation. As we have seen, the argument for new weapons was seriously undermined by the absence of a Soviet threat; and even the 'declining' American defence budget of 1985–99 exceeded the military spending of every other nation by a substantial margin. Clinton, however, spoke boldly in favour of the Pentagon's request for more than $60 billion per year to 'modernise' its existing weapons, and the US Congress enthusiastically supported his initiative. Even the modest budget reduction following 1993's BUR – which ensured that the US spent a mere three times as much on its military as any other country – failed to satisfy Democrats and Republicans, and the US prepared to enter the twenty-first century on another defence-spending spree.[32]

Defence spending makes many large US corporations happy. Although this fact might seem self-evident, it's surprising to note just how many big American companies are boosted by major Pentagon contracts. In the 1998 fiscal year, some $70 billion of business was split between the top 100 Pentagon suppliers. Although obvious companies like Lockheed Martin ($12.3 billion) and Boeing ($10.9 billion) headed this list, hundreds of millions of dollars also went to less likely suppliers, including General Electric ($1.2 billion), CBS ($567 million), MCI Worldcom ($235 million), and Procter & Gamble ($217 million). It is worth remembering the broad base of corporate suppliers when reviewing debates in the US over the size of the military, as well as the need for new weaponry. If the armed forces were substantially reduced in size and funding, these companies (and many more like them) would lose a lucrative and reliable source of income.[33]

Many of the largest Pentagon suppliers have succeeded in converting domestic contracts into international orders – weapons systems designed in the US, with Pentagon money underwriting research and development, are marketed aggressively by American companies to foreign governments. Given the huge Pentagon budget, and the encouragement given by the American government to this arms trade, it should not surprise us that the US is the world's largest supplier of arms to other countries, as well as the biggest spender on its own military. Companies like Lockheed Martin and Northrop Grumman attend and stage weapons trade fairs around the world, often with the encouragement of the State or Defense Departments. In some cases, the government's desire to help the arms industry and to prop up foreign regimes results in a kind of double bail-out: a foreign country is given billions of dollars in 'military aid', which in fact goes to US companies that manufacture planes, tanks or bombs for the foreign beneficiary. At the same time as the American taxpayer has subsidised countries like Israel, Egypt and Colombia to the tune of tens of billions of dollars, the weapons industry in the US has received a giant helping hand.[34]

A cursory consideration of foreign arms dealing suggests two problems. In the first place, an international trade in arms encourages international instability, and allows destructive weapons to reach the hands of undemocratic or oppressive regimes. Although this might seem a major concern in the abstract, the US government has done relatively little to prevent this kind of arms proliferation in recent decades. During the Cold War, the doctrine of anti-communism was used to justify substantial military aid to extremely oppressive regimes around the world. Since 1989, the US has continued to train and supply the armed forces of countries like Indonesia, Turkey and Colombia, each of which has used its military to oppress its own people. Moreover, the earlier, lax policy on proliferation has left a lasting legacy: countries like Iran and Iraq became 'rogue states' only after the US had helped to arm them; and the huge international market in small arms, many of them US-made, has contributed to many casualties, combatant and civilian, especially in the developing world. Statutes which would restrict US arms sales to countries with poor human-rights records do exist in American law, but successive presidential administrations (and Congresses) have lacked the will to enforce them.[35]

The other obvious problem in exporting weapons is that a country might thereby give its technology and secrets to a potential adversary. Some commentators in the US have raised this concern in view of recent US weapons sales to countries like Saudi Arabia, which might undergo a violent regime change and ultimately threaten US forces with their own, technologically advanced weaponry; the solution, some have argued, is to restrict sales of such technology, or to abandon the export of high-tech weapons altogether. Of course, such a cautious approach is incompatible with the plainly commercial imperatives which drive the arms trade: companies and countries in Europe and the US compete with each other for foreign business, and cannot afford the luxury of these scruples if their product (a gun, a tank, a plane, or a mine) is to win 'market share'.[36]

Such caution also ignores the wider context in which technology transfer coincides neatly with the interests of the American arms industry. If the US develops a technologically superior weapon, it will not need another one until other countries catch up. Since the US military budget is so much larger than that of other countries, this should mean that each American weapon enjoys a technical edge for many years, and that US taxpayers are not called upon to fund research into its successor as soon as the weapon enters service. A boon to the taxpayer is anathema to the military corporations, however, who would thereby lose substantial Pentagon research and development funds. Against this backdrop, arms sales to foreign regimes achieve two purposes. First, they maximise the profits of companies like Boeing and Lockheed Martin, which are given access to an expanded international market for their product. Second, and more importantly, they enable those arms companies (and the Pentagon) to argue that new US technology is required, since the 'old' weapons have proliferated around the world. This maintains the flow of development money to the big military contractors, who produce new weapons, export them to foreign regimes, and then begin designing an expensive replacement.[37]

Given the absurdity of this cycle, we should remember that it continues precisely because it brings real benefits to some powerful people, even as it threatens the financial welfare (or even the lives) of others. Defence-based companies like Lockheed Martin, Raytheon and Northrop Grumman profit on a grand scale, as do companies like Boeing and General Electric which mix military contracts with civilian production. Congressional representatives in Washington benefit through campaign donations made by such companies, and are able to claim that they have created or defended jobs at any military plants in their district. The president and the State Department can reinforce or consolidate a foreign ally, or even attempt to buy a new one through the donation of this high-tech hardware; the president can also help the defence industry by increasing foreign arms sales and guaranteeing a domestic market for even newer, more sophisticated weapons. The military, meanwhile, is given a genuine, home-produced threat against which to define its own purpose; and the chance to replace all of its toys before it grows tired of them.[38]

Although we should not discount the significance of the defence industry to tens of thousands of ordinary US workers, the majority of these beneficiaries – stockholders, the military, politicians – enjoy positions of power and privilege. The losers in this game of international arms dealing are less powerful and scattered throughout the world. American taxpayers largely bankroll the process, but are distracted from recognising the iniquities of arms dealing by government references to national security, regional stability, or the importance of the defence industry to safeguarding American jobs. In foreign countries, meanwhile, civilian populations endure the effects of militarisation and 'internal security' without attracting much American attention, save from arms dealers on the lookout for new orders. US-made small arms have driven numerous conflicts in Asia and Africa, while major US arms sales to Turkey and Indonesia have directly abetted the efforts of those governments to oppress and kill Kurds, East Timorese and other civilian populations. It seems hardly coincidental that those who gain most from this international arms business have sought to preserve it, even though they are in a tiny minority when compared to the many millions of people who inadvertently sponsor the trade, or those who suffer directly from its effects.[39]

Binding together the beneficiaries are the consistent threads of money and influence, with corporate and government officials moving easily from the public to the private sector, retired military personnel plugging the merits of new technology to foreign customers and domestic politicians, and a close connection between public institutions and private interests. The NATO summit of April 1999, held in Washington, DC to mark the 50th anniversary of the Alliance, was funded entirely by corporate donations. In return for their largesse, CEOs and salesmen from these companies were given privileged access to the politicians and military representatives of the nineteen NATO member states. Alan John Blinken, an American investment banker who helped to coordinate this corporatisation of NATO, declared proudly to the *Washington Post* that 'the business community was in it from Day One. In a lot of cases, they came to us – we didn't solicit them.'[40]

Given the opportunity to sell high-tech weaponry and communications equipment to NATO members, especially the new entrants from eastern Europe, it is hardly surprising that US corporations should rush for the bunting. The *Post* report went on to describe the activities of former congressman Gerald Solomon, who had left politics to work in the more lucrative business of defence lobbying:

> Solomon, now a private lobbyist, said he traveled through Eastern and Central Europe spreading the message that if the United States was going to be NATO's principal military power, supplying most of its high-tech weaponry, then US defense firms should receive contracts to rearm the former Soviet states.
> 'We wanted them to buy American,' Solomon said.

The boundaries between politics, the military and business have effectively dissolved, leaving increased military accounts for some of the most prominent US corporations, and plentiful employment for former military personnel and politicians in defence projects and lobbying efforts.[41] Even though the rhetoric of national defence makes no reference to profit margins and corporate performance, US defence policy – including the massive trade in American arms – is heavily influenced not by strategic considerations or a drive towards efficiency, but by the simple pursuit of material gain.[42]

Case studies: the F-22 and 'Star Wars'

To illustrate some of these points, I want to look briefly at two high-profile US defence projects of recent years: the Air Force's F-22 fighter programme, designed to replace the F-15, and the 'Star Wars' missile defence system, originally proposed by Ronald Reagan in the 1980s to shield the US from ballistic missile attacks. Each of these projects has suffered major setbacks, technical and political, during its development; the survival of each is testament to the sacred status of expensive defence projects in Washington, and proof that the funding of high-tech weaponry in the US will not be affected by such minor concerns as the usefulness of the weapon, or the chances of making it work in practice.

In the early 1980s, as the US squared off against the Soviet Union, the Pentagon argued that the American military would need four new types of 'next generation' fighter aircraft to maintain America's technical edge. If the need for so many new planes was at all plausible in the 1980s, it seemed highly dubious a decade later. The collapse of the Soviet Union removed the only serious threat to American air superiority, and with it the rationale for these new planes; one might suspect, then, that most or all of the new designs would be cancelled. By 1999, however, three of these four projects had survived, and tens of billions of dollars had been spent on their development.[43] Inevitably, a Congressional committee took notice of this fact, and expressed particular doubts in a July 1999 report about the viability of the Air Force F-22 programme. Congressional efforts to question the F-22's progress met with fierce resistance not only from its manufacturer, Lockheed Martin, but from defense secretary William Cohen and from Bill Clinton. The relatively modest actions of Congress – amounting to a suggestion that one part of the plane's funding be suspended, pending technical results – sent the Pentagon and corporate boardrooms into apoplexy, and a massive counter-campaign was waged against Congressional sceptics. Lobbyists from the Department of Defense and from Lockheed Martin bombarded politicians with promotional videotapes, lined up to write op-ed pieces in major newspapers, and told anyone who would listen that the safety of the nation depended on the completion of the F-22 order.[44]

As we have seen, companies like Boeing and Lockheed Martin love projects like the F-22 for many reasons: they are very large; they create many jobs over a prolonged period; once awarded, they are ordinarily guaranteed to last until production, which could be years or decades after the original research funds reach a company; and they enable corporations to make technological advances at public expense, which can then be utilised commercially. In the case of the F-22, Lockheed Martin is looking to deliver an order of 339 airplanes to the US Air Force, with each plane costing around $200 million – a total in excess of $65 billion. If the programme had been cancelled in 1999, Lockheed Martin would have kept the $18 billion already spent on research and development, but would have lost the additional cash from domestic sales of the finished fighter; not to mention the inevitable foreign sales, which would, in turn, create the need for another 'next generation' fighter. If US taxpayers looked to the Pentagon to contain the greed of defence contractors, the picture was equally grim: fixated by the prospect of yet more high-tech equipment, the Pentagon planners (in the words of former Senator Dale Bumpers) 'want this worse than they want to go to heaven'.[45]

The House Appropriations Committee, in its 1999 report on defence spending, noted that the F-22 had serious technical problems on a variety of fronts: its fuel tank was leaking, its fuselage had shown signs of structural weakness, and its advanced avionics had not even been tested. The Pentagon, however, had decided in December 1998 to put the unfinished plane into production, effectively committing Congress to provide funds for the aircraft indefinitely. Although less than 5 per cent of basic testing on the F-22 had been completed, the Air Force had transferred the incomplete, 'technically challenging' F-22 programme from the development stage to a production track, making it much harder for Congressional representatives to cancel or amend the final order. Although the US media reported that the House Appropriations Committee had voted to kill the F-22 programme, in reality the Committee seems to have been most offended by the underhand way in which the inchoate airplane was being transferred to 'production' status. The Committee therefore denied these production funds, but agreed to another $1.2 billion for the fiscal year 2000 to support the plane's development. Few commentators predicted that the F-22 would actually be scrapped, and a compromise between the Pentagon and Congress reached in September 1999 suggested that the sceptics had been quickly and thoroughly routed.[46]

Even these limited battles between Congress and the Pentagon are rare: the deluge of defence lobbyists on Capitol Hill, and the lure of campaign dollars for politicians prepared to serve the defence industry, largely ensure that Congressional scrutiny of major military 'needs' is kept at bay. The recent furore over the F-22, therefore, may jolt the military and defence contractors from their complacency, and force them to try harder in addressing what the Committee's report tactfully described as 'issues of credibility' in their requests for funding.[47] On the question of the threat against which the F-22 was to be deployed, the report was particularly scathing:

> The Air Force does not have a particularly good record in making straight-forward threat assessments.... In the early 1990s, after the Soviet Union collapsed (and the Air Force's argument for procuring the F-22 with it), the Air Force changed its threat analysis to say that some 35 countries had procured aircraft with capabilities that threatened US air domination. Only later were we surprised to learn that the Air Force included countries like Switzerland, Norway, Israel, Australia, even New Guinea as possible threat countries, all of whom possessed US-built F-16 aircraft that we had sold to them.[48]

If past form is anything to go by, the Pentagon and Lockheed Martin will ignore the suggestions that the F-22 is too costly, technically difficult or irrelevant, and will save the project using familiar methods: exaggeration of the threat from other countries, a scare campaign in the media asking Americans if they are 'ready to lose the next air war', and judicious use of financial inducements to keep Congress in line.[49]

While the F-22 has been a *cause célèbre* for the Air Force of late, the various plans for missile defence in the US have for nearly two decades inspired all branches of the military, and politicians from both major American parties. When Ronald Reagan announced the Strategic Defense Initiative (popularly known as 'Star Wars') in 1983, many scientists and commentators expressed great scepticism over the feasibility of the project. The essential goal of missile defence – to hit one missile with a laser or another missile, at incredible speeds – is extraordinarily difficult to accomplish. The political payoff from a functioning system, however, would be substantial. Ronald Reagan spoke excitedly of a nuclear umbrella, a shield of laser beams which would destroy a Soviet missile attack and keep every US city safe, even in the event of an all-out nuclear war. This noble dream managed neatly to distract from the tricky job of averting such a conflict in the first place, and from the general wisdom that the Strategic Defense Initiative was technically impossible.[50]

Throughout the Reagan and Bush administrations, missile defence was seen as a Republican party project, a hawkish challenge to Russia and a sop to the defence industry. Upon assuming the presidency in 1993, Bill Clinton cut funding to the various versions of missile defence, although different projects continued to receive billions of dollars for research and development. Finally, in 1999, the Clinton administration caved in to Republican pressure and promised to build a system of National Missile Defense (NMD) as quickly as possible. The Democratic Party, which had previously decried Star Wars as a choice moment of Reaganite excess, had now embraced the idea as its own.[51]

Missile-defence projects come in many shapes and sizes, from small systems designed for 'theater use' (i.e. to protect US troops fighting in a particular regional conflict) to the NMD, intended to protect the cities and people of the mainland United States. There are also several technological tracks and approaches, appealing to the big defence corporations which are being paid billions of dollars to conduct the research. Boeing has been busy adapting its 747 jumbo jet to fire lasers at distant missiles (turbulence has, apparently, caused problems with the targeting);[52] Raytheon and its charmingly named 'Exoatmospheric Kill Vehicle' have been trying to harness what Raytheon calls 'hit-to-kill technology' (or, in common language, ramming) to knock out enemy missiles as they pass through space;[53] and Lockheed Martin has taken overall charge of the NMD programme, even as its own Theater High Altitude Air Defense (THAAD) missile chalked up its seventh consecutive failure in May 1999.[54] This diverse family of anti-missile systems does, however, have some common features: all of the programmes are hugely expensive, and none of them seems to work very well.

In many respects, the course of missile-defence spending has demonstrated that the Pentagon's most impressive defensive operations surround its own budget. The cost of the anti-missile systems has been matched only by their ineffectiveness, and the Pentagon has acquired a reputation for subterfuge and obfuscation which it would do well to incorporate in its weapons. The two successful tests of missile-defence technology in the 1980s were later shown to have been rigged by the Defense Department and its contractors. Most notoriously, one 'success' featured the interception of a target missile by the heat-seeking anti-missile system under test; but relied on Pentagon scientists heating the surface of the target missile to 100°C before its launch and interception, thereby making it much easier to hit. Thus the Pentagon proved its ability to contain the threats of 'rogue states', providing the latter were kind enough to heat their missiles before firing them at the US.[55] Even the vaunted successes in missile-defence technology in 1999 (after a string of costly failures) proved little, and serious technical questions await a satisfactory answer even as more money is thrown at these programmes. Huge sums are poured into missile defence each year, and the Pentagon is trying (as with the F-22) to rush these systems into production, thereby to safeguard them from Congressional cancellation. Even if the various programmes were cancelled immediately, their cost to date has been immense: estimates of missile-defence spending since the 1970s range from $60 billion to an extraordinary $110 billion, and the US is still unable to name a date when even a limited system might be deployed over American skies.[56]

Given the obvious technical problems, the tricks and 'creative accounting' of the Pentagon, and the immense cost of missile defence, we are again entitled to wonder why this research and spending enjoys approval across the American political spectrum. Of course, a major answer lies in the desire of defence contractors to maximise their profits, and the Pentagon's willingness to bankroll huge and prolonged projects in return for even the vaguest and most distant hope of success.[57] We should also note, however, that the various plans for missile defence are the most prominent examples of a rather common strain in US thinking, which holds that the putative enemies of the United States can be deterred or overwhelmed by technology. In effect, projects like the NMD are attempts to deal militarily with a threat that would otherwise require a diplomatic response.[58] Given their demonisation of a series of 'enemies' as 'rogue states', it should not surprise us that Bill Clinton and his administration favoured the idea of an NMD. Missile defence suggests that, in the near future, the US will be able to act with complete impunity on the world stage, since it will be impervious to any kind of attack. In the meantime, the US can simply work to 'contain' the 'rogue threat', confident that its military personnel (and patriotic defence corporations) are bravely toiling to condemn this threat to obsolescence. The irony of all this defence spending is that it has, then, a parochial and disengaged aspect as well as a hawkish one: the US has embraced a sort of technological isolationism, which insists on preserving an overwhelmingly powerful and sophisticated US military to obviate the need for real political engagement with the world's most pressing problems.

If the missile-defence strategy promised success, it would hardly seem laudable given the substantial American influence on the global economy and geopolitics: for the US to manage this global situation behind an impregnable shield would not ensure the fairness or responsiveness of the system. The US perspective is more worrying, however, since the shield is hardly impregnable. With the proliferation of nuclear materials from the former Soviet Union, and the diffusion of technical knowledge in weapons-building, the US remains open both to missile attack and, more plausibly, to a terrorist operation conducted from the ground. There is nothing inevitable about this threat to the US – it arises largely from a series of local grievances based on American actions throughout the world, many of which have violated international law and traumatised civilian populations. The American goal should be to minimise these grievances, to engage the disadvantaged in dialogue, and to restore to people throughout the world some influence over the processes which govern their life. In reality, the US appears ready to ignore these grievances and to persuade its citizens that dubious technology will keep them safe. This comforting notion may well explain the persistence of massive defence spending even after the Cold War; but it hardly prepares the US for the challenges and dangers of the next century.

CONFLICT

Although the US military is large, well-funded and frequently deployed, American politicians are constrained by a public reluctance to see US forces in prolonged foreign combat. The spectre of the Vietnam War lingers in many American minds, and remains as an example of the destructive costs of American engagement abroad. However, the debate over the US role in Vietnam has largely confined itself to a discussion of strategy or of overreach: according to this skewed debate, American politicians and soldiers erred in their assessment of the task at hand, or tried too hard to save an ungrateful

Vietnam from the communist 'threat'. These perspectives have ensured that the 'lessons' of Vietnam are more schematic and technical
than political or moral. As we saw in the last chapter, US politicians
have sought to avoid 'mission creep', the commitment of troops in a
dynamic political situation which can lead to escalation of American
involvement; the 'Powell Doctrine' (stemming from Colin Powell's
own experience in Vietnam) holds that US military forces should
only enter conflict with overwhelming superiority in numbers and
firepower; and the 1990s have seen the emergence of 'smart' weapons,
theoretically able to hit targets precisely and to minimise damage to
nearby civilians. These developments, each linked to assessments of
the American failure in Vietnam, have shaped American ideas about
the kind of wars the US should fight, and the ways in which those
wars should be fought.[59]

In this section, I am going to look at how these post-Vietnam
imperatives have shaped American military action, using the examples of the US attacks on Iraq since 1991 and the 1999 assault on
Yugoslavia. In both examples, we can see clearly the American desire
to use overwhelming force, to employ high-tech weapons, and to
reduce US casualties to virtually zero. We can also identify, however,
some drawbacks of these new priorities: the sophisticated weapons
have not always proven so 'smart'; the need to avoid American
casualties has led to confusion over the extent of American commitment to a mission; and the eventual use of overwhelming force has
resulted in spectacular mismatches, and extensive (non-US) loss of
life. These new approaches to warfare also ignore the political
problems which, in the long run, dwarf the difficulties of any military
operation: why should the US go to war? Is war the best way to
achieve your objectives? Will a political problem always submit itself
to a military solution? I want in conclusion to consider some of
these questions alongside the problem of terrorism, and to ask
whether the might of the US military offers substantial protection
against aggrieved nations, groups or even individuals.

Iraq

When Saddam Hussein invaded Kuwait in August 1990, he set in
motion an American military campaign against Iraq that has endured
for a decade. Saddam's own survival, then, seems rather surprising.

The US military has ample resources to level his many residences, and has reminded the Iraqi people on several occasions since 1990 that Iraq's armed forces cannot defend their territory from American encroachment. US politicians have routinely condemned Saddam as a tyrant, called for his removal from power, and pledged to 'contain' Iraq for the duration of his rule. Repeatedly in the 1990s – in 1991, 1993, 1996 and 1998/9 – extensive military power was brought to bear on Saddam, with substantial loss of Iraqi life; and yet he remained in office, showing little sign that his rule had been weakened by the many military attacks. His various weapons programmes continued, without US or UN supervision after 1998, and the Iraqi people continued to suffer under his rule.

Iraq is an excellent example of the costs of applying a military solution to a political problem; and, more generally, indicative of the many ways in which the US can use its extraordinary military power to disguise or distract from its tangled political agenda. In 1990, the problem was relatively simple: Saddam was a former ally of the US in its own fight against Iran, but had stepped out of line by invading Kuwait.[60] Such an action constituted a major disruption to the region, and particularly to the oil lanes in which the US held a substantial interest – the US would therefore make a show of strength to confirm its seriousness to Saddam.[61] When troops began to mass in Saudi Arabia and elsewhere in the Gulf the problem became rather more complicated. Saddam had started to link the withdrawal of his own forces to an Israeli agreement to end its 25-year invasion of the Palestinian territories, an analogy which may have made some sense in international law but which was anathema to the US.[62] Meanwhile, American military planners were eager to take action. In practical terms, the huge number of US forces could not be billeted in the desert indefinitely, and their commanders sought word from the Bush administration on whether the soldiers would be sent into combat or withdrawn. More abstractly, the Pentagon sensed a watershed moment as Saddam defied international calls for an Iraqi withdrawal from Kuwait. After a nervous year of watching the Soviets slump into obsolescence, US planners saw in Saddam a fresh reason for being; and this military enthusiasm in turn persuaded President Bush that a conflict with Saddam was operationally viable and a genuine option.[63]

The US policy towards Iraq began to come unstuck as Bush and other American politicians laid the rhetorical groundwork for the imminent war. In truth, Saddam was a brutish, oppressive leader who largely satisfied the US (in spite of his undemocratic rule) by keeping the Iraqi state together. The State Department had long observed that the Iraqi population consisted not only of Sunni Muslims (the minority from which Saddam himself had emerged) but also Shia Muslims and Kurds. The Shias alarmed State Department and CIA analysts, who predicted a possible, fundamentalist alliance between Shia-dominated Iran and a Shia-controlled Iraq; the Kurds scared American planners, who had been working hard to court Turkey, which had its own Kurdish 'problem' in the south-east of its territory, and would not respond well to Iraqi Kurds trying to form their own independent state. Although these American fears were certainly exaggerated, the possibility remained that in a democratic Iraq these three ethnic or religious groupings might have gone their separate ways; but Saddam, for all his intransigence and bloody oppression, kept the country together. If he could just be persuaded to keep out of Kuwait, and to carry on the good work of facing down Iran, he could still be valuable to the US, as he had been in the past.[64]

Of course, George Bush did not present the issue to the American people in this way, since this brand of realpolitik usually upsets many of them and undermines the noble rhetoric more usually employed to muster Americans to war. Instead, the Bush administration tried to build support for an attack on Iraq by stressing Saddam's many crimes, and claiming that his continued survival constituted a threat to global peace. In the short run, this was a smart tactic: (true) stories of Saddam using poison gas on his own people, of the brutality of his regime, and of its undemocratic make-up established him in American minds as a thug who deserved to be punished. In the long run, however, this rhetorical move brought its own dangers. What about the many other thugs around the world who committed similar crimes, and who were on the American payroll? What about other undemocratic regimes, or other countries (like Israel, the number one recipient of US aid) which had invaded and occupied their neighbours without an American response? Even if Americans could overlook all this, one major problem remained: if Saddam was demonised, US public opinion would find it hard to tolerate his continuing in power when Kuwait had been liberated; and yet American policy in the region depended heavily on the idea of a unified Iraq, and the reality of Saddam's oppressive role in maintaining 'stability'.[65]

We can see, then, that the US allowed itself to be drawn into a conflicted policy on Iraq from the earliest days of the military build-up. This explains, in large part, the muddled appearance of US policy towards Iraq after 1990. When Operation Desert Storm was finally implemented in January 1991, it seemed that the US commanders on the ground would exploit their advantage in equipment and personnel and sweep Saddam from power; moreover, George Bush and American military leaders urged the majority Shia population (and the Kurds) to rise up against Saddam, strongly hinting that US support for any uprising would follow. The State Department and the CIA, however, continued to stress Saddam's usefulness to the US as a 'stabilising' force in the region, even after his Kuwaiti mischief, and the US military was instructed to allow Saddam to survive. In fact, the Iraqi leader was probably strengthened, at least inside Iraq, by the flip-flop in American support for a regime change: the promise that the US would help the rebels to overthrow their leader had emboldened Saddam's critics and brought them to the surface. Saddam, using his troops and his helicopters, calmly imprisoned or killed this resistance movement as the massive US-led military force looked on, deferring to the importance of the 'stabilising' effort.[66]

The years following 1991 have produced a catastrophe for the civilians of Iraq, who have been subjected to military attacks and economic warfare at the hands of the US. Unwilling to use military force to remove Saddam, but eager to 'contain' him and to avoid the possibility of another Kuwait, the US imposed an extremely harsh sanctions regime, which amplified the material damage of the 1991 conflict throughout Iraqi society. Iraq's infrastructure, seriously damaged by the American bombing, was kept in a moribund state by prohibitions on imports and exports; even essential items, such as medical supplies, were kept from the Iraqi people.[67] When George Bush was defeated by Bill Clinton in 1992, all hopes of a change in US policy were swiftly quashed: one of Clinton's first foreign-policy initiatives was to launch a cruise-missile attack on Baghdad, in 'retaliation' for a supposed Iraqi plot to murder his predecessor on a visit to Kuwait.[68] Throughout the Clinton administration, Iraqis had to endure either direct military attack or the catastrophic effects of sanctions. Meanwhile, a strengthened Saddam continued to keep the country together, eliminating his domestic opponents and preserving the 'stability' of the region.

To many observers in the US, American policy towards Iraq has seemed a grand failure. Despite his defeat in 1991, Saddam has outlasted George Bush and seems set to eclipse even Bill Clinton's tenure. Moreover, the UN-authorised (but US-dominated) weapons inspection team in Iraq, UNSCOM, was expelled from the country in the prelude to the major US attack on Iraq in December 1998. US commentators who had accepted their government's descriptions of Saddam's crimes and his 'rogue' status were doubly frustrated by his survival in power and his apparent evasion of an international weapons inspection regime.[69] Behind this version of the US war on Saddam, however, we can uncover a more complex agenda, and we can see that many of the goals of US policy towards Iraq have been achieved in the 1990s. If we accept that American policymakers have placed a premium on a unified Iraq, Saddam's survival seems less a defeat than a victory for US policy in the region. Moreover, the ease with which the US has been able to attack Iraq in the past decade – both in terms of the military's easy access and the absence of international opposition to US strikes – illustrates the success of the American 'containment' policy. The US is hazily suspicious of Saddam himself, but basically realises his resemblance to many other regional tyrants who have happily served American interests over the decades; US policymakers are rather more scared of Shia fundamentalism or Kurdish nationalism, and so they have chosen to keep Saddam in power even as they remind him, with military strikes and sanctions, that they have him surrounded. Spokespeople from the State Department like to boast of how US 'containment' keeps Iraq from bullying its neighbours; in fact, the US fears that Iraq's internal tensions will change the make-up of the Middle East, and so US policy is intended to deter not Iraqi expansion but Iraqi implosion. The US has sought to freeze the status quo, actually bolstering Saddam even as Iraq is cut off from the world.[70]

It is more accurate, then, to see American policy towards Iraq in the 1990s as rather successful, at least on its own terms. The problem lies not in US military weakness, but in the brutishness of an approach to Iraq which punishes those ordinary people least able to affect their destiny. As we've seen, the US encouraged the Iraqi people to overthrow Saddam in 1991, only to stand on the sidelines as Saddam quashed their rebellion. American rhetoric concerning sanctions since 1991 has been equally disingenuous. What can Iraqi civilians do to overthrow either Saddam or the sanctions regime? The State Department often suggests that sanctions are intended to undermine Saddam, an outcome which might provide an opening for a concerted, internal challenge to his rule. However, in reality sanctions have had the opposite effect: they have denied resources to Saddam's enemies, have had little effect on his personal well-being, and have enabled him to reach out to ordinary Iraqis and blame their predicament on the US.[71] Of course, American policymakers are fully aware of these facts, and their continued commitment to the sanctions regime can only mean that they see the survival of Saddam (and the impoverishment of his people) as a desirable goal.

Evidence to this effect was offered by Madeleine Albright in an interview with the CBS television show '60 Minutes' in 1996. The interviewer, Lesley Stahl, confronted Albright with the effects of sanctions on Iraq, noting that 'there is no longer much hope that the sanctions will inspire the people to rise up and topple the government'. Given the apparent failure of the sanctions to produce revolt, and their crippling effects on Iraqi society, Stahl questioned their continued usefulness:

> STAHL: We have heard that a half a million children have died, I mean, that's more children than died when – in Hiroshima. And – and, you know, is the price worth it?
>
> ALBRIGHT: I think this is a very hard choice, but the price – we think the price is worth it.[72]

Of course, the value of this particular arrangement stems from the simple fact that the 'price' is paid by Iraqis, rather than the United States. The US has been able to tighten the economic screw since 1991, or to bomb suspected weapons or radar sites at will; Saddam has survived intact, and any pretensions he might have towards making another foray outside his borders have been dashed. The only losers in this are Iraqi civilians, denied basic health care and food, and enduring a generation of malnourishment and poverty. The US military underpins their misery, enforcing their isolation and standing ready to attack at any time.[73]

Kosovo

When Iraq invaded Kuwait, a vital US interest – the regular flow of oil in the Middle East – was threatened. This certainly explains the expeditious response of George Bush, even if more complex issues of ethnic and religious rivalry have shaped American policy in the subsequent decade. In contrast, the disintegration of Yugoslavia after 1991 threatened few immediate US interests and, as we saw in the last chapter, Bill Clinton was content to keep out of the fighting even as it became clear that Bosnian Muslims were being 'ethnically cleansed' by Serbs and Croats. In the absence of an urgent US motive for involvement, the flip side of the 'Powell Doctrine' was invoked, and American forces played little or no part in the bloody conflict until the limited airstrikes of 1995. Although the 'Butcher of Baghdad' was quickly confronted in the deserts of Iraq and Kuwait, the killers of Belgrade and Pale were left to complete their 'cleansing' without American opposition.[74]

After 1995, this reluctance to engage in the Balkans was challenged by events. The US had brokered the Dayton Agreement, and had therefore acquired a stake in the region, if only at the level of saving face.[75] The American public, meanwhile, was perturbed by new reports of ethnic cleansing, and hardly persuaded that the US and its allies had performed admirably in their 'peacekeeping' efforts before 1995. Finally, the NATO alliance had emerged from the Bosnian war with a serious credibility problem. Although NATO had been installed as a kind of military arm of the UN in 1994, its forces had enjoyed very little success in preventing Serb offensives, or defending the 'safe areas' which had been promised by the UN. The most powerful military alliance in history had failed comprehensively to stop Croatia and Serbia from carving up Bosnia, a fact which hardly recommended NATO as a force for peace and stability in the post-Cold War world. This left NATO looking for a chance to redeem itself, desperate to improve its image in Europe and the US after its earlier humiliation.[76]

Unsurprisingly, the Dayton Agreement did not secure a conclusion to the Balkan conflict. Slobodan Milosevic turned his attention to the small province of Kosovo, formally a part of the Yugoslav federation but traditionally (and politically) a separate entity from Serbia, the federation's dominant member. In 1997 and 1998, troops from the (Serb-controlled) Yugoslav army, as well as Serb paramilitary groups, waged a war inside Kosovo with the Kosovo Liberation Army (KLA), an armed band of Kosovar Albanians seeking independence from Serbia. Kosovo, with 90 per cent of its population being Kosovar Albanians, had been subjected to an increasingly centralised and direct rule from Belgrade, a development which cut against the former autonomy enjoyed by the region and which scared many Kosovar Albanians. By 1998, the Serbs were running a campaign of intimidation against the KLA and many Kosovar civilians, and incidents of violence and reprisal increased accordingly.[77] The US encouraged NATO to threaten Milosevic, and to promise some form of intervention if Serbia continued to undermine Kosovo. As in the Bosnian war, these threats seemed at first to be empty; until the Serbs rejected a peace deal brokered in March 1999, and NATO finally made good on its pledge to intervene. Over the next eleven weeks, the overwhelmingly American forces of NATO launched a huge aerial attack on the Serbs in Kosovo and on Serbia itself, destroying thousands of targets and finally bringing Belgrade to a standstill. In June 1999, Milosevic at last agreed to surrender terms, and NATO forces entered Kosovo on the ground, without opposition from the Serbs.[78]

The American-led intervention in Kosovo created a bitter debate in the US, and produced some unlikely allies amongst commentators. Right-wing politicians urging a more robust response to Serbia were supported by left-leaning activists who were pleased at last to see the US acting on behalf of the powerless.[79] Other commentators on the left, meanwhile, banded with isolationists and suggested that the US would do better to stay out of the conflict altogether.[80] It's fair to say that those on the left of the political spectrum were most divided by the war in Kosovo. Many activists who had bemoaned the American abdication from other conflicts, or US participation on the side of injustice when the American military had been employed, were confronted by a US/NATO operation which seemed to target an unjust power. Could one forget about the US military's assaults on Iraq, Panama or Sudan, and cheer on the effort against Serbia? Was the Kosovo operation a rare but admirable instance of the US backing the right side?[81]

To answer this question, we need to put the Kosovo crisis into a broader context. Although it is hard to decry the new US desire to stand up to Milosevic, it's worth remembering that the US had overseen Milosevic's international rehabilitation at Dayton. Most analysts of the recent Balkan conflicts have heaped blame for the fighting since 1991 on Milosevic's various nationalist and expansionist projects; at Dayton, the US negotiators essentially closed the book on Milosevic's war crimes and treated him as a serious and sincere proponent of peace in the region.[82] I stress this point because the US government and media largely gave Milosevic the Saddam Hussein treatment in 1999, and emphasised his undemocratic and brutal role in the break-up of Yugoslavia.[83] This was common knowledge before the Dayton talks in 1995, but the State Department preferred to deal with Milosevic rather than to isolate him politically or militarily. Since Dayton certainly strengthened Milosevic's position within Serbia, it was disingenuous of the American government to blame him wholly for the mess in Kosovo. From 1991 onwards, Milosevic had been rather consistent in his pursuit of a racist, nationalist and expansionist agenda of ethnic cleansing and war; any inconsistency came from the US, which was prepared to tolerate Milosevic's destructive behaviour for most of the time, while launching into occasional (and often flimsy) condemnation at random intervals. This was not the foundation for the preservation of human rights in Kosovo, and Milosevic can hardly be blamed for thinking that the US would again avert its gaze as he resumed his oppression within Yugoslavia.[84]

If the US played a role in Milosevic's survival after Dayton, it was entirely responsible for the conduct of the Kosovo war and its effects on the Kosovar Albanians. Although Milosevic's forces in Kosovo had substantially honed their intimidatory tactics in the weeks and days before NATO commenced its aerial attacks, the bulk of the Kosovar Albanian population remained inside Kosovo until the shooting began. At this point, the American strategy for pursuing the war had grave and direct consequences for Kosovo's civilian population. Bill

Clinton, with the examples of Vietnam and Somalia lodged imperfectly in his mind, insisted that any US intervention should be limited to an aerial campaign. Although this would certainly satisfy the strategic goal of limiting US casualties, the cost of this achievement was the vulnerability of Kosovar Albanians on the ground. Unsurprisingly, the Serb forces inside Kosovo used the NATO bombing as an excuse to empty Kosovo of its non-Serb majority population, burning homes and killing refugees without any NATO opposition on the ground. Although the US may not have intended or desired this outcome, the expulsion of virtually the entire Kosovar Albanian population was a direct result of the limited military tactics chosen by President Clinton. While US planes soared high above Kosovo, battling poor weather and restrictions on low-level flying (imposed to reduce pilot risk), the Serbs committed ethnic cleansing on an enormous scale, with minimal resistance.[85]

It could be argued that the eventual NATO victory in Kosovo justified the means used to achieve it, and that the completion of the air campaign with virtually no military casualties vindicated the cautious tactics. However, this would be to overlook not only the thousands of Kosovar Albanians who were killed in the various Serb expulsions, but also the unsettled outlook for Kosovo's future after the conflict. The Kosovar Albanians forced into Albania, Macedonia and Montenegro were predictably distraught at their experience, and eventually returned to Kosovo (under NATO escort) with a much-reduced commitment to coexistence with their former Serb neighbours. This brittle circumstance has forced many of the minority Serb population in Kosovo to leave their homes, further inflaming the situation and inspiring more nationalist hatred inside Serbia.[86] Meanwhile, the US-led NATO forces which helped to create the refugee problem made every effort to avoid this difficult task of policing a post-war Kosovo, and the US revived its familiar strategy of dumping intractable problems on the UN. Although the prognosis is not clear, early indications suggest that the ethnic and political tensions which caused the Kosovo crisis remain as strong as ever; and that the US desire for involvement in the region, even after pummelling Yugoslavia for nearly a hundred days, is waning once more. Against this backdrop, it's easier to see the continuity between the established contours of US foreign policy and the 'selfless' American role in Kosovo; and it's harder to praise the US military for its partial, problematic, and unfinished role in the defence of human rights in Kosovo.[87]

Isolationism and terrorism

One of the most striking news stories to emerge from the war in Kosovo concerned the pilots of the B-2 bombers which flew many offensive sorties over Yugoslavia. According to a report in the *Wall Street Journal*, many B-2 crew members based in Missouri flew missions directly from the US to their Yugoslav targets, before returning to Missouri for landing. These pilots could find themselves bombing Milosevic one day, then returning to the US to mow their lawns or take their families for a meal the next. The *Wall Street Journal* noted the surreal effect of this kind of combat, and the contrast between the heat of battle and the absolute ordinariness, even banality, of life in the US. During the Kosovo conflict, there was little sign in the US that the country was fighting a major war; and even the pilots involved in combat could return easily to their undisturbed homes, and familiar surroundings.[88]

This story nicely illustrates the extent to which the US, and especially the American public, is cushioned from the effects of American military action. The size and strength of the US military has not only allowed the US to achieve its objectives quickly, but it has also enabled the American public to enjoy the benefits of isolationism and of military engagement. While US bombs rained down on Yugoslavia, the conflict struggled to make the headlines in American newspapers and on television shows. The low-level war with Iraq, meanwhile, took place throughout 1999 beneath the public radar altogether. Where the US public does exhibit awareness of US military involvement, popular perspectives tend to bear out a series of stories which the Pentagon and the State Department have been selling since the Gulf War: the US uses moderate force, targeted with pinpoint accuracy, to achieve a series of just political goals with minimal civilian casualties. Given the prevalence of these interpretations of US military action, commentators have noted that Americans have been numbed to the effects of war; and are too ready to believe the Pentagon/State Department line on the restraint and effectiveness of US military action. I want to critique these ideas about American military efficiency, and to trace some of the possible consequences of a desensitised US public as we contemplate sources of conflict in the twenty-first century.[89]

The most obvious weakness in the argument for the military's efficiency would simply hold that 'precision bombing' is an oxymoron. Even with the technological advances of recent decades, the 1991 Gulf War still featured huge quantities of 'dumb' weapons, including the use of carpet-bombing techniques which had been the mainstay of air power in World War II and Vietnam.[90] In Kosovo, meanwhile, efforts to avoid 'collateral damage' (civilian casualties) were hampered by several factors. The sheer number of US attacks in or near heavily populated areas was hardly compatible with a safe environment for enemy civilians, particularly since the many cluster bombs and bomblets dropped during the campaign remained a hazard to civilians even after the fighting was over.[91] Conversely, the advanced technology employed in missile guidance systems could not compensate for poor reconnaissance and research, a fact made amply clear by the disastrous US bombing of the Chinese embassy in Belgrade. While the American government has tried to emphasise the possibilities for more humane and accurate combat tactics, the evidence from Iraq and Kosovo suggests that military conflict is as bloody and destructive as it ever was.[92]

The ironic corollary to this persistence of 'collateral damage' is that those who understand the workings of the high-tech US arsenal may be best placed to defend against it. In practice, this can shift the advantage back to an enemy military force, which can use a variety of tactics to outwit the 'smart' bombs and guided weapons. In Kosovo, where the US insisted on keeping its pilots above 15,000 feet, and NATO eschewed the use of ground forces, a great deal depended on the efficacy of the new generation of 'smart' weapons. In the aftermath of the war, however, it appeared that the Serbs had been very effective in disguising their tanks and planes, and in setting up decoy targets for US pilots to waste their expensive missiles on.[93] In fact, the resilience and ingenuity of the Serb forces, which remained in Kosovo even after weeks of intensive NATO bombardment, played a large part in diverting the bombing campaign to Belgrade and other large cities, with the consequent casualties and damage to civilians and their infrastructure. Even given the most recent technology and overwhelming air superiority, the US and NATO could only persuade Slobodan Milosevic to withdraw his forces from Kosovo by threatening to destroy large parts of Belgrade. This logic suggests that 'smart' weaponry has not so much obviated the need for civilian casualties, as postponed or drawn out the threat to non-combatants. The Kosovo example demonstrates that an effective war continues to depend on the killing and intimidation of large numbers of people, many of them civilians.[94]

In addition to these issues of technological effectiveness, there is a broader difficulty with the American notion that a military offensive can provide an immediate or a lasting solution to a political problem. As we have seen, the American military has been used in Iraq to postpone the moment when the US has finally to engage with the political realities of Iraq's diverse population. With the twin weapons of airstrikes and economic sanctions, the US has been able to maintain Saddam's oppressive hold over the country, and to prevent Iraq from emerging as a strong regional power. The cost of this policy has been the alienation of most Iraqis from the US, and the radicalisation of many Iraqis (and other Arabs) who reject this instance of American imperium. In the Balkans, we can see a similar dynamic. Since at least 1993, the US has shown extreme reluctance to deter ethnic cleansing and its proponents, or to employ an effective mixture of political and military pressure necessary to defend the victims of these 'cleansing' campaigns. Even the Dayton Agreement, which represented the first substantial US engagement in the region since the wars began, pandered to Slobodan Milosevic and legitimised his role in a Balkan peace process. Since 1995, the US has been reluctant either to urge the arrest of Milosevic's chief lieutenants, or to counter Serb moves against non-Serbs in and around Serb-controlled territory.[95] Although the attack on Milosevic in 1999 therefore represented a shift in US commitment to the region, it is hard to see the usefulness of American action unless it is backed up by a long-term commitment, political and military, to peace in the Balkans. Given the US track record, it's more reasonable to suppose that the conflict in Kosovo was a short-term measure enacted by the US in the absence of a long-term strategy; and that the problem of an expansionist, nationalist Serbia will persist in the years ahead.[96]

I have been tracing the curious ways in which American technological and military power has allowed many in the US to be simultaneously engaged with and isolated from the world. Given the ability
of the US military to overwhelm enemy forces at relatively little cost
in American lives, the big military operations of the 1990s have
offered Americans a version of war which looks nothing like Vietnam or World War II. Moreover, the requirement that US forces
defeat their enemy quickly and decisively has shifted more of the
cost of war onto those nations which bear the brunt of an American
attack. Even sceptical US citizens can sleep safely in the knowledge
that war with Iraq or Yugoslavia is unlikely to have any effect on
their daily life in New York or Los Angeles. Recent conflicts have
thus made clear the disparity not only between US power and the
strength of other nations, but between the consciousness of war in
some parts of the globe and the awareness of conflict in the US. The
Iraqi people, for example, have spent virtually a decade living in a
state of siege, enduring US bombing and sanctions which many
Americans are barely aware of. The distance between the two
countries can be spanned in a few hours, but this disjunction of
experience is massive.[97]

It seems prudent, then, to note that many people around the
world are frustrated by the complacency and impenetrability of the
US, and that the apparent absence of political solutions to this (such
as a genuinely multilateral and independent United Nations) is likely
to drive many towards more radical and extreme measures. The US
government has paid great attention to the threat from weapons of
mass destruction, and has based its definition of 'rogue states' on the
maniacal desire of some nations to acquire these weapons. In the
case of some of the nations on the US list, however, the motivation
for acquiring a nuclear or biological capability seems more straightforward: from the perspective of Iran, Iraq or Libya, each frozen out
of the international community by American 'containment' policies,
is there another route by which one can bring pressure on the US?
I don't mean to endorse the acquisition or the use of these weapons,
but merely to suggest that the WMD problem has stemmed not
from the mania of the 'rogues', but from the effective breakdown of
meaningful and equitable dialogue with the US. There is a dangerous imbalance here which has exacerbated the problem: the US can

continue to function without interruption when its relations with such countries deteriorate; but, thanks to US economic, military and political power, other nations face effective ruin when the US shifts to a 'containment' strategy. In a genuinely multilateral world, the isolation of supposed 'rogue states' would not produce this intense anger on the part of the civilian population of a 'rogue', and wouldn't focus this rage onto a particular country; but given the overwhelming US influence in political and economic terms, and the relative marginalisation of the UN, such emotions are inevitable. This has created large and dangerous pockets of resentment towards the US around the world, grounded not in fundamentalism or insanity but in a real perception of the imbalance of power, and a real frustration at the impotence of political means of change.

Given the large US military forces deployed around or near many of the 'rogues', the US may be able to 'contain' a WMD threat by starving populations or bombing them at will. A more troubling prospect, from a US perspective, is the threat of individuals initiating terrorist actions against American property, either abroad or within the United States. In 1996, terrorists proved the vulnerability even of the US army as they bombed the Khobar Towers apartment building in Saudi Arabia, killing nineteen American soldiers.[98] In 1998, the US embassies in Tanzania and Kenya were attacked, leaving hundreds dead and thousands injured. The American government's response to each case was hardly encouraging. US forces in Saudi Arabia were moved to a new, fortified base deep in the desert, but the perpetrators of the original attack remained unknown. In response to the embassy bombings, meanwhile, the US launched cruise missile attacks against Sudan and Afghanistan and blamed a Saudi businessman, Osama bin Laden, for all the trouble.[99]

The temptation in the US has been once more to drain terrorism of its political significance and to sell the American public on the idea that lunatic-masterminds are responsible for these actions, before setting out to apprehend or kill them with extensive force. The folly of this approach is substantial. In the first place, the demonisation of figures like bin Laden ignores the extent to which their actions are grounded in political reality. Spinning its attack on bin Laden in Afghanistan, the US claimed that it had bombed a 'terrorist university' in 1998, as if this were a simple act of right squashing wrong.[100] In subsequent months, reports in newspapers began to trickle down and confirm that 'Terrorist University' was actually created by the US in the 1980s, a part of the CIA's covert campaign to arm and train Afghan rebels in their fight with the USSR; and that TU's presumed Dean of Studies, Osama bin Laden, had been on the American payroll at that time.[101] These facts are crucial not only to making sense of what happened in 1998, but to establishing the political (rather than the military, or psychological) foundation for this particular terrorist threat. The facts are largely ignored, however, since their admission would force exactly the sort of broad debate on US foreign policy which many Americans are reluctant to have.

If the avoidance of politics in the US response to terrorism is a bad idea, the speedy resort to military force (as in the cruise missile attacks of 1998) is no better. The unilateral US bombings of Sudan and Afghanistan were in contravention of international law, and hardly seemed an appropriate or measured response to a complex and terrible problem. It's hard to imagine how the US would respond if, say, China bombed two countries in Latin America after declaring that they had sponsored or harboured terrorists. Moreover, the two targets chosen by US planners in 1998 each had its own drawbacks. In Afghanistan, the missiles failed to kill bin Laden, the supposed target of the bombing.[102] In Sudan, the US claimed to have attacked a chemical weapons plant owned by bin Laden and intended to support terrorist operations. It soon transpired that the plant was neither associated with bin Laden nor engaged in the production of chemical weapons. Instead, the US had bombed the most important pharmaceutical plant in Sudan, and had stopped production of vital medicines on which the Sudanese population depended. The fact that thousands of Sudanese died in subsequent months in the absence of these medicines made little impact in the US. The terrorist menace, exemplified by the embassy bombings, had been answered by a show of strength – even if the chief terrorist had escaped unscathed, and yet another civilian population had been made to suffer by the US military.[103]

In the past decade, the US has been able to project its power in these ways at very little cost, and even to preserve an illusion of American isolation which comforts many ordinary people in the US. The American military has overwhelmed its opponents abroad, and an increasing reliance on air power and guided missiles has minimised disruption – or even awareness of these conflicts – at home. Given the increasing pace of technological change, however, it is hard to believe that the US will continue to go undisturbed in its repose over the coming decades. The American failure (or refusal) to engage politically with 'rogue states' or disaffected populations will ultimately encourage a small minority to express their grievances in horrific ways: by attacking American interests abroad, and even targeting cities within the US. In 1993, Egyptian terrorists protested against the iniquities of US foreign policy by bombing the World Trade Center in New York City, a spectacular target in the heart of the world's financial capital. Although the explosion caused relatively minor damage, it raised the prospect of truly calamitous terrorist actions, on a scale never previously seen. The American response, once again, was to stress the fanaticism of the perpetrators, to depoliticise their actions, and to downplay the threat, lest it unnerve the American people and cast doubt on their security.[104]

We can see, then, that the debate over defence and the military in the US has focused on one supposed threat and largely ignored the other. The American military has continued to arm itself with the latest weapons, to knock the 'rogue states' into line, and to generate an aura of invincibility which reassures Americans of their own safety. Floating above American cities, the rhetoric suggests, will be planes, satellites and 'kill vehicles' which can zap any 'rogue' missile and underwrite the security of the American heartland. The US military thus promises a stable environment in return for massive defence spending: on conventional forces to contain and occasionally pulverise 'outlaws'; and on 'Star Wars' technology to insure against any nasty surprises. The American Congress and successive presidential administrations take the military at its word, and channel huge sums of money to the Pentagon and its suppliers to complete this bargain.

Meanwhile, all of this spending offers little or no defence against the individuals or groups who may try to cause havoc inside the US, exploiting the relative freedom of movement within America and employing high technology to wreak terrible devastation. The US military is hardly an effective weapon against such people, and a system of missile defence – however spectacular and expensive – will be unable to contain the threat they embody.[105] The only effective deterrent would involve an effort on the part of the US to rethink its foreign policy fundamentally, and to minimise the many situations in which American military or economic power has led to profound and enduring suffering in other countries. As long as the US remains insulated from the effects of its actions it will have little sense of the true desperation they produce in others; and of the terrible predicament of those – in Iraq, or Sudan, or the Palestinian territories – who can find meaning and promise in an act of recklessness and destruction.

NOTES

1. Delivered on Capitol Hill, Washington, DC, 19 January 1999.
2. For a representative example of this strain of commentary, see Charles Krauthammer, 'The Unipolar Moment', *Foreign Affairs* 70, no. 1 (1991): 23–33. Krauthammer corrected those who had suggested that the post-Cold War world might be grounded in a broad distribution of military and political force: 'The center of world power is the unchallenged superpower, the United States, attended by its Western allies.'
3. In this sketch and what follows, I have drawn on Michael Klare's *Rogue States and Nuclear Outlaws: America's Search for a New Foreign Policy* (New York: Hill & Wang, 1995); William Greider, *Fortress America: The American Military and the Consequences of Peace* (New York: Public Affairs, 1998); and Sanford Gottlieb, *Defense Addiction: Can America Kick the Habit?* (Boulder, CO: Westview Press, 1997).
4. On the military's role in formulating post-Cold War defence strategy, see Klare, *Rogue States and Nuclear Outlaws*, 6–11.
5. For general accounts of the relationship between defence contractors and the Pentagon, see John L. Boies, *Buying for Armageddon: Business, Society, and Military Spending Since the Cuban Missile Crisis* (New Brunswick: Rutgers University Press, 1994); William H. Gregory, *The Price of Peace: The Future of Defense Industry and High Technology in a Post-Cold War World* (Macmillan: New York, 1993); and Ann Markusen and Joel Yudken, *Dismantling the Cold War Economy* (New York: Basic Books, 1992), 33–68. One study undertaken by the RAND corporation in 1994 noted that some defence contractors with a healthy commercial business (like Boeing) were less dependent on the Pentagon than others, but that the 'technology spillovers' from military to civilian projects would keep Boeing in the defence business: Ellen M. Pint and Rachel Schmidt, *Financial Condition of US Military Aircraft Prime Contractors* (Santa Monica, CA: RAND Corporation, 1994). The subsequent takeover of

McDonnell-Douglas (and its large military division) by Boeing suggests that these 'spillovers' were enticing; and the general consolidation in the aerospace and defence industries in the late 1990s has ensured that each major corporation left standing has a substantial defence division. For details of the extent and ramifications of this corporate consolidation, see Donald M. Pattillo, *Pushing the Envelope: The American Aircraft Industry* (Ann Arbor: University of Michigan Press, 1998), 344–66.

6. For an account of the priorities and perspectives of those 'Cold War communities' in the US which have come to depend upon the defence industry, see Markusen and Yudken, *Dismantling the Cold War Economy*, 170–207. On the politics and social effects of military base closures, see Betty G. Lall and John Tepper Marlin, *Building a Peace Economy: Opportunities and Problems of Post-Cold War Defense Cuts* (Boulder, CO: Westview Press, 1992).

7. This was, in essence, Charles Krauthammer's point; see note 2 above. Although Krauthammer's arguments about the 'unipolar' world were popular in the early 1990s, a subtle shift has taken place in policy-making circles since Bill Clinton's arrival in the White House: with no challenge to the US on the horizon, and numerous instances of ethnic or religious conflict demanding some kind of international response, it has become fashionable to stress the relative weakness of the US, even as the American military continues to eclipse any other fighting force in equipment and funding, and continues to intervene when US interests are at stake. See, for example, Robert J. Lieber, 'Eagle Without a Cause: Making Foreign Policy Without the Soviet Threat', in Lieber, ed., *Eagle Adrift: American Foreign Policy at the End of the Century* (New York: Longman, 1997), 3–25; and Richard N. Haass, *The Reluctant Sheriff: The United States After the Cold War* (New York: Council on Foreign Relations, 1997). I will examine this shift in perceptions of American power in Chapter 4.

8. For an early account of the 'Powell Doctrine', see Rick Atkinson and Bob Woodward, 'Gulf Turning Points', *Washington Post*, 2 December 1990. The general himself codified his perspective in a 1992 article: 'US Forces: Challenges Ahead', *Foreign Affairs* 72, no. 5 (1992): 32–45. It should be noted that although Washington insiders referred to a 'Clinton Doctrine' (stressing the desirability of intervening in small conflicts and/or for humanitarian reasons) in competition with the 'Powell Doctrine', neither Democrats nor Republicans seriously questioned Powell's definition of military needs; merely the conditions under which the military should be employed. After Somalia, the 'Clinton Doctrine' was hardly a convincing pillar of US foreign policy. For a recent perspective on the durability of Powell's ideas among policymakers, see Eric Schmitt, 'The Powell Doctrine is Looking Pretty Good Again', *New York Times*, 4 April 1999.

9. Les Aspin, 'Report on the Bottom-Up Review', US Department of Defense, Washington, DC, September 1993. For an analysis of the BUR,

see Andrew F. Krepinevich, *The Bottom-Up Review: An Assessment* (Wash-ington, DC: Defense Budget Project, 1994); and Klare, *Rogue States and Nuclear Outlaws*, 111–19. The goals of the BUR were reasserted in 1997: The 'Report of the Quadrennial Defense Review', US Depart-ment of Defense, May 1997, declared that 'US forces must be capable of fighting and winning two major theater wars nearly simultaneously.'

10. The issue of nuclear weapons was excluded from the BUR, which circumvented debates over their deterrent value (and the consequent obsolescence of a huge conventional military force) and the desirability of reducing the colossal US stocks of warheads; see Klare, *Rogue States and Nuclear Outlaws*, 119–25. Essentially, then, the US has chosen to keep both a large conventional military and a large nuclear arsenal, a strategy which can only be described as overkill. See Lawrence J. Korb, 'Our Overstuffed Armed Forces', *Foreign Affairs* 74, no. 6 (1995): 22–34. Korb elaborated on this topic in a speech at the US Information Agency, Washington, DC, on 11 December 1996, and took issue with the exclusion of US allies from most Pentagon assessments of military planning needs: 'Take a look at the United States, you add NATO's allies, you add Japan, you add South Korea, and you add Israel, we have 80 percent of all the world's military expenditures. (Chuckling) So, I mean, this idea that somehow or another, you know, that we're being jeopardized, I mean, to me just doesn't make a great deal of sense.'

11. Colin Powell warned of the emergence of new 'demons and dangers' at the Pentagon press conference accompanying the release of the BUR, 1 September 1993. Ironically, Powell had told *Army Times* newspaper in April 1991 that 'I'm running out of demons. I'm running out of villains. I'm down to Castro and Kim Il Sung.' Of course, this was before the emergence of those fearsome rogues named by Powell and Aspin in 1993 – Mohamed Farah Aideed and Ratko Mladic – and Saddam Hussein's reassignment to the rogue's gallery; as Powell put it to reporters, noting his earlier remarks on the paucity of 'demons': 'History and central casting have supplied me with new ones along the way.' For this earlier scepticism on Powell's part, see Fred Kaplan, 'Powell Says Cuts Can Be Made', *Boston Globe*, 9 April 1991.

12. On the US demonisation of Saddam, see Dilip Hiro, *Desert Shield to Desert Storm: The Second Gulf War* (London: HarperCollins, 1992), 135–6; John Mueller, *Policy and Opinion in the Gulf War* (Chicago: Univer-sity of Chicago Press, 1994), 40–42; and, for some sense of the bi-partisan nature of the US campaign, Democratic Congressman Stephen J. Solarz's January 1991 essay 'The Case for Intervention', reprinted in Micah L. Sifry and Christopher Cerf, eds, *The Gulf War Reader: History, Documents, Opinions* (New York: Random House, 1991), 269–83.

13. For the Clinton administration's perspective on the 'rogues' (also known as 'outlaws' or 'backlash states'), see the essay by National Security Adviser Anthony Lake, 'Confronting Backlash States', *Foreign Affairs* 73, no. 1 (1994): 45–55. Lake's core group of 'rogues' comprised Cuba, North

Korea, Iran, Iraq and Libya; these nations shared a 'siege mentality', Lake argued, and had 'embarked on ambitious and costly military programs – especially in weapons of mass destruction and delivery systems'. An updated list of 'rogues' (including Syria) was provided by former Reagan adviser Raymond Tanter, *Rogue Regimes: Terrorism and Proliferation* (New York: St. Martin's Press, 1998), in a monograph which essentially endorses the fears and exaggerations of the Clinton administration. The best guide to the hysteria and constructedness of the 'rogue threat' is Michael Klare's *Rogue States and Nuclear Outlaws*, especially 130–68.

14. Of course, the obverse of this fact is that those nations which are governed undemocratically, and which have sought to acquire WMDs, are potential 'rogues' of the future. For an analysis of proliferation and of the likely candidates for future 'roguery', see Klare, *Rogue States and Nuclear Outlaws*, 169–231. Klare makes the important point that US efforts to control the spread of WMDs have been patchy at best; and that an American desire to exclude US stocks of WMDs from any international monitoring has hampered multilateral efforts to control WMD proliferation. The substantial battle in the US Congress over the Chemical Weapons Convention is one example: see Michael Krepon, Amy E. Smithson and John Parachini, *The Battle to Obtain US Ratification of the Chemical Weapons Convention* (Washington, DC: Henry L. Stimson Center, 1997). The US government, under pressure from the American biotech industry, has also shown great reluctance to accept international monitoring of biological WMDs: see Debora MacKenzie, 'Deadly Secrets', *New Scientist*, 28 February 1998.

15. The original roster of 'rogues' was offered by Colin Powell at the 1 September 1993 Pentagon press conference announcing the BUR. Powell's identification of Saddam Hussien, Ratko Mladic and Mohamed Farah Aideed as founding members of this new international guild of roguery hardly allowed for the many differences between them, or their markedly different relationship with (and threat to) the United States.

16. An influential and high-profile demand for better relations with Iran was offered by Zbigniew Brzezinski, Brent Scowcroft and Richard Murphy, 'Differentiated Containment', *Foreign Affairs* 76, no. 3 (1997): 20–31. On Gaddafi's handover of the Lockerbie suspects, see Marlise Simons, '2 Libyan Suspects Handed to Court in Pan Am Bombing', *New York Times*, 6 April 1999. The partial detente between North Korea and the Clinton administration is the subject of Warren I. Cohen's 'Compromised in Korea, Redeemed by the Clinton Administration?', *Foreign Affairs* 76, no. 3 (1997): 106–12.

17. Madeleine K. Albright, 'The Testing of American Foreign Policy', *Foreign Affairs* 77, no. 6 (1998): 50–64. Albright had been using this taxonomy of nations for some time previous to this article, which probably reflects the shift in Clinton administration policy after the Somalia debacle and PDD-25.

18. This figure refers to the number of nations which contributed combat forces to Operation Desert Storm; around twice this number participated in Operation Desert Shield or contributed financially to the Coalition effort. For details of the participants, see Alberto Bin, Richard Hill and Archer Jones, *Desert Storm: A Forgotten War* (Westport, CT: Praeger, 1998), xvii.

19. The first night of the air campaign against Iraq set the tone for the dominant role of the US forces: 93 per cent of the 1,300 sorties flown in the first twenty-four hours involved American aircraft; see Lawrence Freedman and Efraim Karsh, *The Gulf Conflict 1990–1991: Diplomacy and War in the New World Order* (Princeton: Princeton University Press, 1993), 301. Over the course of the entire campaign, US pilots flew around 85 per cent of the sorties, and dropped around 9,000 'smart' bombs in addition to 210,000 'conventional' bombs: Bin et al., *Desert Storm*, 235.

20. For upbeat accounts of the debates surrounding NATO's role in the post–Cold War world, and the eventual decision to push for the expansion of the Alliance, see Gerald B. Solomon, *The NATO Enlargement Debate, 1990–1997: Blessings of Liberty* (Westport: Praeger, 1998); Piotr Dutkiewicz and Robert J. Jackson, eds, *NATO Looks East* (Westport: Praeger, 1998); and Clay Clemens, ed., *NATO and the Quest for Post-Cold War Security* (London: Macmillan, 1997). A rather more critical perspective is offered by some of the essayists in Philip H. Gordon, ed., *NATO's Transformation: The Changing Shape of the Atlantic Alliance* (Lanham, MD: Rowman & Littlefield, 1997); and by George W. Grayson, *Strange Bedfellows: NATO Marches East* (Lanham: University Press of America, 1999). It should be stressed, however, that the overwhelming majority of studies of NATO expansion have warmed to the idea.

21. On some of the reasons for US interest in NATO expansion, see Stanley Hoffmann, 'The United States and Western Europe', in Lieber, ed., *Eagle Adrift*, 178–92; and Grayson, *Strange Bedfellows*, xxii–xxiii. The NATO Expansion Act, HR 4210, 103rd Congress, Second Session, was introduced in the House of Representatives on 14 April 1994.

22. Albright used this term in 'The Testing of American Foreign Policy', 52.

23. Kissinger offered his views to this effect in the hearing on NATO expansion of the Senate Foreign Relations Committee, 30 October 1997. On the prevalence of 'virtually racialist' views of Russia within the US policymaking establishment, see Anatol Lieven, *Chechnya: Tombstone of Russian Power* (New Haven: Yale University Press, 1999), 5–6.

24. The danger of 'recreating a kind of iron curtain' with an expanded NATO is addressed by Hoffman, 'The United States and Western Europe', 183. This was also on the minds of some congressional representatives who were sceptical towards NATO expansion. Note the questioning of Madeleine Albright by Senator Jeff Bingaman at the hearing on NATO enlargement of the Senate Armed Services Com-

mittee, 23 April 1997. Bingaman noted Albright's remark that the Iron Curtain should not be recognised by NATO as a block to expansion, lest such action should validate Stalin's dividing line in Europe: 'But [NATO expansion] does validate the notion that there is going to be a dividing line. And instead of eliminating the dividing line, it essentially sets out to move it. And we are saying that – we're putting the emphasis on moving the dividing line, rather than on eliminating it. And that concerns me.'

25. A detailed (but jargon-filled) summary of the shift towards offensive operations and missions outside NATO's traditional sphere of influence is offered by Charles Barry, 'Combined Joint Task Forces in Theory and Practice', in Gordon, ed., *NATO's Transformation*, 203–19.

26. See Madeleine Albright's statement to the North Atlantic Council, Brussels, 8 December 1998; and her subsequent press conference at NATO headquarters in Brussels. Rather cryptically, she told one reporter that 'we are not trying to get NATO to go global.... What we want is for NATO to be able to act in the area that it now acts in and also to be able to have missions out of area that affect the interests of NATO members.'

27. On European reservations, see William Drozdiak, 'Albright Urges NATO to Take Broader Role', *Washington Post*, 9 December 1998. For a more direct sense of European anxieties over American intentions, see Jonathan Steele, 'Nuking the Neighbours', *Guardian*, 5 January 1999.

28. The context of EU failures or reluctance since 1990 is an important one for NATO expansion; the inability of the EU either to mobilise independently in Bosnia, or to persuade the US to take an interest before 1995, hardly established the EU's claims to a separate European defence policy; while the increasing emphasis on stringent economic criteria for European Union membership largely and indefinitely alienated the former Warsaw Pact nations from the EU, making NATO the next best option for a gesture of Western integration. On NATO membership as a consolation prize, see Hoffmann, 'The United States and Western Europe', 183; on the inability of the EU to organise effectively away from NATO, see Philip H. Gordon, 'Introduction', in Gordon, ed., *NATO's Transformation*, 4–5.

29. See, for example, the remarks of Professor Jack Matlock of the Institute for Advanced Study, Princeton, at the hearing on NATO expansion of the Senate Foreign Relations Committee, 30 October 1997. In the panel discussion that followed Henry Kissinger's appearance, Matlock lamented the perspective of Cold War triumphalists on Russia: 'So to treat [the Russians] now as if they were somehow a defeated enemy and a potential threat to the future would be making the same mistake we made after World War I when we blamed Germany exclusively for the First World War.'

30. Although it is couched in the language of the seasoned US strategy-wonk, Robert Joseph's 'NATO's Role in Counter-Proliferation', in

Gordon, ed., *NATO's Transformation*, 235–55, offers an ominous prospect of NATO's future: 'While the Alliance must retain the option for an effective nuclear response [against possible 'rogue' users of weapons of mass destruction], it is essential to complement NATO's nuclear forces with a mixture of conventional counter-force enhancements and active and passive defences.' Somewhat improbably, Joseph recommends this aggressive posture to combat, among other threats, the danger that North Korea may bomb 'substantial sections' of western Europe 'in the next few years.'

31. Testimony of Henry Kissinger before the Senate Foreign Relations Committee, 30 October 1997.

32. Clinton announced his new policy in the 1999 State of the Nation address: 'It is time to reverse the decline in defense spending that began in 1985.' His policy shift was welcomed by Democrats and especially by Republicans, who controlled Congress and would vouchsafe the extra funds. For some indication of the Republican ardour for military spending, note the widespread opposition to the Kosovo war in Congress in May 1999, followed immediately by a Republican emergency-spending bill which made available an extra $5 billion for 'military programs that the Pentagon never asked for'. Tim Weiner, 'Bill on Emergency Spending Hits $15 Billion at the Finish', *New York Times*, 14 May 1999.

33. These figures are drawn from '100 Companies Receiving the Largest Dollar Volume of Prime Contract Awards – Fiscal Year 1998', US Department of Defense.

34. For an overview of the leading American role in the international arms trade, see Jane E. Nolan, 'United States', in Andrew J. Pierre, ed., *Cascade of Arms: Managing Conventional Weapons Proliferation* (Washington, DC: Brookings Institution Press, 1997), 131–49; Ian Anthony, 'The United States: Arms Exports and Implications for Arms Production', in Herbert Wulf, ed., *Arms Industry Limited* (Oxford: Oxford University Press, 1993), 66–83; and William W. Keller, *Arm in Arm: The Political Economy of the Global Arms Trade* (New York: Basic Books, 1995), especially 51–96. On the importance of foreign sales to US military contractors, see Greider, *Fortress America*, 61–5. Although the 1990s have seen a proliferation of weapons trade fairs around the world, the use of US military equipment in actual conflicts (accompanied by intense interest from the international media) has been the best advertisement for the American products on offer to other countries. Ethan B. Kapstein has described the 1991 Gulf War, for example, as 'the greatest arms sale show on earth'; 'America's Arms-Trade Monopoly', *Foreign Affairs* 73, no. 3 (1994): 13–19 at 15.

35. On the US efforts to dominate the trade in conventional arms, and the political consequences of this policy, see Stephen D. Goose and Frank Smyth, 'Arming Genocide in Rwanda', *Foreign Affairs* 73, no. 5 (1994): 86–96; and the testimony of Holly Burkhalter, program director for Human Rights Watch, before the Foreign Operations Subcommittee of

the Senate Appropriations Committee, 23 May 1995. President Jimmy Carter was responsible for legislation in the US to curb the arms trade, but his efforts met with considerable opposition from the very beginning, and subsequent presidential administrations (and Congresses) have made little effort to comply with the letter of the law. See Joanna Spear, *Carter and Arms Sales: Implementing the Carter Administration's Arms Transfer Restraint Policy* (London: Macmillan, 1995). Burkhalter noted in her testimony that, since the late 1970s, 'weapons have flowed to extremely abusive countries as if this provision of law did not exist, with disastrous consequences for human rights.'

36. William D. Hartung, in his testimony before the 23 May 1995 Foreign Operations Subcommittee, noted that US troops had faced US-developed weapons in Panama, Iraq, Somalia and Haiti; Hartung called this element of American export policy 'the boomerang effect': 'Our "carefully considered" arms transfer policy is batting 1.000 [i.e., 100 per cent] in putting US weapons in the hands of our adversaries in every major war this nation has been involved in during the post-Cold War era.' Hartung's points were reinforced by Lawrence J. Korb in testimony before the same committee: 'Imagine the outcry in this nation if American military men and women are killed by the late model F-15, F/A-18 and F-16 aircraft, Bradley tanks, or Patriot missiles, all of which have been exported in the last 5 years to nations with a history of instability.'

37. As we will see in the debate over the proposed F-22 fighter, the proliferation of high-technology military hardware is a powerful argument for the acquisition of even more advanced equipment. For a recent articulation of this argument, see the essay by Oscar Arias Sánchez, former president of Costa Rica, 'Stopping America's Most Lethal Export', *New York Times*, 23 June 1999. Arias noted the two components of US defense contractors' strategy – to encourage domestic military spending, and exports to 'friendly' regimes – and then linked the two: 'This two-pronged approach serves the manufacturers well: by shipping top-of-the-line arms overseas, they create greater dangers to surmount. They can then argue that continued American supremacy requires the development of even more sophisticated weapons systems – weapons that translate into lucrative defense contracts.'

38. For a sense of the harmony of (elite) interests preserved by this policy, see Gottlieb, *Defense Addiction*, 123–36; at 124, Gottlieb laconically notes that 'everybody gains from this arrangement except the taxpayers.' Greider, *Fortress America*, 11–13, notes that the US has offloaded a 'virtual army' of tanks in the past decade, giving them away to other nations, encouraging local museums to preserve them, and even dumping them in the sea to form artificial reefs for bemused fish. Greider quotes from a 1997 Federation of American Scientists report which notes the coincidence of the early retirement of such weapons and the massive procurement of newer models: 'The services appear to be giving away still useful equipment in order to justify procurement of new weaponry.'

39. Boies, *Buying for Armageddon*, 27–40, offers a detailed account of the entanglement of Congress, the Executive, the Pentagon, and defence contractors, paying particular attention to the web of consultative committees and policy recommendation boards which are staffed by 'experts' who move easily from private to public work. Top officials, even members of presidential cabinets, abide by the 'revolving door' principle and see no conflict of interest in a career which takes them from the corporate boardroom of a military contractor to the Pentagon or State Department, and then back again. Gottlieb, *Defense Addiction*, 113–18, makes the important point that employees of defence corporations did much worse in the 1990s than the shareholders and the executives of those corporations: blue-collar workers enjoyed only a slight share of government 'conversion' assistance (only a quarter of which was dedicated to employee re-training) and were laid off in huge numbers; whilst bosses and shareholders enjoyed huge bonuses and dividends as corporate efficiency and profitability increased, a consistent feature of 'downsizing' across all branches of US industry in the past decade.

40. Tim Smart, 'Count Corporate America Among NATO's Staunchest Allies', *Washington Post*, 13 April 1999.

41. We should also note, in passing, that the military's lengthy affair with corporate America has led some to suggest corporate solutions for the military's problems. David McCormick, a former army lieutenant and now a consultant with McKinsey and Company, suggested in 'The Draft Isn't the Answer', *New York Times*, 10 February 1999, that the armed forces could solve their recruitment problems with performance-related pay. How this would be calculated – the number of bombs dropped, the number of bad guys killed, avoidance of 'collateral damage' – was less clear.

42. Senator John Harkin expressed his scepticism towards NATO expansion at the hearing of the Senate Appropriations Committee, 21 October 1997: 'My fear is that NATO expansion will not be a Marshall Plan to bring stability and democracy to the newly freed European nations, but rather a Marshall Plan for defense contractors who are chomping at the bit to sell weapons and make profits. Billions of dollars in military upgrades are at stake in this agreement.' On the contractors' special deals for eastern European NATO ingénues, and the Pentagon's efforts to assist the new customers for US weapons, see Greider, *Fortress America*, 97–101.

43. On the F-22's development, see James P. Stevenson, 'The Long Battle', *Aerospace America*, November 1998; and Greider, *Fortress America*, 40, 44–5.

44. On the Congressional action, see Bradley Graham, 'House Passes Defense Bill, Omits Funding for F-22 Jet', *Washington Post*, 23 July 1999. Bill Clinton confirmed his support for the F-22 in a press conference at the White House, 21 July 1999. On the frantic efforts of Lockheed and the Pentagon to reverse the funding freeze, see Elizabeth Becker, 'Lockheed

Lobbies Furiously to Restore Financing for the F-22', *New York Times*, 23 July 1999; and 'Air Force Jet in Fierce Fight, in Capitol', *New York Times*, 8 September 1999. The Air Force Association made its own contribution by sending members of Congress the provocatively titled promotional puff *F-22: Does Air Superiority Matter?* Becker notes that Lockheed Martin had spent more than $2 million on lobbyists in the first six months of 1999, and contributed more than $1 million to political candidates of all parties in the 1998 Congressional elections.

45. For an account of the spiralling costs of the programme, see Tim Weiner, 'House is Prepared to Cut Off Funds For F-22 Fighters', *New York Times*, 17 July 1999. On the prospect of F-22 sales to Israel, see Abdel Monem Said Aly, 'The Middle East and the Persian Gulf: An Arab Perspective', in Pierre, ed., *Cascade of Arms*, 253–83 at 261. Bumpers's remark was noted by Becker in 'Air Force Jet in Fierce Fight'.

46. Report of the Committee on Appropriations on the Department of Defense Appropriations Bill, 106th Congress, 1st Session, 20 July 1999. Initial scepticism about the chances of the cancellation of the F-22 programme came from Lawrence J. Korb, 'Why One Vote Won't Kill The F-22', *New York Times*, 26 July 1999; and David A. Fulghum, 'F-22 Headed for Reprieve from Congressional Ax', *Aviation Week and Space Technology*, 9 August 1999. After the Pentagon's furious response to the Congressional hesitation, and Lockheed's expensive lobbying effort, a 'compromise' was reached which affirmed the Pentagon's plan to move the plan to a production/procurement track, even as the military and Lockheed agreed to more F-22 testing. See Juliet Eilperin, 'Hill Compromise Saves F-22 Fighter Jet, Funds Further Testing', *Washington Post*, 1 October 1999.

47. Many commentators noted that the military and its contractors, and even many Congressional representatives, were stunned by the action of the House Appropriations Committee in July 1999; and the rhetoric emanating from the Pentagon and Lockheed all but conceded that the proponents of the F-22 hadn't tried as hard as they could to persuade Congress of the merits of the programme. The speedy Congressional volte-face of September and October 1999 suggests that just a little more alarmist rhetoric and a few more campaign dollars might be sufficient to circumvent Congressional scrutiny. On the surprise of Lockheed and the Pentagon at the Appropriations Committee decision, see Robert S. Dudney, 'Battle of the F-22', *Air Force Magazine*, September 1999. Michael O'Hanlon, a researcher at a think-tank which expressed doubts about the viability of the F-22, complained about the number of Pentagon and defence industry advisers who blanketed Congress with literature supporting the fighter: 'The Pentagon says it's not lobbying, but there's about a half dozen of us in the think-tank world and about a thousand of them talking to Congress.' Becker, 'Air Force Jet in Fierce Fight'.

48. Report on the Department of Defense Appropriations Bill.

49. For a representative sample of the military's scaremongering, see the op-ed piece by acting secretary of the Air Force, F. Whitten Peters, 'Are We Ready to Lose the Next Air War?', *New York Times*, 24 July 1999. The likelihood of any threat to existing US fighters from Russia is very low. Although the Russian firm Sukhoi unveiled its S-37 airplane in 1998, one aerospace commentator noted that it was 'seen more with curiosity than caution by aircraft experts', and that the design would require massive funding (money which Russia does not have) and a decade of development to realise: 'The threat to the West … may be in setting up the S-37 as a 'straw man' in order for Western air forces to obtain scarce funding for weapons to counter it.' Rick DeMeis, 'Russia's Golden Eagle Challenges US Raptor', *Design News*, 2 February 1998.

50. For an account of Reagan's enthusiasm for Star Wars, see Philip M. Boffey et al., *Claiming the Heavens: The New York Times Complete Guide to the Star Wars Debate* (New York: Times Books, 1988). This account was published before the revelation of serious exaggerations and errors in the technical planning of the original laser concepts. For a more critical perspective on the faulty science which went into the Star Wars project, see William J. Broad, *Teller's War: The Top-Secret Story Behind the Star Wars Deception* (New York: Simon & Schuster, 1992). Broad sketches a key role in missile defence for Edward Teller, the inventor of the hydrogen bomb, who kept alive Reagan's hopes of a laser-based system in the 1980s, before switching allegiance (after the discrediting of his views on lasers) to 'kill vehicle' technology in the 1990s. This second strand of Star Wars continued to enjoy billions of dollars of research funding at the century's end.

51. For an overview of the politics in this shift, see Eric Schmitt, 'Missile Defenses Leave Fantasy Behind', *New York Times*, 21 March 1999. Analysts speculated that the Democrats feared their opposition to NMD would expose them to the charge that they were 'soft on defense', and that with the 2000 election in view, they could not afford to allow this impression to go uncorrected. The fact that NMD experiments consistently failed seems not to have bothered either party.

52. For a description of Boeing's work on the laser track, and the problems with this programme, see the United States General Accounting Office report, 'Theater Missile Defense: Significant Technical Challenges Face the Airborne Laser Program', October 1997.

53. On Raytheon's contribution to the NMD, see Michael A. Dornheim, 'National Missile Defense Focused on June Review', *Aviation Week and Space Technology*, 16 August 1999. It's hard to tell if the 'Exoatmospheric Kill Vehicle' was so designated because Raytheon's euphemisms department was on vacation, or to compensate for the fact that the 'kill vehicle' resembles an inverted blender.

54. For details of this failure, see Reuters, 'Antimissile Test is Aborted', *New York Times*, 26 May 1999.

55. On these early efforts to rig Star Wars tests, see William J. Broad, 'New

Anti-Missile System to be Tested this Week', *New York Times*, 24 May 1999.

56. On efforts to rush missile-defence programmes to production tracks, see Bradley Graham, 'Pentagon Gives THAAD a Boost', *Washington Post*, 20 August 1999. After reporting two successful tests of THAAD – after seven consecutive failures – a Pentagon spokesman declared that the US military would now skip more prototype testing 'rather than spending months and millions of dollars on another THAAD prototype launch only to prove a point'. This confidence belied the fact that, with a success rate of around 30 per cent, THAAD had still to prove the point that it could be made to work consistently. Broad, 'New Anti-Missile System', estimates the cost of missile defence in the past few decades at $110 billion; Robert Park, Professor of Physics at the University of Maryland, puts Pentagon spending on missile defence at $60 billion since 1980 in 'Another "Star Wars" Sequel', *New York Times*, 15 February 1999.

57. Joseph Cirincione of the Carnegie Endowment for International Peace told the *Los Angeles Times* that Pentagon planners 'don't want a limited system' of missile defence: 'They want a lot more. That's what's got these contractors salivating.' Paul Richter, 'Deployment of US Missile Shield Looks Ever Likelier', *Los Angeles Times*, 21 March 1999.

58. Although many commentators have observed in the Star Wars programme this privileging of a military over a diplomatic approach, the argument was put most directly by Nobel Prize-winning physicist Hans A. Bethe, who observed the various experiments and research efforts from the beginning: 'These people want to eliminate the danger of nuclear weapons by technical means. I think this is futile. The only way to eliminate it is by having a wise policy.... The solution can only be political. It would be terribly comfortable for the President and the Secretary of Defense if there was a technical solution. But there isn't any.' William J. Broad, 'Star Wars is Coming, But Where is it Going?', *New York Times*, 6 December 1987.

59. A focus for debate on the American recollection of Vietnam was Robert McNamara's *In Retrospect* (New York: Times Books, 1995). For a cogent critique of McNamara and his extremely conditional regrets, see Noam Chomsky, 'Memories', *Z Magazine* 8, no. 7/8 (1995): 28–40. For an account of the skewed lessons learned in Vietnam, as applied to the US–Iraq conflict, see Bruce Cumings's 'No More Vietnams: The Gulf War', in his *War and Television* (London: Verso, 1992), 103–28.

60. On US support for Saddam, even into 1990, see Alan Friedman, *Spider's Web: The Secret History of How the White House Illegally Armed Iraq* (New York: Bantam Books, 1993); Bruce W. Jentleson, *With Friends Like These: Reagan, Bush, and Saddam, 1982–1990* (New York: W.W. Norton, 1994); and Mark Phythian, *Arming Iraq: How the US and Britain Secretly Built Saddam's War Machine* (Boston: Northeastern University Press, 1997).

61. Although many in the US media were complicit in spinning the Iraqi

crisis towards ideas of tyranny, invasion and stability, the obviously undemocratic nature of the Kuwaiti and Saudi regimes, and the unavoidable fact of the oil riches of the region, forced many commentators to accept the truth of American interest. Thomas Friedman, hardly the most critical observer of US foreign policy, told *New York Times* readers soon after Saddam's invasion, and the American response, that 'this is about money, about protecting governments loyal to America and punishing those that are not, and about who will set the price of oil.' Thomas L. Friedman, 'Confrontation in the Gulf: US Gulf Policy – Vague "Vital Interest"', *New York Times*, 12 August 1990.

62. On Saddam's 'linkage' peace plan of 12 August 1990, which would also have required Syrian withdrawal from Lebanon, see Walid Khalidi, 'Why Some Arabs Support Saddam', in Sifry and Cerf, eds, *The Gulf War Reader*, 161–71.

63. For a contemporary account of the pressure on Bush to 'lose or use' his huge army in the Gulf, see Rick Atkinson and Bob Woodward, 'Gulf Turning Points', *Washington Post*, 2 December 1990. On the Pentagon's broader strategic objectives during Desert Shield and Desert Storm, see Klare, *Rogue States and Nuclear Outlaws*, 51–64.

64. On the ethnic and religious make-up of Iraq, and its influence on US foreign policy, see Hiro, *Desert Shield to Desert Storm*, 400–407; Faleh 'Abd al-Jabbar, 'Why the *Intifada* Failed', in Fran Hazelton, ed., *Iraq Since the Gulf War: Prospects for Democracy* (London: Zed Books, 1994), 97–117; and Yitzhak Nakash, *The Shi'is of Iraq* (Princeton: Princeton University Press, 1994), 273–81.

65. For a contemporary view of the shift from demonising Saddam to vouchsafing his survival, see John Pearson et al., 'Gulf Politics Have Bush Treading Softly in Iraq', *Business Week*, 8 April 1991.

66. Until more classified documents come to light, it is difficult to assess the degree to which the events of March and April 1991 were intended by the US. Some facts, however, are clear. For an overview of the shift in US policy, and the fear of instability in a post-Saddam Iraq, see Freedman and Karsh, *The Gulf Conflict 1990–1991*, 410–21; and Andrew Cockburn and Patrick Cockburn, *Out of the Ashes: The Resurrection of Saddam Hussein* (New York: HarperCollins, 1999), 37–41. Freedman and Karsh quote a State Department official as saying (in February 1991, before the uprising) that 'if [Saddam] survives, and is defanged, so what, why worry about it? He can make all the speeches he wants. A weakened Saddam with a weakened political reputation is maybe better for us if he is in power than if he is martyred.' On the encouragement offered by American leaders to the Iraqi resistance, and the rapid collapse of this encouragement when Saddam began his counterattacks, see Nakash, *The Shi'is of Iraq*, 274–5; al-Jabbar, 'Why the *Intifada* Failed', 97; Cockburn and Cockburn, *Out of the Ashes*, 12–13; and John Simpson, *From the House of War* (London: Hutchinson, 1991), 360–61. For a corollary in the Kurdish uprising in the north of Iraq, see Michael

Kelly, *Martyrs' Day: Chronicle of a Small War* (New York: Random House, 1993), 279–280; and Sheri Laizer, *Martyrs, Traitors and Patriots: Kurdistan after the Gulf War* (London: Zed Books, 1996), 30–31. The most direct accusation of US complicity in the massacre of thousands of Kurds and Shia Muslims by Saddam's forces is offered by Ramsey Clark, *The Fire This Time: US War Crimes in the Gulf* (New York: Thunder's Mouth Press, 1992), 55–8. The American belief that the 'stability' of the region depended on a military strongman in charge of Iraq was reflected in the original US hope that a 'palace coup' would simply substitute another military despot for Saddam: see Freedman and Karsh, *The Gulf Conflict 1990–1991*, 415.

67. For general accounts of the effects of sanctions, see Geoff Simons, *The Scourging of Iraq: Sanctions, Law and Natural Justice* (London: Macmillan, 1996); and Sarah Graham-Brown, *Sanctioning Saddam: The Politics of Intervention in Iraq* (London: I.B. Tauris, 1999).

68. For the US justification for this attack, which reached improbably for the self-defence provisions of Article 51 of the UN Charter, see Bill Clinton's 'Address to the Nation', The White House, 26 June 1993.

69. This interpretation of US policy as a failure is exemplified by Caspar Weinberger and Peter Schweizer, 'A Strategy with No End', *USA Today*, 18 December 1998.

70. A rather blunt version of this position was offered by former US ambassador to Iraq, Edward Peck, in a 1996 television interview: 'You get rid of Saddam, and what's going to happen? You know, it isn't that he's a neat guy. He serves as the rather vile totalitarian cork that bottles that place into a country.' Peck dismissed the notion that Saddam posed some external threat – 'He doesn't pose a threat to anybody in the region. We've taken care of that and we're watching very carefully to make sure it won't happen again' – and chose instead to paint a picture of the 'bloodbath' of ethnic violence that would supposedly follow Saddam's demise. As Peck put it, as if the message was not already clear: 'I mean – Can you spell Bosnia?' 'The World Today', *CNN*, 12 September 1996.

71. Most commentators have agreed that, since his suppression of the uprising in 1991, Saddam has consolidated his rule over Iraq; and that the sanctions have enfeebled the Iraqi people. For perspectives on this unfortunate outcome, see Maggie O'Kane, 'The Wake of War', *Guardian*, 18 May 1996; and Graham-Brown, *Sanctioning Saddam*, 92–3, 194–5. Of course, the goal of keeping Saddam 'in his box', as State Department planners have put it, does not necessarily require that the civilian population of Iraq is happy or healthy; quite the reverse. A recent assessment by the Council of Foreign Relations (CFR) suggested that the sanctions regime since 1991 has 'been a success to date', given the containment of Saddam and his inability to threaten his neighbours. The cost of this success – the deaths of hundreds of thousands of Iraqi civilians – is unfortunate, but bearable, at least from an American

perspective. As the CFR report puts it, 'The sanctions have not created conditions enabling forces within Iraq to depose him. (However, this was a desire rather than an explicit objective of the sanctions.)' Eric D.K. Melby, 'Iraq', in Richard N. Haass, ed., *Economic Sanctions and American Diplomacy* (New York: Council on Foreign Relations, 1998), 107–28 at 123.

72. '60 Minutes', *CBS*, 12 May 1996. For details of the US efforts after 1994 to alter the interpretation of the UN resolutions against Iraq to maintain a sanctions regime, see Graham-Brown, *Sanctioning Saddam*, 79–80.

73. On the devastating effects of sanctions, see John Mueller and Karl Mueller, 'Sanctions of Mass Destruction', *Foreign Affairs* 78, no. 3 (1999): 43–65. Noting that US rhetoric frequently employs the threat of WMDs to justify sanctions, Mueller and Mueller argue that the hundreds of thousands of Iraqi civilian deaths under the sanctions regime demonstrate that the sanctions are themselves a WMD: 'If the US estimates of the human damage in Iraq are even roughly correct, therefore, it would appear – in a so far futile effort to remove Saddam from power and a somewhat more successful effort to constrain him militarily – economic sanctions may well have been a necessary cause of the deaths of more people in Iraq than have been slain by all so-called weapons of mass destruction throughout history.' For recent UN estimates which suggest that child and infant mortality rates in Iraq have doubled in the decade since the Gulf War, resulting in hundreds of thousands of child deaths, see 'Child and Maternal Mortality Survey, Preliminary Report: Iraq', UNICEF, July 1999. Even Dennis Halliday, the UN official responsible for humanitarian policy in Iraq, was unable to support the continuing sanctions regime, resigning in August 1998 and lamenting 'our level of complicity in the suffering'. Michael Powell, 'The Deaths He Cannot Sanction: Ex-UN Worker Details Harm to Iraqi Children', *Washington Post*, 17 December 1998.

74. For an explicit comparison between US interests in (and understanding of) the Gulf situation and Bosnia, see Wayne Bert, *The Reluctant Superpower: United States' Policy in Bosnia, 1991–1995* (London: Macmillan, 1997), 108–10; and James Gow, *Triumph of the Lack of Will: International Diplomacy and the Yugoslav War* (London: Hurst & Co., 1997), 203–8. Gow, 208, suggests that the arrival of the Clinton administration, for all its rhetoric of principle and morality in foreign affairs, signalled very little: 'US policy approaches graduated from virtually no action to little action.'

75. Richard Holbrooke has described the various ways in which Dayton has bound the US to Bosnia in his *To End a War*, revised edition (New York: Random House, 1999), 360–72.

76. For a critical perspective on NATO's role in the Bosnian war, and a sceptical treatment of NATO's future as a peacekeeping force, see William G. Hyland, 'Is NATO Still Relevant?', in Clemens, ed., *NATO and the*

Quest for Post-Cold War Security, 154–61. Of course, European governments were also embarrassed by NATO's failure in Bosnia, and more
amenable to the assuaging of their guilt via offensive operations in
Kosovo. See Peter Ford, 'Europe's Kosovo Aim: Redress Bosnia Inaction', *Christian Science Monitor*, 4 February 1999. Within a few days of
the start of the bombing of Kosovo and Serbia in March 1999, the *New
York Times* published an editorial clarifying the benefits to NATO of
this attack: 'The air campaign against Yugoslavia is doing what years of
abstract debate could not. It is beginning to define the role for the
NATO alliance to play in post-cold war Europe.' 'Inventing NATO's
New Role', *New York Times*, 28 March 1999.

77. For a general background on the post-Dayton campaigns of Milosevic
against ethnic Albanians in Kosovo, see Noel Malcolm, *Kosovo: A Short
History*, updated edition (New York: HarperCollins, 1999). 353–6; and
Noam Chomsky, *The New Military Humanism: Lessons from Kosovo*
(Monroe, ME: Common Courage Press, 1999), 28–37.

78. On the diplomatic conclusion to the bombing, see Michael Elliott,
'Getting to the Table', *Newsweek*, 14 June 1999.

79. Susan Sontag argued in favour of NATO intervention in 'Why Are We
in Kosovo?', *New York Times*, 2 May 1999. Responding to critics who
bemoaned US absence from other conflicts, and the 'eurocentrism' of
US concern for Kosovar Albanians, Sontag was icily dismissive: 'If several
African states had cared enough about the genocide of the Tutsis in
Rwanda (nearly a million people!) to intervene militarily, say, under
the leadership of Nelson Mandela, would we have criticized this initiative as being Afrocentric?' Of course, Sontag's jibe overlooked the fact
that many African soldiers were waiting for months in 1994 for the
delivery of US-promised vehicles; but her advocacy of a US right to
take interest in Kosovo was unburdened by such detail. For a collection
of right-leaning views in support of intervention, see Don Feder, 'Why
Right Went Cuckoo Over Kosovo', *Boston Herald*, 14 June 1999.

80. For examples of anti-war sentiment on the right and left respectively,
see Charles Krauthammer, 'We Don't Need to Inflict', *Washington Post*,
26 February 1999; and Chomsky, *The New Military Humanism*.

81. The schism in the American left over Kosovo intervention is described
by E.J. Dionne, Jr., 'Not Munich, But the Holocaust', *Washington Post*,
30 April 1999; and Michael Kazin, 'Culture Wars: For Left, It's Finally
Post-Vietnam', *Los Angeles Times*, 30 May 1999. See also Patricia Cohen,
'Ground Wars Make Strange Bedfellows', *New York Times*, 30 May 1999.

82. Dayton's role in strengthening Milosevic makes the later US appeals to
a 'democratic opposition' in Serbia seem the more disingenuous. Writing
before the Kosovo conflict, Laura Silber and Allan Little were in no
doubt that Dayton had bound the future of the region to the good
behaviour of an expansionist dictator: 'Milosevic controlled all the pillars
of power: the police, the media and finance. In Serbia, there were only
two people who mattered: Slobodan and Mira [Milosevic's wife]. This

was the legacy of Dayton. The West based its peace agreement on Milosevic and his opposite number in Croatia, bolstering their dictatorships at the expense of any support for democracy. That was part of the price of Dayton.' *Yugoslavia: Death of a Nation*, revised edition (New York: Penguin, 1997), 385–6.

83. Bill Clinton, in an effort to explain 'this Kosovo thing' to an audience in March 1999, suggested that Kosovo 'is about our values. What if someone had listened to Winston Churchill and stood up to Adolf Hitler earlier?' 'Remarks by the President to the AFSCME Biennial Convention', Washington, DC, 23 March 1999. One sceptical journalist wondered aloud at a White House press conference about Milosevic's transition from Dayton-statesman to Kosovo-Hitler: 'Joe, in the Bosnian War, there were many more Muslims massacred, perhaps 200,000, which is about 100 times more than have been massacred during the Kosovo offensive. And yet, at the conclusion of that war, Milosevic was brought to Dayton and treated with the respect that's accorded a head of state, and signed the peace agreement. Now he's apparently killed 2,000 people, and President Clinton and Gore are both calling him a junior league Hitler. How do you reconcile that?' Press Briefing by Joe Lockhart, The White House, 29 March 1999.

84. For a summary of the inconsistencies and vacillation of Washington's policy on Kosovo after Dayton, see William G. Hyland, *Clinton's World: Remaking American Foreign Policy* (Westport: Praeger, 1999), 44–7.

85. On the NATO tactics, see Richard J. Newman et al., 'Making War From 15,000 ft', *US News and World Report*, 10 May 1999. Although the State Department tried to pass off these tactics – including the prohibition on low-level flying – as reflecting the nervousness of their European NATO allies, many commentators in the US easily traced them to the Clinton administration's desire to avoid any American casualties, whatever the cost in Kosovar Albanian lives. See Blaine Harden and John M. Broder, 'Clinton's Aims', *New York Times*, 22 May 1999; and 'Messy War, Messy Peace', *Economist*, 12 June 1999. The *Economist* editorial noted that 'this was a war to stop ethnic cleansing, but the main effect was to intensify it. The bombing campaign accelerated the killing ... and it accelerated the emptying of the population at large. In humanitarian terms, the Kosovo campaign turned into a disaster.' See also the entertaining exchange between Pat Buchanan and Senator Joseph Lieberman, 'Meet the Press', *NBC*, 25 April 1999. Buchanan, contending that 'we ourselves have ignited this debacle', noted that 'the massive NATO ethnic cleansing has been caused – is a consequence of air strikes and Rambouillet' (Rambouillet was the French town in which the US-led, abortive Kosovo peace accord was proposed in early 1999). Viewing this blunder, Buchanan wondered if 'there's anybody here who would not accept immediately the status quo ante?' Lieberman responded in double-talk: 'This is an outrageous claim. The status quo ante *was about to be* Milosevic moving into Kosovo and doing exactly what he's done,

slaughtering the Kosovars [stress added].'

86. On the difficult relations between returning refugees and Serb civilians in Kosovo, see Karl Vick, 'Rage Fuels Reprisals in Kosovo', *Washington Post*, 1 July 1999. Three months later, around 100,000 Serb civilians had left Kosovo, and the UN police commissioner Sven Fredriksen was forced to admit that 'the hate is enormous'. Jeffrey Smith, 'Grenade Blast in Market Kills 2 Kosovo Serbs', *Washington Post*, 29 September 1999.

87. On the hasty transition from NATO/the US to the UN, see William Shawcross, 'The Cleanup Crew', *Newsweek*, 21 June 1999. The Pentagon not only dropped the job of policing Kosovo onto the UN, it actually blamed the UN for not moving quickly enough to take up the slack. See Eric Schmitt, 'UN Drags Feet in Kosovo, Pentagon Leaders Declare', *New York Times*, 21 July 1999; and, for the UN's testy response, Judith Miller, 'UN Says it's NATO that Lags in Kosovo', *New York Times*, 22 July 1999. Given that the US and its NATO allies had happily marginalised the United Nations prior to this 'clean-up' mission, the haste with which Pentagon chiefs criticised the UN over its policing operation was seen by many as unseemly: see David Hannay, 'Balkan Scapegoat', *Financial Times*, 16 July 1999.

88. See Thomas E. Ricks, 'These B-2 Pilots', *Wall Street Journal*, 19 April 1999. The wife of one pilot noted that her husband's long-distance commute was 'very strange – to drop bombs and then come home and watch my son's soccer game'. One defence analyst observed that this preference for the relatively detached method of air warfare had some precedent: 'You do it nice and cleanly. Nobody gets their feet muddy. A pilot flies over at 15,000 feet, kills only those people that need to be killed, flies home and has a cold beer with a beautiful young lady. This is not a new concept.' Harden and Broder, 'Clinton's Aims'.

89. On the implications of this sustained use of US forces, see Steven Lee Myers, 'Bomb. Missile. Bomb. Hey, It Looks Like a War', *New York Times*, 21 February 1999; and, for details of the military offensive against Iraq, Steven Lee Myers and Tim Weiner, 'Weeks of Bombing Leave Iraq's Power Structure Unshaken', *New York Times*, 7 March 1999; and Philip Shenon, 'US Quietly Intensifies Attacks on Iraq', *New York Times*, 5 May 1999.

90. For accounts of the 'dumb' weapons in common use in the Gulf, see note 19 above.

91. Evidence of the destructiveness of these weapons arrived swiftly after the fighting: civilians and military personnel in Kosovo and Yugoslavia were killed by unexploded cluster 'bomblets' in the first month of the ceasefire. The Pentagon grimly confirmed that at least 11,000 NATO 'bomblets' might remain active throughout Kosovo and Yugoslavia, each one capable of killing civilians. Mark Fineman and Valerie Reitman, 'The Path to Peace', *Los Angeles Times*, 23 June 1999.

92. After NATO jets bombed a column of Kosovar Albanian refugees inside

Kosovo, killing more than seventy people, Bill Clinton admitted that 'you cannot have this kind of conflict without some errors like this occurring. This is not a business of perfection.' Bill Clinton, 'Remarks to the American Society of Newspaper Editors', San Francisco, 15 April 1999. NATO forces killed Kosovar Albanian and Serb civilians both mistakenly (in the case of the refugee column, and the bombing of a train in April) and through planned attacks on Belgrade. For details of and perspectives on civilian casualties, see Chris Bird et al., 'After the Bombs, the Blame', *Guardian*, 15 April 1999; Robert Fisk, 'NATO Stained with Blood of Civilians', *Independent*, 15 April 1999; and Alexander Nicoll, 'The War Intensifies', *Financial Times*, 17 April 1999.

93. See Eric Schmitt, 'Bombs are Smart, but People are Smarter', *New York Times*, 4 July 1999. Serb forces built fake tanks from wood, and placed barrels of water inside them (which would warm in the sun) to trick the thermal sensors of attacking NATO planes. This may explain the modest rate of attrition of Yugoslav tanks in Kosovo – around 200 of the 300 which entered Kosovo were unharmed at the ceasefire, despite being targeted persistently by the most powerful and sophisticated air force in the world.

94. For the view that the NATO victory was finally effected through the bombing of Yugoslav civilians, see Paul Richter, 'Crisis in Yugoslavia: Officials Say NATO Pounded Milosevic into Submission', *Los Angeles Times*, 5 June 1999.

95. The US has pursued a two-track strategy on the most notorious Serbian war criminals – those who have been indicted by the International War Crimes Tribunal (including Radovan Karadic and Ratko Mladic, leaders of the Bosnian Serbs during the Bosnian war) have been allowed to come and go inside the NATO protectorate without arrest; and those major players, like Milosevic, who have not been charged with war crimes have been treated as statesmen and diplomats when this approach is amenable to American strategy. On the failure to arrest Karadic and Mladic, or to pursue Milosevic even after his indictment by the International War Crimes Tribunal, see Michael Scharf, 'Indicted for War Crimes, Then What?', *Washington Post*, 3 October 1999. Journalists at a White House press conference in March 1999, having heard Clinton administration officials apply *reductio ad hitlerum* to Milosevic over Kosovo, wondered if his simple acceptance of the Rambouillet agreement would wipe the slate clean (again): 'Joe, if I could just follow up on that interesting notion. If Milosevic did quit Kosovo and did sign Rambouillet, is he not a war criminal anymore?' Press Briefing with Joe Lockhart, The White House, 29 March 1999.

96. Milosevic survived the NATO bombardment, and may even have consolidated his political hold over Yugoslavia in the face of the US-led attack. See Scott Peterson, 'Serbia's Fracturing Opposition', *Christian Science Monitor*, 23 August 1999.

97. On the apathy or ignorance of most Americans towards the ongoing

war with Iraq, see Myers, 'Bomb. Missile. Bomb'. Although the Kosovo situation had been discussed at length in the media in the weeks leading up to the NATO assault, public awareness remained low. One television producer in Florida told the *New York Times* of a flood of calls from viewers watching President Clinton's declaration of war, however: 'We kept receiving calls to the station asking us when President Clinton was going to stop speaking to the nation. These people wanted their show back on and they were really annoyed.' Rick Bragg et al., 'For Jane and Joe Public, Wariness and Ignorance', *New York Times*, 26 March 1999. The influence of public opinion in the US will be treated in more detail in the next chapter.

98. On the attack on Khobar Towers, see Christopher Dickey, 'Target: America', *Newsweek*, 8 July 1996; and Brian Duffy et al., 'Terror in the Gulf', *US News and World Report*, 8 July 1996.

99. On the relocation of US forces to a fortified base deep within the desert, see Douglas Jehl, 'US Military in Saudi Arabia Digs into the Sand', *New York Times*, 9 November 1996. US resentment at the slow progress of the (Saudi) criminal investigation was evident in Congressional hearings in 1998 and 1999; see the remarks of Arlen Specter to the hearing of the Senate Judiciary Committee on US counter-terrorism policy, 105th Congress, 2nd Session, 3 September 1998. On the bombings in Tanzania and Kenya, and the US government's attacks on Sudan and Afghanistan, see Madeleine Albright and Samuel Berger, press briefing, The White House, Washington, DC, 20 August 1998.

100. Several administration officials helped to dub bin Laden's Afghanistan camps as 'Terrorist University': see, for example, the op-ed article by Defense Secretary William Cohen, 'We Are Ready to Strike Again', *Washington Post*, 23 August 1998. On the contribution of the CIA to the construction of the 'university', see Tim Weiner, 'Afghan Camps Hidden in Hills', *New York Times*, 24 August 1998.

101. On CIA funding to the Mujaheddin and bin Laden, see Michael Dynes, 'Hunted Leader Trained By the CIA', *Times* (London), 22 August 1998.

102. The bombings probably strengthened bin Laden, in fact, and solidified his (previously shaky) claims to represent a genuine bulwark to American dominance in the Middle East. See John Barry et al., 'Making a Symbol of Terror', *Newsweek*, 1 March 1999. A similar boost was given to the government of Sudan, which had been mired in bitter domestic dispute and a de facto civil war: see Scott Peterson, 'US Attack is "Best Gift" for Sudan', *Christian Science Monitor*, 31 August 1998.

103. Serious reservations over the targeting of the al-Shifa plant were expressed in the days following the bombing: see Hassan Ibrahim et al., 'The Missiles, the Bungling Pentagon, and the Nerve Gas Factory that Never Was', *Observer*, 30 August 1998. By mid-1999, the US government had conceded that the al-Shifa plant manufactured ibuprofen and other medicines rather than nerve gas. See Vernon Loeb, 'A Dirty Business', *Washington Post*, 25 July 1999. A year after the attack, experts estimated

that the demolition of the factory – which produced around 90 per cent of Sudan's medicines – had led directly to a shortage of medicine and thousands of preventable deaths in the following months. See Jonathan Belke, 'Year Later, US Attack on Factory Still Hurts Sudan', *Boston Globe*, 22 August 1999.

104. The 'mastermind' of the World Trade Center bombing, Ramzi Yousef, told the court which sentenced him to 240 years in prison that he had employed violence against the US because 'this is the only language which you understand. It is very painful to innocent people and very painful for anyone to lose a close relative or a friend, but it was necessary. This is what it takes to make you feel the pain which you are causing to other people.' Yousef made specific reference to US support for Israel, the plight of the Palestinians, and to the effects of American-imposed or US-led economic sanctions against the civilian populations of Cuba and Iraq. The judge in the case, Kevin Thomas Duffy, brushed aside these political remarks and maintained that Yousef was 'an apostle of evil'. See Benjamin Weiser, 'Mastermind Gets Life for Bombing of Trade Center', *New York Times*, 9 January 1998.

105. Oddly, American commentators seem fully aware of this threat, but have chosen largely to marginalise or ignore it, especially in their effort to promote missile defence and other high-profile military projects. *New York Times* pundit William Safire, in a puff for Star Wars spending in 1998, offered a bizarre rationale for disregarding the threat from terrorists working on the ground: 'Opponents of missile defense then tried a different argument: a shield in the sky would not stop a terrorist from sneaking a bomb into the US in a suitcase. True enough, and methods of detecting smuggled nuclear and germ weapons need refine-ment. But nations like China, Iran, Iraq, North Korea, India and Pakistan have not been investing heavily in suitcases.' William Safire, 'Stop the "Incoming!"', *New York Times*, 11 June 1998. Safire's core argument for missile defence rests on the idea that 'rogue' governments have spent more money on long-range missile research than on luggage; a position which may reflect reality on one level, but which also ignores the fact that the threat of a 'suitcase bomb' would reside in its relatively cheap cost and the ease with which it might be brought into the US. (And, of course, the fact that statistics for the purchase of suitcases are not closely observed by Western intelligence services.)

CHAPTER 4

AMERICAN MISSIONS

> My fellow Americans, this is our moment. Let us lift our eyes as one nation, and from the mountaintop of this American Century, look ahead to the next one – asking God's blessing on our endeavors and on our beloved country.
>
> William Jefferson Clinton, 1999 State of the Union address[1]

In the previous chapters, I have tried to give a sense of the shape and direction of American foreign policy at the end of the twentieth century. In order to tell this complex story in such a small space, I have largely pushed to one side the many interpretations and frameworks offered within the US to describe the course of American foreign relations. My aim in this final chapter is to redress this deficiency, and to set out some of the principal interpretations (and interpreters) of US foreign policy. I want also to give a sense of the settings in which American analysis takes place – and especially to consider the nexus of academia, think-tanks and government office which shapes the career of many policy 'experts'. Although the predominant explanations for American foreign relations are seriously flawed, and occasionally absurd, we would do well to grasp these arguments, and to concede the fact that their proponents are often sincere in their advocacy.

In the first section, I am going to deal mostly with academic interpreters of foreign policy, though it should be remembered that the boundary between academia and government service in the US is extremely porous. I will consider some of the most popular and resonant ideas of the past decade, before looking broadly at what the various analysts agree upon and share – in their careers and lifestyles as well as their thinking. In the second section, I want to look in more detail at the rhetoric and ideology of government officials, and to examine the political context (including the relationship between the president and Congress) in which policy is made. I will also consider the role and perspective of the media, and finally the influence of public opinion on foreign-policy decisions. My aim in all this is not to give a complete picture of American politics or society, but instead to outline some of the obstacles that stand between US commentators and a clear-sighted view of American actions abroad. I've been arguing up to this point that US foreign policy is seriously flawed in its execution; to get a fuller sense of the problem, we have also to explore the problems of interpretation which have kept many Americans from a sober assessment of the US relationship with the rest of the world.

THEORIES

'The need to be discriminating': foreign policy after the Cold War

Although thousands of American academics and policy analysts had been fixated upon the USSR for more than forty years, surprisingly few of them managed to predict the demise of the Soviet Union in the late 1980s. Consequently, the first responses to the 'new world order' were breathless and excited. The most famous interpretation was offered by Francis Fukuyama, an academic and occasional State Department adviser. According to Fukuyama, the bloodless resolution of the Cold War presaged the 'end of history', at which time all the nations of the world would coalesce in a Western, liberal model of democratic capitalism. Fukuyama argued that the most significant debate in world history had ended with the Soviet bloc: although this meant that world affairs would henceforth seem more mundane, even boring, the 'end of history' also suggested quiet and peaceful times ahead for American foreign policy.[2]

In the last chapter, we looked in some detail at the ways in which this optimism upset the American defence establishment, and at Saddam Hussein's rude interruption of the new idyll. Fukuyama's perspective, however, was more attractive to some policy analysts. On the one hand, commentators like Charles Krauthammer celebrated the 'unipolar moment', viewing the world as a stage cleared of rival actors, and amenable to the uses and preferences of American power.[3] On the other hand, Bruce Russett, Tony Smith and others charged the US with a responsibility to promote democracy around the world, even suggesting that democratic countries were much less likely to go to war with each other than undemocratic nations.[4] The 'democratic peace' thesis attained a wide currency and the public approval of the Clinton administration; some commentators even revived the memory of Woodrow Wilson and spoke of a new US-led internationalism, with a commitment to the spread of democracy abroad as the cornerstone of American foreign policy.[5] Proponents of a new 'Wilsonianism' could take heart from the 'unipolar moment', which suggested that the US was now in a position to shape the world in any way it pleased. The speedy and comprehensive American victory in Iraq hardly discouraged this line of argument, especially as George Bush had framed the struggle in the abstract terms of democracy and rule of law, rather than the tangible American interest in oil and Middle East 'stability'.[6]

In time, however, this euphoria subsided, and foreign-policy analysts outlined a more modest American role on the world stage, whilst simultaneously downplaying the ability of the US to solve the world's problems. It's not altogether surprising that commentators adjusted their expectations in these ways. If the US was truly the dominant power in a unipolar world, other governments and peoples might look to the US for assistance in dealing with their problems. Similarly, the 'democratic peace' argument might compel the American government to support democracy in parts of the world – such as Africa – where few US interests were affected. Both perspectives threatened to commit American money and troops to regions of little strategic importance, with no obvious gain for the US. Beneath the resurgent, 'Wilsonian' rhetoric of democratisation and altruism, then, stronger currents of self-interest and isolationism swept away visions of a new era in foreign relations.[7]

After the US intervention in Somalia in 1993, Richard Betts complained that US foreign policy had been distorted by the 'delusion of impartial intervention', and suggested that the US should either intervene heavily in foreign conflicts, or let 'the locals fight it out'; American forces might then enter an area only after the 'locals' had experienced 'exhaustion from prolonged carnage'. Sensing that the

Clinton administration was poised uncomfortably between the strict pursuit of US interests and putatively humanitarian gestures, Betts essentially provided a justification for American detachment and local 'carnage'. Other analysts have tried to formalise this mandate for detachment, urging caution towards the previously fêted notion of democratisation. In a 1997 article, Thomas Carothers attacked the idea that the promotion of democracy should be the lodestar of US foreign policy, claiming that those who had espoused this idea (including members of the Clinton administration) had overestimated American power:

> [O]nly in a very limited number of cases is the United States able to mobilize sufficient economic and political resources to have a major impact on the political course of other countries.

If Betts questioned the ability of the US to make a difference in foreign conflicts, Carothers provided an argument for avoidance of overseas engagement based on the intractability of other nations' problems. These views reinforced each other, and undermined the more optimistic assumptions about the American role after the Cold War: that the US had the means to intervene abroad, and that American intervention could make a difference.[8]

Noting that the end of the Cold War had produced in the US the 'attractive idea' that 'US moral and pragmatic interests abroad were fusing', Carothers countered that the rest of the world was not destined for democracy, nor would other countries necessarily respond to US encouragement in this area. Fareed Zakaria, in an essay which was highly praised by his analyst peers, even argued that democracy itself might be the problem. Noting the rise of regimes which are nominally democratic, but actually repressive or recalcitrant, Zakaria suggested that the world was increasingly dominated by 'illiberal democracy', political systems which allowed for popular elections but which failed to guarantee the rule of law. For Zakaria, 'illiberal' democratisation would be a foolish goal for the US to pursue; in fact, he suggested that undemocratic countries like Singapore, Malaysia, Thailand, and even China offered more opportunities to their citizens than those nations with free and fair elections, but a volatile social or legal climate. By this logic, the US might actually help regions or nations by denying them democratic rule, a policy which would seem familiar to State Department veterans who remembered US support for undemocratic regimes during the Cold War. In Zakaria's work, the US agenda had come full circle, and the rationale for a new and dynamic American foreign policy had vanished entirely.[9]

The analyses of Betts, Carothers and Zakaria contributed to the notion that Fukuyama's optimism was misplaced: crucially, however, these commentators argued that international conditions dictated a more modest role for the US abroad. By exaggerating the risks of intervention, and especially by impugning the prospects or the quality of democracy in other countries, these theorists tried to shift the debate from an assessment of US interests to an assessment of US capabilities: dissociating themselves from the 'unipolar moment' and the 'end of history', analysts downplayed the potential of American action even as they emphasised the discord and instability which characterised the post-Cold War world. More optimistic or internationalist perspectives have thus given way to 'realistic' strategies for US foreign policy, largely revolving around the simple pursuit of American interests. Michael Mandelbaum, in a 1996 article, lambasted the idea of 'foreign policy as social work', pointing out that 'the world is a big place filled with distressed people', and cautioning against an American commitment to alleviation of their suffering. In Mandelbaum's view, the 'American public' supports assistance to 'poor, distant' countries only 'on behalf of traditional American national interests', a perception which leads to an 'inevitable conclusion': 'the promotion of domestic interests is the default strategy of American foreign policy'.[10] Meanwhile, Mandelbaum's colleague at Johns Hopkins University, John L. Harper, applied 'realism' to the question of American alliances and partnerships abroad, concluding that 'the one indispensable factor in forming reliable partnerships is not democracy or the lack of it, but self-interest, and there is not the slightest reason to think that will change.' Both Mandelbaum and Harper used this pessimistic vision of world affairs to license American self-interest, with predictable implications for non-Americans: Harper's realpolitik might legitimise American support for undemocratic or dictatorial regimes, while Mandelbaum's distaste for 'social work' confirmed the US abandonment of humanitarian crises throughout the globe, unless 'domestic interests' were coincidentally threatened.[11]

The culmination of this line of thinking is Richard N. Haass's *The Reluctant Sheriff: The United States After the Cold War*. Haass argues that the end of superpower rivalry and the threat of nuclear war has created a 'deregulated' world, in which many countries enjoy much greater freedom to pursue their interests, or their grudges against each other. Haass contends that the US should try to 'regulate' this world in two ways: by deterring aggression between countries, and by encouraging participation in the global economy. The key to Haass's thesis, however, is his terminology. The US cannot be a global policeman, enforcing order and laws wherever they are threatened, but must accept a more modest role:

> A sheriff must understand his lack of clear authority in many instances, his need to work with others, and, above all, the need to be discriminating in where and how he engages.[12]

Although Haass's various prescriptions seem eminently sober and sensible, they depend on the idea of the US as a kind of honest broker, and on a vision of the post–Cold War world which resembles the Wild West: we are offered a picture of a benign sheriff facing a lawless terrain (and, presumably, hordes of restless natives), reliant on his own best guesses and the occasional friend to keep the peace whenever possible. Unashamed of the metaphor, Haass even praises the 1991 Gulf War coalition as an example of American 'foreign policy by posse', recommending similar vigilante outfits for future hot spots and conflicts. In fact, Haass's framework merely codifies the recent efforts to justify US self-interest by exaggerating the instability of the rest of the world. The result is a prescription for a 'discriminating' foreign policy which would ignore instances of suffering and need, and underwrite the traditional pursuit of American interests.[13]

We should note two lines of criticism which are absent from this reconfiguration of US policy and the global environment. In the first place, American commentators were disinclined to probe the 'democratic peace' thesis, and especially reluctant to question the sincerity with which the Clinton administration advanced this policy. As we have seen, the evidence suggests, at best, an extremely brittle and meagre American commitment to 'state-building' or humanitarian resolve in Bosnia and Somalia; however, the abortive American actions in each were largely held up by US critics as evidence of the folly of intervention, rather than the folly of a very limited and fragile interest in seeing the job through.[14] Consequently, the shambolic American efforts fuelled the attempts of commentators to stress the volatility of the new world order, and the relative inability of the US to make a difference. Similarly, the inchoate and often underfunded UN operations of the 1990s, frequently upset by American vetoes or US-induced budgetary restraints, were used by American commentators to marginalise the role of the UN in world affairs, and to suggest that a multilateral approach to instability and conflict was doomed to failure. We can therefore observe a reluctance on the part of these commentators to interrogate the American government's 'internationalist' impulses, or the external efforts to find multilateral solutions to the world's problems. This inevitably hardened a new 'realism' in policymaking circles, and ensured the evaporation of the optimism of 1989 within a decade.

The 'wild bazaar': selling global capitalism

During the Cold War, foreign policy 'experts' in the US tended to be drawn from university departments of politics or international relations: these analysts were steeped in ideas of diplomacy and balance-of-power, inclined to make references to Thucydides or Hobbes or the Westphalian system, and reliant on traditional frameworks for understanding interactions between sovereign nation-states. In the 1990s, as we have seen, these analysts quickly distanced themselves from the more optimistic or progressive visions of a post-Cold War order, and realigned their thinking along traditional lines: the world was composed of nation-states – some better, some worse; some of more importance to the US, some of rather less importance. The task of US foreign policy was to define American interests against this variegated backdrop, and not to tarry on the improvement of the whole.[15]

These traditional accounts have been challenged of late, however, by commentators from a new field of expertise: global capitalism. Francis Fukuyama's 'end of history' essay was less a prediction of social justice than a suggestion that the many nations of the world were moving towards participation in a single, interlocking economic system. Following Fukuyama's lead, a new breed of foreign-policy analysts has emerged in recent years, with very different perspectives and biases than the old guard which had traditionally counselled the US government. These 'globalists' comprise not only professors of politics but also journalists, international lawyers, consultants, management gurus and economists. Given the onward march of global capitalism in the 1990s, the globalists have also tended to sound much more optimistic, even triumphalist, than traditional commentators. While Haass and others have outlined a policy of cautious and selective American engagement with the rest of the world, the globalists have identified and celebrated the extensive and complex US involvement in the global economy.

The first contention of the globalists is that the old foreign-policy framework of competing nation-states is nearing obsolescence. After centuries of exchange, interaction and conflict based on competing sovereignties, the world is now defined by international and multinational interests and initiatives. In her 1997 essay 'Power Shift', Jessica Matthews argued for 'the rise of global civil society', suggesting that the peoples of the world would look beyond their national governments not only for goods and services, but in the process of self-identification and in an effort to improve their status. 'Nation states', opined Matthews, 'may simply no longer be the natural problem-solving unit.' The implication of this demise in national sovereignty is clear: American policymakers (and CEOs) should not become obsessed with national governments as the entryway into foreign societies, but should instead concentrate on the various non-governmental points of access and influence. Matthews looked hopefully to the business community, non-governmental organisations (NGOs), and other 'non-state actors' to circumvent foreign governments and to speak directly to the would-be capitalists of the world, the latter presumably eager to participate in a transnational economy.[16]

Following directly from the identification of economic change as the world's most powerful force, globalists have plainly urged the American government to dedicate its foreign-policy resources to the promotion of American business abroad. Jeffrey Garten, who served as under-secretary of commerce in the Clinton administration, described the reorientation of traditional diplomatic goals which he had undertaken with his boss, trade secretary Ron Brown:

> We had a mission: Brown called it 'commercial diplomacy', the intersec-
> tion of foreign policy, government power and business deals. We used
> Washington's official muscle to help firms crack overseas markets. The
> culture was electric: we set up an economic 'war room' and built a 'trad-
> ing floor' that tracked the world's largest commercial projects.

Garten, in terms that would undoubtedly alarm traditional policy
experts, claimed that the promotion of business was a logical basis
for foreign policy 'now that we don't have a military enemy'. Moreover, he held firm even against those who questioned the probity of
the business deals (many involving high-level US government officials)
which he had encouraged in office: 'If you open a wild bazaar, as we
did, you have to expect the occasional pickpocket.'[17]

Alongside the notion that American foreign policy should concentrate on 'commercial diplomacy' by default, the globalists have tried
hard to define the interests of the ordinary citizens of the world as
coincident with those of American corporations. Josef Joffe has argued
that the continued dominance of the US in the years after 1989
proves exactly this point: even if the US reaps greatest advantage
from the world economy, other nations respect the fact that 'the
United States is the ultimate guarantor of the global free trade system'.
As we saw in the first chapter, this contention has little basis in fact;
however, Joffe and others continue to argue for a harmony of interests between US corporations and people throughout the world, a
belief which leads to such sententious aphorisms as Joffe's 'great powers remain great if they promote their own interests by serving
others'.[18] Jeffrey Garten has developed this link between US interests
and 'altruism' more fully:

> America's economic interest in improving the lives of people in emerging
> markets goes well beyond enhancing their incomes so they can purchase
> more goods and services – important as that may be. The issue is the rule
> of law. If foreign governments do not seek to protect basic human rights,
> they are more likely to ignore or circumvent other basic laws of great
> commercial importance, such as those that protect intellectual property
> rights, combat corruption, and mandate the disclosure of critical financial
> information.[19]

It's interesting to note here the double displacement of any respect
for human rights in the abstract. The argument that human rights
should be respected for their own sake – and that this respect may

have the attendant benefit of creating more numerous and contented consumers in a particular country – is a familiar one. For Garten, however, the abstract respect is for the creation of more consumers, with the happy corollary of a better legal climate in which US corporations can do business. Given the Clinton administration's willingness to trade with countries that violate basic human rights – like China – it's fair to assume that 'more products and services' will hardly lead to the improvement of political conditions in 'emerging markets'; and that Garten's focus on income generation and the maintenance of standards for business transparency will not address chronic problems of wealth inequality and oppression. These reasonable assumptions have eluded Garten and many other globalists entirely, however, with the unfortunate consequence that 'globalism' is regarded by many as a kind of missionary enterprise, an American-led effort to enlighten those backward regions of the world which have yet to embrace the global market.[20]

From a historical perspective, Daniel Yergin and Joseph Stanislaw have provided an account of the world since 1945 which catalogues the spread of the free-market creed. In their 1998 book *The Commanding Heights*, Yergin and Stanislaw attempt to write the history of the world in the past fifty years as a battle between government management of national economies and a free-market approach. For Yergin and Stanislaw, the pioneers in this story are the economists (Friedrich von Hayek, Milton Friedman) and the politicians (Margaret Thatcher, Ronald Reagan) who beat back regulation, the demands of labour and the welfare state, leaving behind a world of choice, individual responsibility and multiple freedoms – including the freedom to fail rather badly and to live beneath the poverty line. *The Commanding Heights* is a key text in the new literature of globalism precisely because of its sweep and its easy conclusion that free-market capitalism has triumphed around the globe. The book is also an affront to the more traditional schools of foreign-policy study, since Yergin and Stanislaw plausibly suggest that one could write a world history in the late twentieth century almost entirely in terms of economic relations, rather than strategic imperatives. By the book's conclusion, a reader could be forgiven for thinking that Fukuyama's 1989 thesis had been triumphantly vindicated in the 1990s: the countries of the world, according to Yergin and Stanislaw, are bound together more

closely than before, and they face little distraction from any competing ideology which might divide them or weaken their free-market
resolve.[21]

Perhaps the most widely read US proponent of 'globalism' is
Thomas L. Friedman, foreign-affairs columnist for the *New York Times*.
Friedman's 1999 book *The Lexus and the Olive Tree* reads as an extended
meditation on the themes discussed by Yergin and Stanislaw. Friedman
is an unapologetic globalist; but he is careful to admit that globalism
will face opposition, and may need its champions and defenders if it
is to succeed. Friedman's title is derived from his own sense of what
is at stake in global politics today: on the one side, the Lexus, a
luxury car, represents a consumer product which the good globalist
can't fail to desire. On the other side, the olive tree symbolises a
dedication to a particular piece of land or ideology which the good
globalist correctly realises is worth very little (and can distract from
the sensible pursuit of Lexus ownership). For Friedman, the central
goal of US foreign policy should be to promote the Lexus at the
expense of the olive tree – to encourage countries throughout the
world to adopt the latest models of free-market capitalism, and to
discourage debate and conflict over territory or dogma. The result
will be more globalists, more Lexuses, and perhaps even a role for the
'olive tree' as a kind of ancillary comfort, taking its place not in
opposition to globalisation, but as a kind of salve to its harsher effects.[22]

Another useful offshoot of globalism will be a more settled international climate. Noting the arguments in more traditional policymaking circles over the 'democratic peace' thesis, Friedman offers his
own 'Golden Arches Theory of Conflict Prevention', which holds
that countries with McDonald's franchise restaurants never go to war
with each other. To some, the equation of a hamburger outlet with
the prospects for international peace might seem trite or bathetic;
Friedman, however, is quite serious in his belief that the economic
integration implied by the expanding McDonald's franchise will dis-
suade nations from fighting each other. Friedman's faith in the eirenic
potential of Ronald McDonald has survived even the Kosovo conflict,
in which NATO's burger-eating forces attacked Yugoslav cities in
spite of the latter's unguarded Big Macs and defenceless McNuggets.
According to Friedman, the Serbs eventually capitulated to NATO
because 'they wanted McDonald's reopened more than they wanted

Kosovo reoccupied'. This fast-food interpretation of Serbian surrender overlooks the possibility that Serb civilians simply didn't enjoy seeing the rest of their city destroyed, but it at least preserves the 'Golden Arches' theory from an assault by the facts of what happened in Yugoslavia.[23]

Friedman's book is engagingly written, filled with easy metaphors and a heavy reliance on language derived from technology.[24] It rests on two broad assumptions. First, Friedman is passionately committed to the idea that unfettered capitalism provides the best chance of global prosperity, and he is therefore sceptical of any alternative model:

> I doubt we will see a new, coherent, universal ideological reaction to globalization – because I don't believe there is one that can both truly soften the brutality of capitalism and still produce steadily rising standards of living.[25]

Friedman's second, and more ambitious, assumption is that most people around the world agree with him. He communicates this belief by narrating stories of budding globalists from many different countries: local politicians in China struggle to defeat each other in elections by advocating the latest telecommunications technology; ordinary people in Hanoi crowd the streets to sell their wares in the hope of (one day) driving a Lexus; a street-vendor in Bangkok chats to Friedman about her stock portfolio.[26] In Friedman's view, these people are evidence of the sacred status of free-market capitalism: 'globalization emerges from below, from street level, from people's very souls and from their very deepest aspirations.'[27] It should not surprise us, then, that Friedman's presentation of globalism has a missionary zeal: for globalisation to work, he concludes, 'America not only can be, it must be, a beacon for the whole world.'[28] Against the conservative injunctions of more traditional commentators, who would urge the American 'sheriff' to intervene in international affairs only sparingly, Friedman and the globalists have the nobler aim of civilising the wilderness, winning over the rest of the world to the ideal of US capitalism.

'It is human to hate': the clash of civilisations

The final image in *The Lexus and the Olive Tree* presents an African-American teacher dressed as Santa Claus leading a group of American children (drawn from many races and religions) in a Jewish holiday song. This sight brings tears to Friedman's eyes, and he offers it to his readers as evidence of the possibilities for cultural harmony and societal (i.e. free-market) progress: the shared economic system of Americans has enabled them to come together despite their ethnic or cultural differences, and even to celebrate those differences with a festive glee.[29] A sharper eye might pick out the details of the story and view the scene with more scepticism – the teacher and children are performing in Bethesda, Maryland, one of the most affluent suburbs in the US, and a favoured home for wealthy commuters to Washington, DC. By the same token, we might view with caution the gathering of world leaders in Switzerland for the annual Davos Economic Forum, since the alpine bonhomie of governing elites cannot simply be imputed to the far-flung populations that these leaders represent. As we saw in the first chapter, the unevenly distributed gains of globalisation make it easy for a commentator to find international harmony or cross-cultural cooperation, providing he or she limits the search to locations of power and privilege. The general picture, however, hardly bears out the stereotype.

We can easily find grounds, then, for disagreement with the 'globalists', and we can question whether their vision of a techno-capitalist millennium is viable. Moreover, the more traditional policy analysts have a vested interest in doing so. Their attempts to define a new 'realism' after the Cold War are directly challenged by the perspective of Friedman et al., whose belief in the centripetal power of free markets implies the obsolescence of more venerable, strategic approaches to the study of international relations. Foreign-policy experts in the US, in government service or in academia, have traditionally relied on the tension between US interests and foreign interests in the formulation of their advice: if the globalists are correct, this tension no longer exists (or is, at most, a fraction of what it once was), and so the best course for American policy is clear: the US should keep markets open, keep capital flowing, and advocate free trade. The challenge for 'realist' thinkers, then, has been to attack the globalists' utopian visions without seriously assailing American capitalism, which is overwhelmingly supportive of the globalist rhetoric. 'Realist' thinkers face the same dilemma as right-wing protectionists: they want to prop up a nationalist view of the world at a time of unprecedented international integration, but are unable to offer a serious critique of capitalism, or to draw attention to its shortcomings.[30]

Benjamin Barber, a professor of political science at Rutgers University, mapped out one possible route for 'realists' in his 1995 book *Jihad vs. McWorld*.[31] As the title suggests, Barber's vision of globalisation is polar: the homogenising forces of American-led capitalism are ranged against the reactionary allies of local culture and traditional enmities. Barber's book, in spite of its trite title, manages to avoid endorsing either of the 'sides', and makes some useful arguments about the emptiness of global capitalism which distinguish his perspective from that of Friedman. In particular, Barber expresses serious doubts about the democratising potential of missionary capitalism, and notes that the benefits of economic liberalisation will not be evenly distributed throughout those societies which 'convert' to free markets. The details of his scheme, however, are hostage to the sensational framework within which he tells his story and, especially, his notion of 'jihad'. Barber plucks a word with specific connotations within Islam, and uses it to categorise a myriad of protests against global capitalism: for Barber, the word connotes 'a generic form of fundamentalist opposition to modernity that can be found in most world religions'.[32] Although he seems interested in detail and nuance at various points in his analysis, Barber here collapses the diverse forms and causes of discontent into a single 'fundamentalist' movement, and then gives it a name which enshrines its inaccessibility and irrationality (especially when ranged against 'modernity'). Barber's legacy to other 'realists' is therefore an inadvertent one: a sense that the battle against global capitalism is based not on the economic injustice of free markets and the dismantling of government services, but on anti-modern, fundamentalist tendencies which are culturally determined.

The United States has, since its earliest days, relied on cultural constructs in the formulation and legitimation of foreign policy. The dispossession of native Americans was grounded in the notion that their forms of hunting and agriculture were inimical to progress, and undeserving of the land which they occupied; in the 1840s, American perceptions of Mexican racial inferiority encouraged and then checked the extent of US expansion; and racial theorists in the 1890s counselled American readiness for a coming race war, in which the various racial 'types' of the planet would engage in Darwinian conflict to decide the destiny of the world.[33] Although these concepts have held less sway in the twentieth century, the temptation to describe the prospects of the world in racial terms has persisted. It should not surprise us, then, that 'realist' thinkers have made speedy recourse to cultural difference (often a euphemism for racial difference) to describe the inevitability of conflict between nations, and to prescribe a strong defence for the US even after the collapse of the USSR. Since 1990, 'experts' like Fouad Ajami and Bernard Lewis have issued urgent reports on the 'Arab predicament' or the dangers of 'political Islam';[34] Aaron Friedberg and Jacob Heilbrunn have looked towards China with growing suspicion, casting doubt on its ability to embrace both capitalism and democracy;[35] and old hands like Henry Kissinger have urged caution in dealing with Russia, ignoring the plight of its impoverished population to revive the old shibboleth of 'ancient Russian imperial drives'.[36] These various American perspectives have presented problems and discontent throughout the world as forms of cultural inflexibility, calling for the curtailment of globalist evangelising and a more hard-headed American assessment of the world.

One influential proponent of the view that ethnic and religious rivalries threaten to bring anarchy to large parts of the world is the journalist Robert D. Kaplan. In 1991, Kaplan's account of his travels in and around Yugoslavia, *Balkan Ghosts*, was published to great acclaim in the US; moreover, the subsequent disintegration of Yugoslavia suggested that his gloomy view was actually visionary, and that policymakers should take heed of this new pessimism in formulating a response to (or packaging their apathy towards) the Balkan crisis.[37] Bill Clinton, whose own rhetoric in 1993 stressed the 'ancient hatreds' which barred a useful US role in the region, came to his conclusions after reading *Balkan Ghosts*; and the US stood on the sidelines as the Serbs and Croats carved up Bosnia, thus fulfilling the morbid prophecies in Kaplan's book.[38] Kaplan himself, while admitting that the putative influence of his book on the Clinton administration was 'disconcerting', continued to generate visions of disaster based on his travels around the world. In 1994, he produced a doom-laden essay for the *Atlantic Monthly* entitled 'The Coming Anarchy', which

suggested that inter-ethnic strife in West Africa 'provides an appropriate introduction to the issues, often extremely unpleasant to discuss,
that will soon confront our civilization.' Noting that those people
untouched by the 'Western Enlightenment' are inclined to 'find
liberation in violence', Kaplan inexplicably suggested that the
problems of West Africa would inevitably spread to the rest of the
world. The US, it seemed, could only ready itself for this challenge
to its 'civilization', praising Kaplan in the meantime for his timely
warnings.[39]

The most complete and influential version of this racial/cultural
'realism' is Samuel Huntington's *The Clash of Civilizations* (1996), a
remarkable book which might easily have been written (and praised)
in the US a century earlier. Huntington divides the world into eight
(or possibly nine) 'civilizations', each covering a specific geographical
area and holding particular values and priorities to be important.
These 'civilizations' are a thinly veiled euphemism for cultures and
races: in Huntington's scheme, the inhabitants of a particular part of
the world will imbibe the norms and goals of that 'civilization', and
will prove commensurately resistant to persuasion or coercion by
other civilizations. During the Cold War, suggests Huntington, the
tense and prolonged standoff between the US and the USSR sup-
pressed these civilisational differences; in the 1990s and beyond, however, they are the determinants of international relations and the
basic fact of any reasonable foreign policy.[40]

In viewing the argument and reception of Huntington's book, it
is hard to know whether to be more amazed by its thesis or by its
apparent acceptance in US policymaking circles. Admiring readers,
from Kissinger to Fukuyama, praised its 'grasp of the intricacies of
contemporary global politics' and its 'challenging framework'.[41] In
view of the panegyrics, we should identify some of its more obvious
deficiencies. In the first place, Huntington's definition of 'civilizations' is wildly subjective, depending on a series of historical guesses,
misreadings and occasional inventions. Historians of, say, Brazil would
ponder over its inclusion in an entity called 'Latin American civilization'; many European nations, as well as Australia and New Zealand,
might question the integrity and homogeneity of the 'West' to which
they supposedly belong. More tellingly, Huntington draws his racial/
cultural map as if the massive population movements of the late

nineteenth and twentieth centuries had never happened. Given the large numbers of Afro-Caribbean peoples in the United Kingdom, or North African Muslims in France, or Southeast Asians in the United States, does it make any sense to talk of Europe or North America as 'Western'? If these migratory movements represent the mixing of different civilisations, why have they taken place at all?[42]

Huntington largely ducks these questions, or resorts to sensationalist (and deeply inflammatory) predictions of race wars *within* those countries with large immigrant populations. This leads to the calm statement that 'while Muslims pose the immediate problem to Europe, Mexicans pose the problem for the United States'. The solution is to fold race fears into domestic and foreign policy: the US should be prepared to fight its Latino citizens for control of a Latino-dominated American south-west; and the Departments of State and Defense should ready American forces for the 'clash of civilizations' abroad, heeding Huntington's warning that 'relations between groups from different civilisations will be almost never close, usually cool, and often hostile'.[43] Huntington's vision is extremely pessimistic, and calls on American policymakers to abandon their more upbeat assessments of the international climate while there is still time to prepare for the 'clash'. At the base of his thinking is a remarkably depressing acceptance of 'the ubiquity of conflict' which determines every expectation of social interaction:

> It is human to hate. For self-definition and motivation people need enemies: competitors in business, rivals in achievement, opponents in politics. They naturally distrust and see as threats those who are different and have the capability to harm them. The resolution of one conflict and the disappearance of one enemy generate personal, social, and political forces that give rise to new ones.[44]

Ironically, hatred is the one quality which Huntington seeks to universalise in his analysis; for all his concessions of civilisational difference, his interpretation depends on the notion that human beings are invariably inclined to hate one another. Unsurprisingly, then, Huntington's predictions for the twenty-first century bear no resemblance whatsoever to those of the globalists, and his recommendations for a reconfiguration of American foreign policy are profound and extreme.

The emergence of a more hysterical body of 'realist' thinking in the US, grounded in notions of cultural difference and civilisational clash, is an angry counterpoint to the upbeat 'globalism' of commentators like Friedman, and the putative internationalism of the Clinton administration. One of the more bizarre consequences of the new 'realism', then, is that it juxtaposes outlandish claims of a coming civilisational war with unnervingly accurate attacks on globalism. Huntington's 'The Lonely Superpower', a 1999 essay from *Foreign Affairs*, launched a devastating assault on US foreign policy in the 1990s. The article contended that 'the US has found itself increasingly alone, with one or a few partners, opposing most of the rest of the world's states and peoples.' With an acuity and directness that is usually unthinkable in American foreign-policy journals, Huntington attacked the US for trying to:

> enforce American law extraterritorially in other societies; grade countries according to their adherence to American standards on human rights, drugs, terrorism, nuclear proliferation, missile proliferation, and now religious freedom; apply sanctions against countries that do not meet American standards on these issues; promote American corporate interests under the slogans of free trade and open markets; shape World Bank and International Monetary Fund policies to serve those same corporate interests; intervene in local conflicts in which it has relatively little direct interest; bludgeon other countries to adopt economic policies and social policies that will benefit American economic interests; promote American arms sales abroad while attempting to prevent comparable sales by other countries; force out one UN secretary-general and dictate the appointment of his successor; expand NATO initially to include Poland, Hungary, and the Czech Republic and no one else; undertake military action against Iraq and later maintain harsh economic sanctions against the regime; and categorize certain countries as 'rogue states,' excluding them from global institutions because they refuse to kowtow to American wishes.[45]

This extraordinary attack gives a clear sense of the disenchantment of many American foreign-policy analysts with US rhetoric and motives in the 1990s; but the queasy alternative of 'civilizational clash' hardly suggests a better way of seeing the world or directing American policy. The most obvious critique of 'globalism' – that its benefits accrue to a narrow segment of society, and that it disenfranchises more people than it empowers – is largely missing from the debate, leaving a skewed typology of free-market 'idealists' and xenophobic 'realists'. Since neither side plays its part very convincingly, each lands easy blows on the other: the globalists scoff at the sensationalism of civilisational clash, while the 'realists' point out the hypocrisy and the limits of the free-market idyll.[46] All the while, more persuasive and measured critiques of American foreign policy are largely excluded from this axis of realism and idealism, and US commentators continue to debate in narrow and confusing terms.

'The complacent, the rich, and the indifferent': US 'experts' and their surroundings

In tracing some of the debates and tensions within US foreign-policy analysis, we should note some important shared assumptions and perspectives which influence commentators of all stripes. In the first place, American analysts are largely in agreement on the missionary nature of US foreign policy, even if they doubt the efficacy of this mission in practice. A truism of American history holds that the US has been the harbinger of Christianity, liberty and democracy to a needy world, frequently acting from a sense of altruism rather than self-interest. Although the historical record hardly supports such a romantic interpretation, we should not underestimate the hold of this view in American political life, and even in the putatively dispassionate recommendations of other 'experts'. To dismiss the advocates of 'American mission' as phony or delusional is to disengage from an important debate over the history and purpose of American foreign relations.

If we pay close attention to the ubiquitous belief in an American mission, we can see more clearly the odd context in which 'realist' and 'idealist' visions of foreign policy interact. Henry Kissinger's *Diplomacy* (1994) is useful in this regard. In his academic and political work, Kissinger subscribed to 'realism' in international affairs: nation-states would compete for power and influence, and would contain or challenge each other through alliances and standoffs. In *Diplomacy*, a kind of textbook of international relations, Kissinger carefully introduces Theodore Roosevelt and Woodrow Wilson as representatives of a 'realist' and an 'idealist' strain in American foreign policy; proponents of realpolitik and of altruistic mission, as it were. In a chapter entitled

'The Hinge', Kissinger suggests that successive American governments in the twentieth century have moved from one vision to the other, but that both are authentically American and worthy. Moreover, even a 'realist' (as Kissinger would describe himself) would admire the goals of Woodrow Wilson, and seek to attain them whenever possible: 'The fulfillment of American ideals will have to be sought in the patient accumulation of partial successes', as Kissinger puts it. His blend of realism therefore infuses self-interest and realpolitik with a kind of moral edge, the sense that the US would behave still more generously if the rest of the world deserved such treatment.[47]

Debates over US foreign policy more typically concern the extent of American idealism than the presence of any 'missionary' impulse: an American mission is taken for granted. 'Realists' like Richard Haass or Henry Kissinger make no serious effort to question the good intentions of the US, but merely to doubt whether the American government has sufficient resources to pursue them abroad. Samuel Huntington has made a more radical suggestion that the rest of the world is ill-fitted to appreciate the American gift, but his portrait of civilisational rejectionism is so extreme that few Americans will challenge their own values in the face of this supposed relativism. The 'idealists', meanwhile, are those who believe that the US has sufficient power and persuasion to make the world in its own image. Inevitably, these commentators – like Jeffrey Garten or Thomas Friedman – are cheerleaders for global capitalism, which has been synonymous in the minds of American policymakers with human rights, improved standards of living, and democracy.

What is missing in all this is a substantial engagement with American 'idealism', and a more fundamental assessment of the trajectory and rationale of American policy. The uncritical acceptance of Woodrow Wilson as a mascot for US altruism would be a good starting point for such a re-examination: and especially Wilson's disastrous confusion of an American mission with a global good.[48] One of the themes of this book has been the schizophrenic American relationship with the United Nations, and an understanding of the pervasiveness of American missionary thinking may offer a clue to making sense of this relationship. American policymakers are alternately supportive and dismissive of the UN because they see the US as not simply a member nation, but a parallel or rival force for good:

a global power dedicated to improving the world, acting more from altruism than self-interest. In this sense, the US thinks that it *is* the UN, and it is understandably perturbed when the Security Council or General Assembly reaches decisions which expose that mistaken assumption. The UN, by its very existence as an organisation of many states, demonstrates the fallacy of seeing the US as a multilateral force, a global 'honest broker'; and so American governments have responded harshly, content to keep the UN in a marginal, if not a moribund condition. All the while, US 'experts' have provided the intellectual armament necessary to defend the ideal of American altruism: even when the US chooses to stay out of a conflict, the righteousness of its cause – and its right to intervene in some future conflict – is assured.

The other context for understanding American 'experts' is more prosaic, but no less important. With virtually no exceptions, the principal voices of foreign-policy expertise shuttle between academia, government service and the corporate world, enjoying homogeneous and privileged lives which are hardly representative of the average American, let alone citizens of less wealthy and powerful countries. We can return to some of the figures introduced earlier for specific examples of this career path. Francis Fukuyama holds a professorial chair at George Washington University in Washington, DC, has done policy research for the government-funded RAND corporation on several occasions, and served in the Reagan and Bush administrations. Richard Haass has worked at think-tanks (the Brookings Institution, the Council on Foreign Relations) and was a special assistant to President Bush. Henry Kissinger left his academic post at Harvard to work for Richard Nixon and Gerald Ford, before returning to academia and pursuing parallel careers in publishing and corporate consulting. Jeffrey Garten worked on Wall Street for thirteen years in investment banking and corporate raiding, served in the Clinton administration in the 1990s, and eventually became Dean of the Yale University School of Management. Samuel Huntington left Harvard in the 1970s to work in the Carter administration, before returning to Cambridge, Massachusetts, to direct the John M. Olin Institute for Strategic Studies.[49]

These stories of career achievement demonstrate that academia, government service and corporate America are linked by a revolving door – virtually every major analyst of US foreign policy has also been (or is currently) on the government payroll, either in the White House or the State Department, or in a government-funded think tank. Although it might be argued that this experience of power has enriched the work of the various commentators, the easy passage from government practice to analysis of government action suggests a serious conflict of interest.[50] If academic posts in International Relations or Strategic Studies are linked to positions within the US government, are young (or even established) students of foreign policy likely to risk their careers by questioning the basic assumptions of the 'experts'? The ostensibly detached perspective of a university professor may even persuade the US government that it has listened to dispassionate and serious criticism merely by hiring a figure like Madeleine Albright, who used to teach International Relations at Georgetown University. The cosy relationship between academia and policymaking may therefore seem normal and proper to government officials, with the unfortunate consequence that a privileged few in American society simply talk amongst themselves about the direction of US foreign policy.[51]

It is also worth remembering that the 'experts' enjoy a quality of life which marks them out from the majority of US citizens, and which bears no resemblance to the lives of the majority of the world's people. This is particularly relevant when we consider that the experts' visions of foreign policy always have a domestic corollary: the promotion of free markets abroad, for example, is likely further to enrich those affluent Americans who have done so well in the Clinton years. What's surprising, however, is the lack of embarrassment or anxiety that surrounds the experts' occasional admissions of privilege. Fareed Zakaria, editor of Foreign Affairs, was hardly nervous in telling a New York Times profiler in 1999 about his privileged lifestyle and his vision of the good life:

> [Zakaria] is a wine columnist for Slate, the Internet magazine, speaks and dresses elegantly, but has an American approachability and a very specific American fantasy. 'The immigrant in me,' he said, 'wants to go off to some Northeastern dock and sail off in topsiders and a polo shirt.'

The 'upper-class' Zakaria went on to confess his alienation from the 'more authentic, Indian India' of the 1990s, preferring the 'somewhat Anglicized India of the 1960s and 1970s' in which he grew up. Fortunately, this dislocation from modern India was no bar to his advance in American policymaking circles, and the *Times* indulged in heavy speculation that Zakaria would soon be drafted to a Republican presidential campaign as foreign-affairs adviser.[52]

Thomas Friedman's acceptance of his own comfortable lifestyle as universal is alternately narcissistic and hilarious. When Friedman accepted the *New York Times*'s invitation to write its 'Foreign Affairs' column in 1994, he became the first writer in the column's sixty-year history to base himself in the US, rather than abroad.[53] Although Friedman has travelled widely, the evidence from his book, *The Lexus and the Olive Tree*, suggests that he has rarely ventured beyond 'Marriott culture', relying mostly on the counsel and perspective of global elites.[54] Friedman is hardly apologetic about this: in the acknowledgements to his book, he thanks investment bankers, business school professors, economists, hedge-fund managers, Fareed Zakaria, and even the Clinton Treasury team of Robert Rubin and Lawrence Summers. His acknowledgements also shed light on why so many of his chapters seem like straightforward advertisements for globalisation and its leading corporate advocates:

> The reader will notice that I quote a great deal from two outside sources. One is *The Economist*, which has been far, far ahead of every other news organization in understanding and reporting on globalization. The other is ads from Madison Avenue. For some reason, advertising copywriters have a tremendous insight into globalization, and I have not hesitated to draw on their work.[55]

There is a delicious naïveté about this: Friedman's awed appreciation of the 'tremendous insight' of the people trying to sell globalization is eclipsed only by his unhesitating acceptance of their campaigns. Again, one might argue that Friedman's extensive list of connections gives him an insider's perspective on economic change and foreign policy; however, the closeness of those connections also blunts the force of any critique, turning Friedman's subjects into his friends, and vice versa.[56]

It is hard to read Friedman without the sense that he fervently believes in his vision of the world; and that both he and many other commentators on foreign policy suffer from a kind of personal and professional myopia which remains unaffected by a visit to a Japanese

car factory, or a cup of coffee in a Jordanian internet café.[57] Friedman
is happy to boast of his own Lexus, or to share tales of his skiing
trips, because he seems unaware that this reality is far removed from
the conditions and prospects of most people on the planet.[58] Globalists
like Friedman continue to counsel free-market reform even after the
dislocation in Asia, Russia and Brazil in 1997/8. 'Realists' like Richard
Haass or Samuel Huntington believe, instead, that the US can choose
its engagements with the rest of the world sparingly, and defend
itself from a chaotic landscape of ethnic tensions and irrevocable
hatred. In many respects, the study of US foreign policy oscillates
between complacency and indifference, underpinned by the wealth
and privilege of the 'experts'. Stanley Hoffmann has drawn attention
to this phenomenon:

> We live in a world in which apathy about what happens in 'far away
> countries of which we know nothing' can all too easily lead – through
> contagion, through the message such moral passivity sends to trouble-
> makers, would-be tyrants, and ethnic cleansers everywhere – not to the
> kind of Armageddon we feared during the Cold War but to a creeping
> escalation of disorder and beastliness that will, sooner or later, reach the
> shores of the complacent, the rich, and the indifferent.[59]

Although Hoffmann clearly hopes that US policymakers and analysts
may yet overcome their apathy or complacency, our brief survey
suggests that a genuine shift in American policy is unlikely to come
from the current crop of 'experts' and their comfortable surroundings.

PERSPECTIVES

As we have seen, many academics and other commentators on foreign
policy have crossed over into government service at various points in
their careers, and we should be careful not to draw a major distinction between policymakers in the US and policy analysts. These two
roles are performed largely by people from the same background,
who have received similar training and who live in the same areas
and circumstances. In this final section, however, I want not only to
suggest some of the ways in which the politicians in Washington,
DC (Congressional representatives as well as the president and his

advisers) think and operate, but also to extend our focus to include the media and public opinion beyond Washington's beltway. Although these are extremely complex and varied subjects for study, I want (at the risk of generalising) to give at least a sense of their contribution to, and influence on, the formation of foreign policy.

Politicians

The central fact of American political life is money. Although the US takes pride in the longevity and vitality of its democratic institutions, federal elections – for president and Congress – have been hijacked by the need to raise and reward big money donations from individuals and corporations.[60] In the 1996 presidential election, Bill Clinton and his Republican challenger, Bob Dole, spent more than $40 million on their campaigns, ensuring obligations to their sponsors which they would be expected to honour in office.[61] For Bill Clinton, some of these debts were to foreign donors, including businessmen from China and Indonesia, and encouraged the notion that the president had put US foreign policy up for sale. Clinton's political opponents repeatedly charged that his administration's policy – especially its pursuit of economic engagement with China – was directly linked to his acceptance of foreign campaign finance, a charge that both he and his vice-president, Al Gore, struggled to refute.[62]

Although the issue of foreign influence through federal campaign funding is important, the malign influence of money on American political life is hardly limited to the 1996 controversy.[63] In recent decades, presidential and Congressional candidates have been forced to raise large sums of money to have any chance of 'democratic' election, hoping to buy advertisements or to stage political events and thereby to present their message to the electorate. As a consequence, virtually every politician in Washington is beholden to one or more 'special interests', and will serve these interests after election with a view to earning more money for a re-election campaign. The special interests vary somewhat, but are basically grouped around corporate needs and priorities. Although some national or ideological interests – like the pro-Israel lobby – have substantial leverage to influence elections (especially at the Congressional level), the major players in campaign finance are corporations. Most have a definite

domestic agenda, but with the extension of global markets many also
have a vested interest in foreign policy. Boeing and Lockheed Martin,
predictably, are major donors, and their dollars clearly persuade 'their'
Congressional representatives to look favourably on defence spending.
US corporations with major overseas operations – for example, the
oil, mining and fruit industries – have been especially successful in
focusing the attention of Congress and the president on their interests
abroad, persuading the US to turn a blind eye when corporate
interests would be compromised by criticism of a corporate-friendly
dictatorship.[64]

Perhaps the most significant source of campaign funding in the
Clinton era, however, has been the financial services industry.
Clinton's foreign policy has been properly criticised as reactive and
inconsistent, but his dedication to the export of neoliberal policies
around the world has been unwavering. Although Clinton and his
Cabinet undoubtedly believe in neoliberalism to a large extent, the
relationship between Wall Street and the Democratic Party has been
underwritten by financial donations.[65] Banking corporations, investment banks and insurance firms have poured money into Democratic coffers, and the Democrats have kept their side of the bargain:
not only have they removed domestic legislation impeding corporate
consolidation and pressured foreign governments to open their economies to US firms; they have even allowed one of Wall Street's captains
– Robert Rubin – to oversee the changes in person.[66] It's worth
noting that, although the influence of banks and the financial industry
is hardly a new phenomenon in US history, Bill Clinton's 'New
Democrats' have extinguished any scepticism on the part of the
formerly left-leaning Democratic Party towards some of the most
wealthy and speculative interests in the US. While many older Democrats lamented the takeover of their party by Rubin and his rich
friends, the palace coup appeared secure: the only Democratic
challenger to Clinton's anointed successor, Al Gore, in the 2000
election was Bill Bradley, who managed to raise even more campaign
money from Wall Street than his opponent.[67] The promise of more
dollars from the financial industry suggests that neither major party
will dissent from the neoliberal consensus, and so the continued
march of globalisation is unlikely to meet much resistance from within
Washington's political circles. Campaign-finance reform, meanwhile,

has proceeded in halting and uncertain steps, with neither of the major political parties keen to alienate themselves from their sponsors.[68]

In addition to money, the relationship between the president and Congress is an important influence on the formation of foreign policy. Under the US Constitution, Congress is obliged to play a large role in American policymaking, and the president is dependent on the approval of Congress for any major foreign-policy initiatives.[69] In practice, however, Congressional involvement in foreign affairs has been sporadic. With the exception of those politicians with links to defence corporations or other interested parties, most Congressional representatives have fixed their attention on domestic issues and conceded foreign policy to the president.[70] This trend has had unfortunate consequences since the end of the Cold War: the president has rushed into military situations without Congressional debate and approval, and Congress has reacted with suspicion and hostility towards international organisations and treaties which require the support of the legislature. In 1999, Bill Clinton launched the bombing of Yugoslavia and Kosovo in spite of Congress's deep-seated reservations over the legitimacy and aims of the American action; later in the same year, Congress rejected the Comprehensive Test Ban Treaty, intended to outlaw nuclear testing and to head off a new international arms race. The effective marginalisation of Congress in times of war contributes directly to its suspicion of international agreements which might underpin peace: presidents (especially Bill Clinton) have isolated Congress from the decision-making process over foreign intervention, and have then reacted with surprise when Congress is sceptical of, say, the Test Ban Treaty or UN funding.[71]

Because Congressional representatives are elected by voters from a specific region of the US, it is easy to conclude that their focus is local, or that their approach to foreign policy is reflexively isolationist. In fact, we would do better to think of Congress as espousing what has been dubbed 'independent internationalism': the notion that the US can and should shuttle between internationalism and self-interest, depending on its own assessment of its best interests.[72] US politicians have framed their opposition to the Test Ban Treaty in terms of the special, even unique, US responsibility to save the rest of the world:

The world community ... are [*sic*] not people that we want to make
United States national defense policy. Their goals are not the same as our
goals. We have an obligation, as the leader of the free world, to insure that
our nuclear deterrent is safe and reliable. They don't. We may have to do
things that they could never dream of doing, including nuclear testing to
insure the safety and reliability of our nuclear stockpile. They don't have
to worry about that. But we do.[73]

While Bill Clinton and his Cabinet understand that the 'free world'
is reluctant to make these concessions to American foreign policy,
many Congressional representatives are serious and sincere in their
belief that the US has an exceptional mission to protect itself and
other nations, and that the responsibilities and obligations bound up
in this mission are best determined by America alone.

It could be argued that Congress operates at one remove from the
formation of foreign policy, and therefore that these messianic visions
of the US role in the world depend on seclusion from the actual
dictates and effects of American conduct abroad. According to this
line of argument, the idea that the US truly leads the 'free world', or
complies with a special responsibility to promote peace and justice
beyond its borders, is tenable only if one averts one's gaze from the
disastrous effects of US policy in Kosovo, Iraq, Rwanda and elsewhere. It is ironic, then, to note that those Clinton administration
officials with first-hand experience of the effects of their decisions
embrace this same missionary idiom. Moreover, the notion that one
can combine missionary concern with a more hard-headed 'pragmatism' has become a sort of badge of honour in Washington, particularly for Democrats. Behind this lurks the same assumptions about
'realism' and 'idealism' that we saw earlier, the same effort to combine
a selfless 'Wilsonianism' with the 'toughness' of Teddy Roosevelt,
and to ignore the fact that either president could invade other
countries or overwhelm other governments with impunity.

In an interview with the *New York Times* magazine in 1995, Bill
Clinton's national security adviser, Anthony Lake, admitted to 'some
degree of missionary impulse' in his approach to foreign policy. His
own career casts doubt on the success with which he carried out any
altruistic mission: Lake served in the American embassy in Vietnam
during the mid-1960s, and was Henry Kissinger's assistant during the
covert US bombing of Laos and Cambodia in the early 1970s.

Although he eventually (and quietly) resigned over Kissinger's extension of the war in Indochina, there is little evidence of any altruism in his counsel to Clinton: Lake's tenure coincided with the disastrous intervention in Somalia, the US vacillation over Bosnia, and the genocide in Rwanda. In the *Times* interview, however, Lake summarised his career and beliefs as 'pragmatic neo-Wilsonian', an unwieldy description which nonetheless conveys Lake's hope that he blended 'realism' with 'idealism'. Lake, along with other members of the Clinton administration, framed his thinking about the US role in the world with a strong idea of what was possible and what was impossible. The response of the 'pragmatic idealist' to the charge of inaction or injustice is to claim that the US has done its best. If the political climate of another country has been adversely affected by US intervention, or hundreds of thousands of people have been killed in the absence of international support, the US is much more inclined to accept these losses as 'realistic' than to question its own role in incurring them.[74]

In considering the motivation and psychology of US policymakers, then, we should remember that they have developed a sophisticated way of disengaging from the horrific consequences of US foreign policy, and even of characterising themselves as 'idealists' or 'Wilsonians' (albeit of the 'pragmatic' persuasion) as they do so. George Stephanopoulos, a Clinton aide, offered an insight into this mentality in his contribution to the *New York Times* profile of Lake, his former colleague:

> The easiest way to say it is he's moral without being a moralist. There's this quote by Camus, something like perhaps we can't stop killing children but we can limit the number of children killed. It's always struck me that Tony's internalized that message. He's deeply moral and deeply realistic at the same time.

The definition of a pragmatic idealist, then, is clear: he or she recognises from the outset that children must be killed, and tries merely to limit the cull somewhat. Even though the US has displayed its ability to intervene decisively around the world, pragmatic idealists have internalised the notion that the American reach is limited; and may even believe in the necessity of 'killing children', if we are to maintain a 'deeply realistic' view of the world.[75]

Of course, policymakers often become associated with particular emphases or philosophies, which can seem like the bedrock of their awareness and thinking. Madeleine Albright, for example, was fond of distinguishing herself from other State Department folk by stressing her belief in moral intervention: 'My mind set is Munich. Most of my generation's is Vietnam.'[76] The typical pattern, however, is for such bullish assertions to subside in the face of the 'realism' that we have been tracing; or, to put it in Albright's terms, American officials have aimed to combine 'principles with pragmatism'.[77] What is particularly interesting in the American context is that policymakers continue to insist that they are behaving in moral or principled ways even as they concede the mitigating influence of 'pragmatism'. Those closest to power may suffer most acutely from this delusion: Dick Morris, a key adviser to Bill Clinton, described the American president in 1996 as a 'secular, global pope', a perspective which suggests that Morris has spent more time in American policymaking circles than amongst the ordinary people of the world.[78] Although we can clearly trace its intellectual and moral inconsistencies and inversions, we should note that 'pragmatic idealism' remains the standard framework in which US policymakers position themselves and present their ideas; and that this framework has proven durable and extremely resistant to the unpleasant facts it has created outside the US.[79]

The media

Just as American political life has become increasingly dominated by money, the American media is now fully integrated within a framework of corporate ownership and profit. Newspapers and television stations are obliged to maximise their revenue returns, and the advertising on which they depend necessitates political conservatism and a careful pruning of controversy. Moreover, the conglomeration of the media and various entertainment corporations has created uncomfortable juxtapositions between serious news organisations and more ephemeral (albeit very rich) bodies: ABC, one of the largest American television networks, is now owned by Disney; Fox, another network, is part of News International, an entertainment and media giant comprising a movie studio and sports franchises as well as newspapers and television news channels; CNN, perhaps the most familiar

American news source to international audiences, is part of the Time–Warner company, which has recently merged with the Internet giant America On-Line (AOL). The new corporate behemoths are inclined to sell the news as if it were any other product. This inevitably has consequences, not only in the soft-pedalling of particular issues sensitive to business, but in the clumsy or cursory presentation of complex and subtle political problems, at home or abroad.[80]

Public television, established in the 1970s as a bulwark against the increasing corporatisation of the media, has struggled against government reluctance to provide funding, and has gradually succumbed to corporate suitors eager to make up the shortfall, in return for advertising and an exemption from public scrutiny. By the end of the century, public radio and television was saturated with commercials for corporate sponsors, and the content and tone of public broadcasting had lost much of its critical edge. Although smaller organisations have continued to report the news from a more progressive perspective, the vast majority of Americans still consult the major corporate networks (or corporate-funded public broadcasting) for news reporting.[81]

In addition to a corporate agenda, news organisations in the US also depend on government access and, occasionally, government censors for their stories. Although the press is nominally free to write anything about American foreign policy, in practice foreign correspondents form a cadre which travels and works alongside government officials. The more compliant journalists are more likely to be given access to the president and his advisers, a bargain which may offer a reporter an exclusive even as it undermines his or her ability to write critically about it. During armed conflicts, the situation is even more claustrophobic: in the Gulf War, all reporting in the US (and other Western countries) was subjected to military censorship, and reporters were forced to work in pools and to restrain their criticism of the military or the war.[82] In Kosovo, the NATO operation was carefully presented to and for the press, with a team of PR officials on hand at NATO headquarters in Brussels to gloss over any awkward mistakes (like the Chinese Embassy bombing) or 'collateral damage' (the bombing of refugee columns). Advances in technology have made it possible for US commanders to present their war to the media at a safe distance, relaying the shooting and destruction through slides, laptops and video which emphasise its cleanness and precision. Fattened on this feast of packaged information, the American media have become especially sedentary, the consumers of Pentagon news releases rather than the gatherers of the news.[83]

When the media take an interest in a story, the pressures of time and the perceived need to iron out complex detail can create confusing or misleading reports. The usual pattern of media involvement is well established: reporters lean on a story very heavily in its opening phase, making it newsworthy and forcing it to the top of the agenda; and then editors and producers drop the story precipitously, even though it continues to develop and mutate away from public view. The television coverage of the Somalia intervention is a good example: US reporters introduced the Somalis as a desperate, starving people in need of American salvation; when US forces arrived, much more attention was paid to their 'relief' efforts than to their long-term strategy. The initial media presentation of Somalis, stressing their simple suffering, drained them of political agency and established them in the minds of many Americans as needy, about-to-be grateful innocents. When Somalia returned to the headlines almost a year later, Americans had no means of understanding the transition from gratitude to (violent) rejection: the initial media blitz had fixed the Somalis in a particular frame, and editors had largely neglected the changing situation as the US 'peacekeepers' began their war against Mohamed Aideed.[84]

I want to offer two examples to illustrate some of these points about the media's role in framing foreign policy. The first is a long article from *Time* magazine (a part of the AOL–Time–Warner empire, along with CNN) profiling Madeleine Albright and her role in the Kosovo crisis. Its title – 'Madeleine's War' – is intended to establish Albright's personal stake in the campaign against Milosevic. The author of the article, Walter Isaacson (*Time*'s managing editor) is so deferential towards Albright that her prose becomes his, and the Clinton administration line on Kosovo is simply parroted by the reporter:

> So the war in Kosovo, and Albright's determined vision of it, has become more than just another regional conflict. It has become ground zero in the debate over whether America should play a new role in the world, that of the indispensable nation asserting its morality as well as its interests to assure stability, stop thugs and prevent human atrocities.[85]

AMERICAN MISSIONS 209

Of course, the sentiment is Albright's, as is some of the language ('indispensable nation'). Isaacson, however, erases the line between himself and his subject, adopting her vision and even her anxieties. In one hilarious passage, Isaacson looks on admiringly as Albright tries to marginalise Kofi Annan and the United Nations in the formulation of Kosovo policy:

> Most important were two calls to UN Secretary-General Annan. A potential problem was brewing: Annan, who had remained on the sidelines, was suggesting that he appoint a group of negotiators to deal with Belgrade. Annan had been reliable from the outset in supporting the NATO position, which Albright appreciated. But the last thing she wanted was a pod of UN-anointed diplomats pushing compromises. 'Kofi, we don't need negotiators running all over the place,' she said.

Our 'critical' profiler has no difficulty in seeing Kofi Annan as another 'problem' to be dealt with, or sharing Albright's fear that the UN could 'broker with Belgrade in a way that could compromise NATO's positions'. In his effort to understand Albright's perspective, Isaacson actually adopts it and thereby forestalls the more obvious questions about the NATO campaign.

In addition to Isaacson's essential acceptance of Albright's self-justification, his article more subtly encourages readers to sympathise with its subject in its design and layout. The pictures are carefully chosen to emphasise Albright's various (appealing) qualities: she reaches out her hand to greet smiling US soldiers; she flashes her teeth in a meeting as General Wesley Clark, NATO's commander, looks on admiringly; she helps herself to cafeteria food in a US airbase, about to share a meal with the troops; and she looks on, rapt with attention, as a soldier discourses over (and reassuringly pats) a very large missile. The photos seem to belong to a paid advertisement for Albright; part of a carefully coordinated campaign to entice the public. Across the top of each page, presumably to keep the interest of the casual reader, the *Time* editors have printed numbers and facts: '6:' declares one, 'Number of languages she understands'; '4: Number of times she received the "teacher of the year" award at Georgetown University.' Predictably, the statistics are all favourable to Albright: '500,000+' refers to the 'number of miles she has flown since becoming Secretary of State', rather than the number killed in Rwanda after the US vetoed an international response to the genocide. The effect of the montage is to bring us closer to Albright and to the administration, to make us see them as simultaneously statuesque and human. When Bill Clinton finally appears, he is 'relaxing in a Shetland sweater in his airborne office', no doubt ready to pour us a drink as he explains how bombing Kosovo 'served our interests as well as our values'.

The *Time* article offers ample evidence of the pitfalls of getting too close to one's subject: travelling with the president or secretary of state, it's tempting to snap a photo of them 'relaxing' in an airplane seat, or eating with the troops, and to write copy which conveys the sensitive side of a government official. As journalists and policy-makers occupy the same space, so their interests begin to fuse, and critical perspectives fall away. As we have seen, American government officials are inclined to tell upbeat stories about the congruence of American interests and values, and journalists are inclined to believe them. Thomas Friedman, 'Foreign Affairs' columnist for the *New York Times*, inadvertently offers an example of the toothlessness and self-regard of the media in the final chapter of *The Lexus and the Olive Tree*. Friedman selects a single episode from Madeleine Albright's visit to Rwanda in 1996, a photo opportunity for the State Department staff at Kigali airport, and pores over its significance:

> As a reporter on the trip, I didn't think I belonged in the picture, so I stood over to the side and watched the Rwandan ground crew watching the American picture-taking session. The Rwandans had a slightly quizzical look. I couldn't help wondering to myself what they were making of this scene, which represented America at its best: the spirit of community, the melting pot, the willingness to help faraway strangers in need, the free-dom and opportunity for each individual to work his way to the top and, most important, a concept of citizenship based on allegiance to an idea, not a tribe. As a picture, it represented everything that Rwanda was not. Rwanda had just emerged from an orgy of tribal warfare – Rwandan Hutus against Rwandan Tutsis – in which a million people were killed, some of them brutally hacked to death with machetes. Rwanda was all olive trees and no Lexuses, a country that was all gnarled roots choking one another, and no flowering branches.[86]

Although Friedman steps out of the photo, his perspective is deter-minedly parochial: the Rwandan onlookers, doubtless mired in their tribal hatreds, cannot hope to understand an American delegation which represents 'everything that Rwanda was not'. There is an extraordinary arrogance and insensitivity in these observations, coupled with a blithe acceptance of the American 'willingness to help faraway strangers in need', which could hardly seem less appropriate given the American response to the genocide. Might the Rwandan ground crew be pondering the irony of American arrival some eighteen months too late? Might they have wondered at the self importance and pomposity of this delegation, and expressed cynicism at the new-found US interest in their country? Friedman could have asked them; but instead he puts his own thoughts into their heads, confirming a story of American mission even where the evidence to support its existence is least abundant. We might simply pass this off as bad journalism, but we should remember that Friedman has won the Pulitzer prize for international reporting on two occasions, and is the principal commentator on American foreign policy for the most influential newspaper in the United States.[87]

Public opinion

Before we generalise about public opinion in America, we would do well to note that this is an especially difficult thing to sketch or to quantify. The US population is extremely heterogeneous, with important tensions and affinities along lines of race, class and region. The preponderance of immigration in American history has led many Americans to retain an active interest in other parts of the world, but the intensity and specific focus of this interest varies widely. In this final section I am going to suggest some of the principal contributions of the public to foreign-policy debates, and to balance the general picture of apathetic or reactionary popular feeling with a recent, more successful example of public engagement.[88]

The natural resources, size and location of the United States have traditionally supported not only the idea of an American mission to the rest of the world but also the feeling that the US can successfully disengage from foreign politics and survive happily on its own. Madeleine Albright helpfully summarised these twin impulses – of mission and of isolation – in a 1998 interview:

> Americans are unbelievably fortunate to be between two oceans and have two friendly neighbors. Often, as I've traveled around and the President has made this comment a lot I imagine what it's like to have been invaded

by Napoleon or by Hitler. That has created a very different mindset in a lot of the world's peoples. Americans have never been invaded and occupied. I say this because I'm not a born American: it makes Americans feel invulnerable in a way that other countries do not.[89]

This feeling of invulnerability translates into a sense that the US can choose when, where and how to engage with the outside world; and so it is a source of missionary rhetoric and also of disengagement, depending on foreign events and American priorities.

The idea that the US could easily closet itself from the world, and still exist in prosperity and peace, tends to reinforce the notion that any kind of overseas action must be altruistic. Although the US is closely (and properly) linked in the minds of many to the spread of global capitalism, even this phenomenon has been presented as an American gift to the world, a force for civilisational progression or societal development. Those with a less optimistic sense of the receptiveness of the rest of the world tend to focus on domestic American missions: Pat Buchanan and others have won over a large following to the view that the US might best work out its altruistic impulses within its borders. The public is thus encouraged either to think highly of the rest of the world – other nations are deserving of and amenable to American overtures – or to give up on it, but in each case to imagine the US as a munificent and even a disinterested force in world affairs, sure of its own place in the world and happy to help other nations if they are willing.[90]

If this gives a sense of the ideological climate in which many Americans find themselves, the media play a crucial role in directing public attention towards specific regions and situations. The level of public awareness of particular countries or international issues is initially low; the media then generate a wealth of information about the matter at hand, and present the issues to the public in simplified form. This typically creates the basis for public support, and the president acts accordingly. The cycle begins and ends with the government: the State Department and president ordinarily shape the information reported by the media, which is bounced off the public and often manifests itself in opinion polls which are trotted out by the government to justify decisive action. In Iraq, then, the State Department was effusive in its press releases on Saddam's crimes; with Rwanda, on the other hand, State Department officials issued cautious and evasive statements for as long as they could, reluctant to name names or place blame on any side lest the public demand action to stop the genocide. Although we should be careful not to depict Americans as completely beholden to government-controlled information, this dynamic of state influence on the perception of foreign affairs is a cornerstone of policymaking.[91]

The bombing of Yugoslavia in 1999 offers a useful frame in which to think about the workings of public opinion. We reviewed the facts behind American involvement in Kosovo in the last chapter, but we might summarise some of the major difficulties in winning public support for NATO's action as follows: it was hard to present Milosevic as a tyrant since he had been recognised by the US as a force for stability and peace at the Dayton talks in 1995; it was hard to argue for American involvement after the Clinton administration had established a precedent for nonintervention in Bosnia and especially Rwanda, stepping aside even during massacres and human-rights abuses which dwarfed those in Kosovo; it was hard to blame Milosevic entirely for what had happened in the first weeks of the war since the mass deportation of Kosovar Albanians only began after the NATO bombing, suggesting that NATO had itself played a role in spurring the exodus; it was hard to maintain public enthusiasm as the war dragged on into its third month, in spite of the initial American expectation that the bombing would bring swift results.

Some Americans needed no prompting to abdicate from the debate entirely. As one department store worker told the *New York Times*, 'I don't like to worry about the world's problems. I'm a happier person if I stay centered on myself.' More common was the sense that ethnic cleansing was taking place, and support for the putative American effort to deal with it. An apple farmer from New Hampshire told the *Times* that, in spite of the risks of intervention, 'cleaning out villages, killing the men and making the women and children refugees – that seems like a pretty terrible thing to let anybody get away with.' Faced with a media blitz showing displaced families in Kosovo, and their government's employment of an impassioned rhetoric of US values and responsibilities, many Americans overlooked or remained unaware of the fact that Milosevic had been 'cleaning out villages' with impunity before the Dayton agreement; and that the refugee problem in Kosovo grew to enormous proportions only after the NATO bombing had begun.[92]

Perhaps the most bizarre element in the public reaction to Kosovo was the way in which the issue almost disappeared from newspapers and television programmes after the first few weeks of bombing. Although the occasional waywardness of NATO ordnance would make the front pages, the daily round of bombing quickly became routine.[93] A group of residents in White Plains, a suburb of New York City, were interviewed by the *New York Times* at various points during the Kosovo campaign. Their responses clearly indicated an impatience not only with the Serbs but with the entire issue, particularly given the perceived ability of the US to kill Milosevic if it really made the effort. David Gammons, an artist, put the point succinctly:

> I haven't been watching TV.... It's still going on, I know; but just shoot the man and be done with it. It's enough already. It's news that went on and went on and what else is new?[94]

Although this yearning for a terminal solution to the problem of Milosevic was not widely voiced, similar sentiments about the ongoing annoyance of Saddam Hussein suggest that the American public is ill-informed and therefore ill-equipped to deal with the complexity and longevity of many foreign-policy problems.[95] Although the speedy US demolition of Iraq in 1991 gained high (if fleeting) poll ratings for George Bush, the lengthy and monotonous pounding of the Serbs produced an impatience or apathy in the American public: fewer than 50 per cent, according to polls taken at the end of the war, shared Clinton's boast of a 'victory for a safer world, for our democratic values and for a stronger America'.[96]

I have been tracing a pessimistic view of US public opinion, suggesting that popular support for overseas action is easily manipulated by government and by the media; or that the public becomes sceptical towards American action only through a combination of self-interested insularity and a short attention span. I want to conclude on a more optimistic note by admitting that many Americans, in spite of government spin and complacent media, are still ready and able to think critically about foreign policy, and to point out the obvious contradictions and inconsistencies in the official version of events. One New Yorker expressed scepticism in the first few days of the Kosovo bombing campaign over the logic of the US role:

> I don't think we should stand by idly. But there have been massive human rights violations everywhere – Tibet, Rwanda, Tiananmen Square. They say we need a stable Europe for our national security. But I'm not sure why a stable Africa or a stable Asia isn't just as important.[97]

Americans who raise such objections are often dismissed by policy-makers as naifs or amateurs, unaware of the complexity of the situations that they presume to judge. As Madeleine Albright put it when asked why the US would intervene in Kosovo but not in Rwanda, 'I don't think you can make a very simple matrix.' In truth, however, the US government almost always tries to win public support by presenting foreign situations in a 'simple matrix', and a large number of Americans are sufficiently aware to point out the gulf between the simplified rhetoric and complex reality.[98]

The Clinton administration did manage to have its war in Kosovo without a full-scale haemorrhage of public opinion, but the fear that the public would either lose interest in the war, or question its parameters and legality, seems justified by the ambivalent popular reaction to NATO's victory. Alongside the ranks of Americans who don't care about what happens abroad, or reflexively rally to the flag over any foreign contention, a substantial number of ordinary people are keen to assess the motives of their government and the logic of its stated policies. Perhaps the best example of this from the Clinton administration came in February 1998, as the US readied the media and the public for a new round of bombing in Iraq. Clinton's foreign-policy team correctly perceived that the public – aware of the effects of US sanctions on Iraqi civilians, but sceptical of their influence on Saddam – was not persuaded of the need for more punitive military action, and so the top policymakers in the administration were sent into the American 'heartland' to drum up support. Given the Clinton administration's ardour for media spin, folksy parochialism and globalisation, the event which emerged from this public-relations offensive was a CNN one-hour special: 'Showdown with Iraq: An International Town Meeting' was held in Columbus, Ohio and featured Madeleine Albright, William Cohen and national security adviser Sandy Berger. The audience of six thousand local people, gathered in a cavernous basketball arena at Ohio State University, was complemented by viewers and telephone callers from around the US and the rest of the world. The administration put its faith in its star performers, given the need to deliver a positive message to sceptical Americans – and the event promised both a large television audience and jealous glances from other television networks, envious of CNN's exclusive coverage.[99]

From its opening moments until its conclusion, the meeting was marked by loud protests from demonstrators in the audience, but also by numerous questions from Ohio residents which wrong-footed and embarrassed Clinton's team. The first question set the tone for what followed: 'The American administration has the might and means to attack the Iraqi state, but does it have the moral right to attack the Iraqi nation?' Even the transcript of the meeting reveals the growing horror in the voices of the 'experts', their surprise and annoyance that these 'ordinary Americans' (as CNN put it) could have the temerity to challenge the Washington insiders. Predictably, their responses were flustered:

> Q: I'm an ER physician here in Columbus. My question is, this administration has raised concerns about Iraq's threats to its neighbors, yet none of these neighbors seem too threatened. They haven't asked for help and, in fact, have come out publicly against the bombings [cheers] – furthermore, the international community has been opposed to the bombings. If nobody's asking us for their help [sic], how can you justify further US aggression in the region? [Applause, shouts]
>
> ALBRIGHT: It is very clear that the problem here is one to the region [sic]. Saddam Hussein has invaded another country before, he continues to try to develop weapons of mass destruction, [shouts from hecklers] and I have been to the region. I have talked to the neighbors. They are concerned about what is going on here.[100]

The pattern of the questioning mixed more aggressive challenges to the policymakers with deceptively simple questions: why did the UN Security Council have doubts about the planned American bombing? Why didn't the US simply remove Saddam from power? If the US didn't know the locations of Saddam's alleged weapons of mass destruction, what would more bombing achieve? Why was the US pursuing a policy against Saddam which inflicted greatest pain on innocent Iraqi civilians? Against the swirl of anti-war chants and more militant protests, the straightforward questions stood out in harsh relief; and the inability of the US officials to answer them seemed especially stark.

One particularly heated exchange between an audience member and Madeleine Albright was widely broadcast on other television news programmes, and reported in the press. Exasperated by the persistence of protests throughout the auditorium, the CNN moderator took a spontaneous question which had not been vetted in advance:

> Q: Why bomb Iraq, when other countries have committed similar violations? Turkey, for example – [interrupted by cheers and applause]. Can I finish? For example, Turkey has bombed Kurdish citizens. Saudi Arabia has tortured political and religious dissidents. Why does the US apply different standards of justice to these countries? [Cheers, applause.]
>
> ALBRIGHT: Let me say that when there are problems such as you have described, we point them out and make very clear our opposition to them. But there is no one that has done to his people or to his neighbors what Saddam Hussein has done – or what he is thinking about doing [sic]. I am very [interrupted by hecklers].
>
> Q: What about Indonesia? Well, you've turned my microphone off.

Albright's typical response to this kind of question – that such relativism or scepticism implied a defence of Saddam – was roundly dismissed by the questioner, when his microphone was eventually switched on again:

> Q: I'm not defending [Saddam] in the least. What I am saying is that there needs to be consistent application of US foreign policy [applause, cheers]. We cannot support people who are committing the same violations because they are political allies. That is not acceptable. We cannot violate UN resolutions when it is convenient to us. You're not answering my question, Madame Albright [cheers, applause].

This extremely unusual show of dissent was embarrassing to the Clinton administration, and reverberated through Washington and around the country. The *New York Times* described administration officials as 'stiff and stranded'; the *Boston Globe* noted that 'the "showdown with Iraq" quickly turned into a showdown with Clinton's team'; *Newsweek* was more direct: 'it was a public relations disaster'.[101]

Although the Clinton administration had hoped to use the Ohio meeting as a springboard to war, the protests and the reasoned scepticism actually undermined the plan before a large television audience, and may even have contributed to the decision not to launch an attack. (Iraq would gain a reprieve until December, when the bombing finally went ahead.) Having placed great emphasis on their ability to manufacture public consent through a high-profile media event, Clinton's advisers were dealt a sharp rebuke by a public able to think independently and to question the blind use of American power.[102]

Although the Ohio episode is an inspiring (if isolated) example of an engaged and critical public response to government policy, we should remember that policymakers will try to avoid such confrontations if at all possible. Reporting on the Ohio event, the *Financial Times* outlined the dilemma for the US government:

> It is not a handful of militant anti-war activists who have rattled the Clinton administration. The most worrying conclusion from this week's effort to explain US policy on Iraq to the people is that ordinary Americans have some tough, intelligent questions about the purpose and likely outcome of the impending clash.[103]

Of course, from a government perspective it is perfectly logical to see popular awareness and scrutiny as 'worrying', particularly if a reinvigorated public begins to challenge some of the more durable and effective American myths about mission, values and the like. If the squirming of the television anchors at CNN's Ohio meeting is any indication, the media will more likely side with the government in the battle over information and policymaking. An editorial in *Newsweek* surveyed this ground after the Ohio debacle:

> [The public] cannot be just told what is good for them. They need to be convinced. That is the case for sending high officials to suffer jeers and catcalls on a basketball court. The tricky question is whether this truth makes the world a safer place. On the one hand, public diplomacy makes political leaders accountable for their decisions − it acts as a rein on what might otherwise be a breakneck gallop to war. On the other hand, any country's national interest will sometimes require the use of force, and it is inherently dangerous for the world's only superpower to be constantly hamstrung by the need to satisfy public opinion − in advance − that such force is necessary.[104]

The immensity of the task, then, is clear. The American public has not only to break out of its apathy and its dependence on the media (and the government) for information about the world; Americans must also combat the suspicion that their dissent is 'inherently dangerous', and remind their leaders that the 'need to satisfy public opinion' is non-negotiable in a democratic state.

NOTES

1. Delivered on Capitol Hill, Washington, DC, 19 January 1999.

2. Fukuyama originally advanced his thesis in 'The End of History', *National Interest* 16 (1989): 3–18. He reworked and expanded this original article into *The End of History and the Last Man* (New York: Free Press, 1992). For critical perspectives on the thesis, see Timothy Burns, ed., *After History? Francis Fukuyama and His Critics* (Lanham, MD: Rowman & Littlefield, 1994).

3. Charles Krauthammer, 'The Unipolar Moment', *Foreign Affairs* 70, no. 1 (1991): 23–33.

4. See Bruce Russett, *Grasping the Democratic Peace* (Princeton: Princeton University Press, 1993); Tony Smith, *America's Mission: The United States and the Worldwide Struggle for Democracy in the Twentieth Century* (Princeton: Princeton University Press, 1994), and 'In Defense of Interventionism', *Foreign Affairs* 73, no. 6 (1994): 34–46.

5. The clearest expression of the Clinton administration's interest in the 'democratic peace' thesis came from Deputy Secretary of State Strobe Talbott, 'Democracy and the National Interest', *Foreign Affairs* 75, no. 6 (1996): 47–63.

6. The 'democratic peace' construct has a historical and a philosophical focus: political philosophers are inclined to reach back to Kant for the intellectual foundations of the thesis, while historians have looked to Woodrow Wilson. For a philosophical perspective, see Michael W. Doyle, 'Kant, Liberal Legacies, and Foreign Affairs', in Michael E. Brown, Sean M. Lynn-Jones and Steven E. Miller, eds, *Debating the Democratic Peace* (Cambridge, MA: MIT Press, 1996), 3–57. Tony Smith's *America's Mission* frames 'Wilsonianism' in quasi-historical (albeit wildly upbeat) terms at 84–109, then returns in conclusion to describe a 'Wilsonianism Resurgent' at 311–45. On the Bush administration's embrace of the 'democratic peace' thesis, see Russett, *Grasping the Democratic Peace*, 127–9.

7. We should note that even the most optimistic boosters of the 'democratic peace' thesis had built a little caution into their original enthusiasm – note Tony Smith's suggestion that the world's dependence on 'determined

American leadership' should not make Americans forget Machiavelli's dictum: 'Men always commit the error of not knowing where to limit their hopes, and by trusting to these rather than to a just measure of their resources, they are generally ruined.' *America's Mission*, 345.

8. Richard K. Betts, 'The Delusion of Impartial Intervention', *Foreign Affairs* 73, no. 6 (1994): 20–33; Thomas Carothers, 'Democracy Without Illusions', *Foreign Affairs* 76, no. 1 (1997): 85–99.

9. Fareed Zakaria, 'The Rise of Illiberal Democracy', *Foreign Affairs* 76, no. 6 (1997): 22–43. A rather more detailed exploration of the same argument is offered by Edward D. Mansfield and Jack Snyder, 'Democratization and the Danger of War', in Brown et al., eds, *Debating the Democratic Peace*, 301–34.

10. Michael Mandelbaum, 'Foreign Policy as Social Work', *Foreign Affairs* 75, no. 1 (1996): 16–32.

11. John L. Harper, 'The Dream of Democratic Peace', *Foreign Affairs* 76, no. 3 (1997): 117–21.

12. Richard N. Haass, *The Reluctant Sheriff: The United States After the Cold War* (New York: Council on Foreign Relations, 1997), 6. In addition to his Wild West terminology, we should note the economic subtext in Haass's scheme – his picture of a politically 'deregulated' world, and the inevitability of this movement, can be easily mapped onto the literature of neoliberalism and globalisation which we examined in the first chapter.

13. For a critique of Haass's terminology, and the suggestion that his 'reluctant sheriff' model is 'useful for only a fraction of foreign policy concerns', see Gaddis Smith, 'Saddle Up!', *New York Times*, 3 August 1997. Haass at least practised in office the same 'discriminating' philosophy which he preached as a policy commentator – Andrew Cockburn and Patrick Cockburn narrate the story of Haass's refusal to meet with Kurdish leaders in the immediate aftermath of the Gulf War, when the population of Iraq had been led to believe that the Bush administration supported a democratic uprising. Haass, then director for Middle East Affairs at the National Security Council, fumed at a hapless Senate staffer who had sponsored the Kurdish overtures: 'You don't understand. Our policy is to get rid of Saddam, not his regime.' *Out of the Ashes: The Resurrection of Saddam Hussein* (New York: HarperCollins, 1999), 37.

14. John Harper's 'The Dream of Democratic Peace' specifically attacks Strobe Talbott's 'Democracy and the National Interest' without touching on the details of Clinton administration policy, or questioning whether the activities of the US government in the 1990s might stem from any source other than altruism.

15. For critiques of the prevailing theories of international relations (IR), see Justin Rosenberg, *The Empire of Civil Society: A Critique of the Realist Theory of International Relations* (London: Verso, 1994), especially 1–8; and Jim George, *Discourses of Global Politics: A Critical (Re)Introduction to International Relations* (Boulder, CO: Lynne Rienner, 1994). George, 73, complains that IR 'continues to be characterized by a crude

essentialism centered on a cast of caricatured historical figures'.

16. Jessica T. Matthews, 'Power Shift', *Foreign Affairs* 76, no. 1 (1997): 50–66.

17. Jeffrey E. Garten, 'The Root of the Problem', *Newsweek*, 31 March 1997. Garten defended his remarks in a subsequent interview, confirming that President Clinton had himself suggested that 'we had to shift our foreign policy much more in the direction of economic and commercial relations', and that the inevitable consequence was some 'scandals': 'In a commercial culture, where there are lots of deals going on and lots of new markets opening, inevitably some people try to get on the train and they're not the people that you want.' Interview with Jeffrey Garten, 'All Things Considered', *National Public Radio*, 25 March 1997.

18. Josef Joffe, 'How America Does It', *Foreign Affairs* 76, no. 5 (1997): 13–27.

19. Jeffrey E. Garten, 'Business and Foreign Policy', *Foreign Affairs* 76, no. 3 (1997): 67–79 at 75.

20. Garten is, in fact, an exception to this rule of globalists – he tends more towards scaremongering over the US economy, and the relative weakness of the domestic sector, in his efforts to persuade Americans to engage with the 'big emerging markets'. See his *The Big Ten: The Big Emerging Markets and How They Will Change Our Lives* (New York: Basic Books, 1997).

21. Daniel Yergin and Joseph Stanislaw, *The Commanding Heights: The Battle Between Government and the Marketplace that is Remaking the Modern World*, updated edition (New York: Touchstone Books, 1999). Although their perspective is broadly triumphalist, the updated paperback edition of *The Commanding Heights* contains some entertainingly hasty throat-clearing about the need for 'measured prudence' and 'legitimacy' in the market system – prompted by the disastrous financial crises in Asia and Russia in 1997 and 1998. Yergin and Stanislaw's admission, 398, that 'few people would die with the words *free markets* on their lips' suggests that the new masters of the 'commanding heights' are not yet sure of their victory.

22. Thomas L. Friedman, *The Lexus and the Olive Tree* (New York: Farrar, Straus & Giroux, 1999). The eponymous metaphor is introduced at 25–9.

23. Ibid., 195–217.

24. Friedman is particularly keen to make use of computer-speak – he writes of a country's 'hardware' (its factories and economic base) and its 'software' (its macro-economic policies), which allows him to make bad puns – for example, the suggestion that the US and the UK are 'running' 'DOScapital 6.0'. Ibid., 128–9.

25. Ibid., 273.

26. Ibid., 60–61, 285–6, 288.

27. Ibid., 285.

28. Ibid., 378. There is, in all this, more than a hint of the founding

document of American missionary enterprise, John Winthrop's 1630 sermon 'A Modell of Christian Charitie', written aboard the *Arabella* in transit from England to America. Winthrop, the first governor of the Massachussets Bay colony, noted that 'Wee shall finde that the God of Israell is among us, when ten of us shall be able to resist a thousand of our enemies.... For wee must consider that wee shall be as a citty upon a hill. The eies of all people are uppon us.'

29. Friedman, *The Lexus and the Olive Tree*, 378.

30. One obvious weakness in the globalist vision of America and the world is that the US itself is hardly the most consistent or thorough promoter of free trade in its handling of the domestic economy – in terms of extensive government investment in the technology and aviation sectors, tariff barriers to cheap foreign goods, and the huge subsidies handed out to agriculture at the federal level, and to a wide variety of businesses at the state and local levels. 'Realists' have largely avoided this fundamental inconsistency in American free-trade rhetoric, however.

31. Benjamin R. Barber, *Jihad vs. McWorld* (New York: Times Books, 1995).

32. Ibid., 205.

33. On the early intellectual rationale for the dispossession of native Americans, see Barbara Arneil, *John Locke and America: The Defence of English Colonialism* (Oxford: Clarendon Press, 1996). On the influence of racial prejudice and theorising on US expansion in the nineteenth century, see Reginald Horsman, *Race and Manifest Destiny: The Origins of American Racial Anglo-Saxonism* (Cambridge, MA: Harvard University Press, 1981). Walter LaFeber discusses the proponents of racial imperialism in *The American Search for Opportunity, 1865–1913* (Cambridge: Cambridge University Press, 1993), 43–4. A good example of 'Anglo-Saxon' racial expansionism is Josiah Strong, *Our Country* [1885], edited by Jurgen Herbst (Cambridge, MA: Harvard University Press, 1963).

34. Bernard Lewis adopts a clear distinction between 'Western' and 'Islamic' or 'Middle Eastern' civilisations in his *Islam and the West* (New York: Oxford University Press, 1993). Fouad Ajami has based a successful career in the US on noting (and lamenting) the resistance of many Arabs to certain phenomena in the Middle East which Ajami takes as given: American power, Israeli expansion and liberal economics. See, for example, *The Arab Predicament: Arab Political Thought and Practice since 1967*, updated edition (Cambridge: Cambridge University Press, 1992); and *The Dream Palace of the Arabs: A Generation's Odyssey* (New York: Pantheon Books, 1998). Both Lewis and Ajami are frequently praised (by Americans) for their insights into the Arab 'character' or 'mind'. For a cogent critique of this practice, and Ajami's acquiescence in it, see Bruce Cumings, *War and Television* (London: Verso, 1992), 107.

35. See Aaron L. Friedberg, 'Ripe for Rivalry: Prospects for Peace in a Multipolar Asia', *International Security* 18, no. 3 (1993): 5–33; and Jacob Heilbrunn, 'The Next Cold War', *New Republic*, 20 November 1995. Both commentators envisage a very similar end-point for Chinese

economic development: 'By 2010 China will probably have gone from being the world's fourth largest economy to its biggest. If the historical correlation between extraordinarily rapid internal growth and external expansion holds, the implications for Asian stability will be troubling indeed' (Friedberg); 'But there's no sound reason to assume that economic advances will lead to a more docile China; on the contrary, rapid economic growth has traditionally resulted in rapid expansion abroad' (Heilbrunn). For more extensive surveys which reach many of the same conclusions, see John Bryan Starr, *Understanding China: A Guide to China's Economy, History, and Political Structure* (New York: Hill & Wang, 1997); and Richard Bernstein and Ross H. Munro, *The Coming Conflict with China* (New York: Alfred Knopf, 1997). These fears of nefarious Chinese designs reached new heights in 1999, as the Republican leadership in the US Congress orchestrated a furious campaign alleging that China had stolen vital nuclear secrets from US labs.

36. See the sources in note 23 of Chapter 3, and 'Beware: A Threat Abroad', *Newsweek*, 17 June 1996; and 'The New Russian Question', *Newsweek*, 10 February 1992.

37. Robert D. Kaplan, *Balkan Ghosts: A Journey Through History* (New York: St. Martin's Press, 1993).

38. For an account of the effect of Kaplan's book on Clinton's thinking, see Elizabeth Drew, *On the Edge: The Clinton Presidency* (New York: Simon & Schuster, 1994), 157–8.

39. For Kaplan's 'disconcerting' remark, see his 'After Balkan Ghosts', *Weekly Standard*, 18 December 1995. See also 'The Coming Anarchy', *Atlantic Monthly* 273, no. 2 (1994): 44–76 at 46, 72, 76. Kaplan sharpened his Cassandrising in *The Ends of the Earth: A Journey at the Dawn of the 21st Century* (New York: Random House, 1996). Perhaps after the Bosnian debacle, Kaplan has realised that the key to achieving success as an author is to point to real problems (such as wealth inequality and competition for resources), but to suggest that neither the US nor the UN can do anything about them – this leads to such aphorisms as 'We are the world and the world is us'; or 'No one can foresee the precise direction of history, and no nation or people is safe from its wrath.' *The Ends of the Earth*, 437, 438.

40. Samuel P. Huntington, *The Clash of Civilizations and the Remaking of World Order* (New York: Simon & Schuster, 1996), 26–7, 33, 40–55.

41. These reviews were reprinted on the 1997 paperback edition of the book (New York: Touchstone, 1997).

42. Many commentators have questioned the usefulness of Huntington's categories, especially his 'Latin American civilization'. See Bruce Nussbaum, 'Capital, Not Culture', *Foreign Affairs* 76, no. 2 (1997): 165; and 'The Man in the Baghdad Café', *Economist*, 9 November 1996. Remarkably few reviewers – even those generally critical of Huntington's thesis – drew attention to his dubious efforts to exclude large and well-established immigrant populations in Europe, North America and

Australasia from his definition of 'Western civilization'. Some commentators were at least able to group Huntington with the present generation of anti-immigration right-wing politicians in 'Western' countries – for a juxtaposition of Huntington's thesis with the current debate over immigration in Australia, see 'A National Identity Crisis', *Economist*, 14 December 1996.

43. Huntington, *The Clash of Civilizations*, 206, 204.

44. Ibid., 130. This extremely gloomy diversion into philosophy seems also to have escaped the attention of Huntington's critics.

45. Huntington, 'The Lonely Superpower', *Foreign Affairs* 78, no. 2 (1999): 35–49 at 38.

46. The globalists have responded acidly to Huntington through predictable avenues: see 'In Praise of Davos Man', *Economist*, 1 February 1997 ('Businessmen may accidentally be making the world safer.'); and Christopher Power, 'Hatfields and McCoys – On a Global Scale', *Business Week*, 25 November 1996. ('Another problem is Huntington's dismissal of business as a force of change.')

47. Henry Kissinger, *Diplomacy* (New York: Simon & Schuster, 1994), 29–55, 835.

48. Since World War II, most historians of 'Wilsonianism' have been notoriously loath to examine their subject in a critical light. Although an earlier historiography had exposed the inconsistencies and strategic miscalculations of Wilson's 'internationalism', the experience of another world war seems largely to have quelled this critical tendency. The most warmly received recent study, Thomas J. Knock's *To End All Wars: Woodrow Wilson and the Quest for a New World Order* (Princeton: Princeton University Press, 1992), explicitly states that 'globalism' (of the Cold War and post-Cold War kind) is the 'illegitimate' heir to Wilsonianism. Knock, 274, describes US foreign policy since 1945 as 'anti-Wilsonian', since its commitment to internationalism seems fleeting and self-interested. N. Gordon Levin, Jr.'s *Woodrow Wilson and World Politics: America's Response to War and Revolution* (New York: Oxford University Press, 1968), 3, argues more convincingly that post-war US policy was shaped in Wilsonian terms: 'For Wilson, then, American national values were identical with universal progressive liberal values, and an exceptionalist America had a mission to lead mankind toward the orderly international society of the future.'

49. The biographical details for Huntington, Garten and Fukuyama are taken from the university websites of Harvard, Yale and George Washington University. Richard Haass's resumé is summarised on the dust jacket of *The Reluctant Sheriff*. Kissinger's colourful career has attracted the attention of several biographers, the most recent being Walter Isaacson, *Kissinger: A Biography* (New York: Simon & Schuster, 1993). Briefer and more recent profiles of Kissinger have been offered by Nigel Farndale, 'Regarding Henry', *Jerusalem Post*, 12 February 1999; and Simon Hattenstone, 'Cold Warrior', *Guardian*, 1 July 1999.

50. We should also remember that corporate cash can create the conditions for a scholarly conflict of interest – one of the most extensive rebuttals to the 'democratic peace' thesis concludes that the US must be prepared for 'great power challenges from states like Japan and Germany', and must not allow itself to drop its military guard. Its author, Christopher Layne, is described in the contributors' notes as 'an unaffiliated scholar' who is 'presently a consultant to the government contracts practice group of the law firm of Hill, Wynne, Troop and Meisinger, which represents major firms in the defense industry'. Layne, 'Kant or Cant: The Myth of the Democratic Peace', in Brown et al., eds, *Debating the Democratic Peace*, 157–201.

51. For a description of Albright's 'Georgetown foreign policy salon', and some creepily prescient speculation over Albright's post-Georgetown career prospects, see Molly Sinclair, 'Woman On Top of the World', *Washington Post*, 6 January 1991. Albright's career, in spite of her academic position, remains 'a singularly Washington one,' according to her biographer. Michael Dobbs, 'Becoming Madeleine Albright', *Washington Post*, 2 May 1999. Dobbs also establishes Albright's perfect 'New Democrat' credentials: after her divorce from newspaper magnate Joseph Albright, 'she got the Georgetown house, a 370-acre farm near Dulles International Airport, and a stock portfolio that would be worth $3.5 million by the time she joined the Clinton administration in 1993'.

52. Elizabeth Bumiller, 'At 34, Worldly-wise and on His Way Up', *New York Times*, 24 September 1999.

53. For details of the history of the *Times*'s 'Foreign Affairs' column, see Patrick Smith, 'Globalism's Pen Pal', *Nation*, 14 June 1999. Smith notes that Friedman 'travels with a heavy bag of ready-made notions', and that his decision to base himself in the US had immediate consequences for his perspective on the world: 'Friedman moved the column to Washington and more or less dispensed with listening – the exceptions being the American elite and the sound of his own voice.'

54. 'Marriott culture' was coined by Janine Wedel to describe the Western environment which grew up around (and because of) the 'experts' who promoted neoliberalism in the former Warsaw Pact countries in the late 1980s and 1990s. Friedman is an unapologetic and happy guest – see *The Lexus and the Olive Tree*, 35. Friedman's inability to mention a hotel without identifying its corporate owner contributes to the sense that his book is an epic commercial for the Fortune 500: for some examples, see ibid., 207–8, 220.

55. Ibid., 381.

56. Some reviewers, at least, were discomfited by Friedman's 'startling' parroting of Madison Avenue copy. See David Rieff, 'The View from Davos', *Los Angeles Times*, 23 May 1999: 'The pity is that while hype is a copywriter's job, it should not be that of the chief foreign-affairs columnist of the New York Times.'

57. *The Lexus and the Olive Tree*, 26, 279–81. Even the reviewer for the

Financial Times, extremely sympathetic to the project of peddling globalism, lost patience with Friedman's generalisations, strained analogies and 'folksy metaphors': 'I confess that by the second chapter I was getting pretty irritated by Thomas L. Friedman. After a canter through the general characteristics of the global market economy, he is soon telling us about his amazing mom, playing bridge across the internet with a man in Siberia. Then comes a rambling story about how difficult it is to satisfy his passion for whole oranges in a Tokyo hotel. From this he deduces that "life is like room service".' Max Wilkinson, 'Global Warnings', *Financial Times*, 15 May 1999.

58. *The Lexus and the Olive Tree*, 378, 320–21, 377.

59. Stanley Hoffmann, 'In Defense of Mother Teresa: Morality in Foreign Policy', *Foreign Affairs* 75, no. 2 (1996): 172–5.

60. For general accounts of campaign finance and the influence of corporate funding on elections, see Elizabeth Drew, *The Corruption of American Politics: What When Wrong and Why* (Secaucus, NJ: Carol Publishing, 1999); Dan Clawson, Alan Neustadtl, and Mark Weller, *Dollars and Votes: How Business Campaign Contributions Subvert Democracy* (Philadelphia: Temple University Press, 1998); and Robert K. Goidel, Donald A. Gross and Todd G. Shields, *Money Matters: Consequences of Campaign Finance Reform* (Lanham, MD: Rowman & Littlefield, 1999).

61. The actual total spent on the presidential campaigns of Dole and Clinton was many times this amount, but the byzantine rules (and loopholes) on funding deter estimates of an exact figure. Although the candidates raised around $30 million in personal contributions, their campaigns relied on commercials and logistical support from their respective political parties, and the so-called 'soft money' (mostly from corporations) which sustains them. For a guide to the financing of the 1996 election, which broke all spending records, see Brooks Jackson, 'Financing the 1996 Campaign: The Law of the Jungle', in Larry J. Sabato, ed., *Toward the Millennium: The Elections of 1996* (Boston: Allyn & Bacon, 1997), 225–60. *Newsweek* estimated the total money raised and spent by Clinton and the Democrats during the 1996 campaign at a staggering $200 million: Howard Fineman et al., 'Strange Bedfellows', *Newsweek*, 10 March 1997.

62. For a brief summary of '1996 Democratic scandals', including the acceptance of money from Asian sources, see Clawson et al., *Dollars and Votes*, 199–202; Jackson, 'Financing the 1996 Campaign', 246–8.

63. One of the reasons why the foreign funding issue became so prominent after 1996 was that the Republicans sensed that they could attack the Democrats on this point without appearing untenably hypocritical; any broader critique of campaign finance would certainly implicate both parties equally.

64. On the direct connections between corporate 'soft money' and political influence, see Clawson et al., *Dollars and Votes*, 107–38. Investigations into 1996 election scandals continued throughout the following years;

for the specific issue of Chinese influence (and of Boeing's eagerness to use political contacts to increase its sales in China), see Paula Dwyer et al., 'The Boeing Connection?', *Business Week*, 31 March 1997; and Owen Ullmann, 'A China Connection that Could Trip Clinton Up', *Business Week*, 1 June 1998.

65. On the influence of Rubin and co. on the Clinton administration, see John B. Judis, 'The Second Rubin Administration', *New Republic*, 10 February 1997; and Karen Breslau, 'Clinton Goes Corporate', *Newsweek*, 17 February 1997. Rubin's former colleagues, the partners of Goldman Sachs, were the most generous donors to Clinton's cause during his presidency: see Howard Fineman et al., 'It's Dole Inc. vs. Clinton Inc.', *Newsweek*, 8 April 1996. Goldman Sachs may also send more of its employees to enforce the 'New Democracy' in person – Rubin's protégé at the firm, Jon Corzine, launched an expensive, self-funded campaign to capture the Senate seat in New Jersey in 1999. Corzine ('New Democrat' credentials – $300 million personal fortune) was admiringly described by the *New Republic* as 'unusual' but 'part of a tradition of upper-class progressives that goes back nine decades'. Judis, 'Gold Man', *New Republic*, 15 November 1999. Goldman Sachs, in return for its support of the 'New Democracy', was assured enormous profits from the Clinton-led normalisation of US relations with China, particularly as American investment banks were invited by the Chinese government to assist in the massive privatisations of former state-owned enterprises in China. See Mark L. Clifford and Brian Bremner, 'Goldman's Big Bet on China', *Business Week*, 6 December 1999.

66. One of Rubin's greatest triumphs, the repeal of the Glass–Steagall banking legislation intended to control financial institutions and to prevent them from consolidating their activities and acting recklessly (as they had done before the Great Depression), was eventually pushed through Congress just as Rubin himself had returned to Wall Street – to head the world's largest financial corporation, Citigroup. Asked by the *New York Times* if he would be earning more in his new job than his old post as treasury secretary, he 'deadpanned': 'That's a fair assumption.' A more precise figure for his personal gain would be somewhere between $10 million and $27 million annually, although his services to the financial industry during his tenure in the Clinton administration suggest that he has earned his reward. Joseph Kahn, 'Former Treasury Secretary Joins Leadership Triangle at Citigroup', *New York Times*, 27 October 1999. Even the business press noted that Rubin's role in all this left a 'slightly unsavory odor': 'Rubin favored dismantling Glass–Steagall when he was in the Administration. Now, he appears to be benefiting personally from its repeal.' Robert Kuttner, 'A Requiem for Glass–Steagall', *Business Week*, 15 November 1999.

67. Bill Bradley resigned from the Senate in 1996, claiming that 'politics is broken'; he immediately set out to fix his own bank balance, at least, by accepting a $327,000 consultancy with investment bank J.P. Morgan.

It was not surprising, then, that he should take Wall Street by storm in his campaign for the presidency in 2000. See John M. Broder, 'Bradley Relies on Wall Street to Raise Funds', *New York Times*, 24 October 1999. The *Times* affected surprise at the Street's solid backing of Bradley given his earlier espousal of policies which would not promote business interests, such as an increase in capital gains tax. Meanwhile, investment banker Louis Susman reminded *Bloomberg News* that Bradley was a reliable player in the much bigger game of neoliberal globalisation: 'I've followed Bradley's career and he's been thoughtful and visionary about the economy on a global basis.' Holly Rosenkrantz, 'Street Bankrolls Bradley', *Bloomberg News*, 8 November 1999.

68. The 2000 presidential election threatened to break even the 1996 records on fundraising and campaign spending. The Republican challenger, George W. Bush, was actually smashing previous campaign finance records by as much as 300 per cent in 1999. 'The Costliest Race in the World', *The Economist*, 31 July 1999. *Business Week* even suggested in 1997 that campaign finance reform was more likely to come from corporate donors, frustrated that their enormous 'soft money' cheques to political parties and committees might escape their control after they'd been cashed. 'The lack of accountability is the big complaint about soft money', grumbled one corporate lobbyist. Another promised that 'We're exploring other avenues for our soft dollars.' Mary Beth Regan and Amy Borrus, 'The Fed-Up Golden Goose', *Business Week*, 23 June 1997.

69. The major exceptions to this rule are foreign-policy situations that demand a rapid response, and minor incidents and skirmishes which are seen as the presidential preserve. See Bruce W. Jentleson, 'Who, Why, What, and How: Debates Over Post-Cold War Military Intervention', in Robert J. Lieber, ed., *Eagle Adrift: American Foreign Policy at the End of the Century* (New York: Longman, 1997), 39–70.

70. See Barbara Hinckley, *Less Than Meets the Eye: Foreign Policy Making and the Myth of the Assertive Congress* (Chicago: University of Chicago Press, 1994); and Stephen R. Weissman, *A Culture of Deference: Congress's Failure of Leadership in Foreign Policy* (New York: Basic Books, 1995).

71. On Yugoslavia, and the tied vote over the execution of the war in Kosovo, see Alison Mitchell, 'Deadlocked House Denies Support for Air Campaign', *New York Times*, 29 April 1999. On the Comprehensive Test Ban Treaty defeat, see Eric Schmitt, 'Senate Kills Test Ban Treaty in Crushing Loss for Clinton', *New York Times*, 14 October 1999.

72. 'Independent internationalism' was coined by Joan Hoff Wilson in her *American Business and Foreign Policy, 1920–1933* (Boston: Beacon Press, 1973), x–xi. Emily Rosenberg has argued that the concept is particularly germane to US foreign policy in the 1920s and 1930s: see *Spreading the American Dream: American Economic and Cultural Expansion, 1890–1945* (New York: Hill & Wang, 1982), 115–17. More recently, however, Joan Hoff has reasserted her belief that American policy throughout the 'American century' has been guided by independent internationalism:

'The American Century: From Sarajevo to Sarajevo', *Diplomatic History* 23, no. 2 (1999): 285–319.

73. The remarks were made on the Senate floor by Jon Kyl, the Republican Senator from Arizona, and reprinted in 'Beyond Testing: Five Senators' Views on US Role in World', *New York Times*, 9 October 1999.

74. Jason DeParle, 'The Man Inside Bill Clinton's Foreign Policy', *New York Times*, 20 August 1995.

75. This may explain Lake's bizarre and disturbing (or, in the words of the *Times* interviewer, 'idiosyncratic') suggestion that 'Mother Teresa and Ronald Reagan were both trying to do the same thing – one helping the helpless, one fighting the Evil Empire. One of the nice things about this job is you can do them both at the same time and not see them as contradictory.' DeParle, 'The Man Inside Bill Clinton's Foreign Policy'.

76. Owen Harries, 'Madeleine Albright's "Munich Mindset"', *New York Times*, 19 December 1996.

77. John F. Kennedy, Jr., 'Interview with Madeleine Albright', *George*, 21 January 1998.

78. Dick Morris, *Behind the Oval Office: Getting Reelected Against All the Odds*, updated edition (Los Angeles: Renaissance Books, 1999), 341.

79. We should note the corollary to this ideology in the presentation of domestic policy. Bill Clinton's chosen successor, Al Gore, offered a new variant of the theme as he opened his campaign for the presidency in 1998: 'practical idealism'. Not to be outdone, leading Republican candidate George W. Bush offered 'compassionate conservatism' as his political compass. Katharine Q. Seelye, 'Gore Floats 2000 Theme: "Practical Idealism"', *New York Times*, 3 December 1998.

80. On the creation of enormous entertainment/media conglomerates, see Dan Steinbock, *Triumph and Erosion in the American Media and Entertainment Industries* (Westport, CT: Quorum Books, 1995); and Edward S. Herman and Robert W. McChesney, *The Global Media: The New Missionaries of Corporate Capitalism* (London: Cassell, 1997). On the connections between the media's news agenda and revenue creation (including advertising), see Bartholomew H. Sparrow, *Uncertain Guardians: The News Media as Political Institution* (Baltimore: Johns Hopkins University Press, 1999), 73–104. Media corporations have also donated huge sums to political campaigns and parties in recent years; by one estimate, more than $31 million between 1995 and 1998. Sheila Kaplan, 'Payments to the Powerful', *Columbia Journalism Review* 37, no. 3 (1998): 54–6. A general perspective on the decline of international news coverage and the deleterious influence of transnational corporate ownership of the media is offered by Garrick Utley, 'The Shrinking of Foreign News', *Foreign Affairs* 76, no. 2 (1997): 2–10.

81. For a general perspective, see James Ledbetter, *Made Possible By...: The Death of Public Broadcasting in the United States* (London: Verso, 1997), especially 154–9 for the influence of corporate sponsorship on the news

coverage of public broadcasting.

82. Cumings, *War and Television*, 103–28.

83. In Kosovo, according to Patrick J. Sloyan of *Newsday*, 'the media once more were asked to sort out a few kernels of fact from a barrage of distortions and half-truths from government information manipulators.' 'The Fog of War', *American Journalism Review* 21, no. 5 (1999): 32–4. On the introduction of Tony Blair's chief 'spin-doctor', Alistair Campbell, to NATO headquarters, see Edward Stourton, 'Spinning for Victory', *Observer*, 16 October 1999. Robert Fisk of the London *Independent* argued that 'most of the journalists at NATO headquarters were so supine, so utterly taken in by NATO's generals and air commodores that their questions might have been printed out for them in advance.' 'Taken In by the NATO Line', *Independent*, 29 June 1999.

84. On the media's role in Somalia, see Michael Maren, *The Road to Hell: The Ravaging Effects of Foreign Aid and International Charity* (New York: The Free Press, 1997), 212–14; Warren P. Strobel, *Late-Breaking Foreign Policy: The News Media's Influence on Peace Operations* (Washington, DC: United States Institute of Peace Press, 1997), 131–42; and Peter Young and Peter Jesser, *The Media and the Military: From the Crimea to Desert Strike* (London: Macmillan, 1997), 204–25. Although these sources differ over the extent to which media reporting influenced US intervention (Strobel in particular claims that the majority of the reporting on Somalia took place after US government initiatives), these authors agree that the media's coverage focused narrowly on the humanitarian, rather than the political elements of Somalia's predicament. Young and Jesser, *The Media and the Military*, 224, suggest that '[f]rom beginning to end in Somalia, entertainment took priority over informed analysis. The initial media optimism, based on the media's own narrow view of the situation and fed by unrealistic American predictions of a quick resolution, soon turned to a disenchanted attribution of blame to the United Nations when expectations were not met.' For a general account of the media's effort to turn complex foreign policy situations into 'human interest' stories, see Susan Moeller, *Compassion Fatigue: How the Media Sell Disease, Famine, War and Death* (New York: Routledge, 1999).

85. Walter Isaacson, 'Madeleine's War', *Time*, 17 May 1999.

86. Friedman, *The Lexus and the Olive Tree*, 349–50.

87. The *New York Times* hardly distanced itself from Friedman's book. Not only did it print a lengthy extract in its Sunday magazine ('A Manifesto for a Fast World', *New York Times*, 28 March 1999), devoting its cover to Friedman (his article was introduced, with no apparent irony, by a full-page photo of a clenched fist painted in the colours of the Stars and Stripes), but it also printed *two* laudatory reviews: Josef Joffe, 'One Dollar, One Vote', 25 April 1999 ('a brilliant guide'); Richard Eder, 'The Global Village is Here', 26 April 1999 ('a breathtaking tour').

88. On the influence of immigration and immigrants on US foreign policy, see Alexander DeConde, *Ethnicity, Race and American Foreign Policy*

(Boston: Northeastern University Press, 1992).

89. Kennedy, Jr., 'Interview With Madeleine Albright'. I am grateful to Andrew Graybill for correcting Albright's statement – *native* Americans, of course, were 'invaded and occupied' on a massive scale by European settlers from the late fifteenth century onward.

90. For examples of 'America First' thinking, see Patrick J. Buchanan, 'America First – and Second, and Third', *National Interest* 19 (1990): 77–92; and his *A Republic, Not an Empire: Reclaiming America's Destiny* (Washington, DC: Regnery, 1999). The latter aroused much controversy in the American media for suggesting that the US might have kept out of the Second World War; Buchanan, ever the anti-communist, was supportive of American intervention in Vietnam, however.

91. For a general account of the misleading of the public over foreign policy, see Eric Alterman, *Who Speaks for America? Why Democracy Matters in Foreign Policy* (Ithaca: Cornell University Press, 1998). On the expeditious creation of Saddam as a monster in the second half of 1990, see William A. Dorman and Steven Livingston, 'News and Historical Content: The Establishing Phase of the Persian Gulf Policy Debate', in W. Lance Bennett and David L. Paletz, eds, *Taken by Storm: The Media, Public Opinion, and US Foreign Policy in the Gulf War* (Chicago: University of Chicago Press, 1994), 63–81. On the State Department's evasions over Rwanda, see Chapter 2 above, notes 93 and 94 and accompanying text.

92. The first quotation is from Todd Hunter Weiss; the second, from Mike Cross. See Rick Bragg, Carey Goldberg and Barbara Stewart, 'For Jane and Joe Public, Wariness and Ignorance', *New York Times*, 26 March 1999.

93. Bill Clinton and Tony Blair complained in May 1999 that reporters had ignored the refugee crisis in Kosovo after only a few days of coverage; Susan Moeller saw this as indicative of the media's short attention span: 'Kosovo can be preempted just like any other news story can be preempted – and when it gets preempted, it goes off the air as if it never existed.' 'Compassion Fatigue', *Christian Science Monitor*, 24 May 1999. On the difficulty of selling the Kosovo campaign, and keeping the public interested, see Michael Powell, 'How to Bomb in Selling a War', *Washington Post*, 27 May 1999. Powell quotes a San Francisco advertising executive on the unfortunate persistence of the conflict: 'It's like the NHL [National Hockey League] playoffs: People get hurt and it goes on too long.'

94. Susan Sachs, 'While Some Americans are Saying, "Just Shoot the Man"', *New York Times*, 25 May 1999.

95. An opinion poll conducted in November 1997 suggested that 61 per cent of Americans supported a military solution to the persistent problem of Saddam Hussein. See Charles Laurence, 'Tired of Words, Americans Want End to "Beast of Baghdad"', *Daily Telegraph*, 13 November 1997. The most prominent advocate of the extrajudicial murder of Saddam

was the *New York Times* pundit Thomas Friedman: 'Given the nature of world politics today, and given America's feckless allies, the US will get only one good military shot at Saddam before everyone at the UN starts tut-tutting and rushing to his defense. So if and when Saddam pushes beyond the brink, and we get that one good shot, let's make sure it's a head shot.' 'Head Shot', *New York Times*, 6 November 1997. It was left to a *Times* reader to point out that Friedman's suggestion was a violation of (tut-tutting?) international law: 'Yes, Saddam Hussein is a bad man. International politics is full of bad men. But there is still a law against murder.' 'Letters to the Editor' (Stanley N. Futterman), *New York Times*, 12 November 1997.

96. John M. Broder, 'Laurels Elude President as Public Judges a War', *New York Times*, 22 June 1999.

97. This comment was made by Bill Burrows, interviewed in Bragg et al., 'For Jane and Joe Public'.

98. The question of the consistency of American intervention was raised by Walter Isaacson in his otherwise hagiographical 'Madeleine's War'. Isaacson printed Albright's reply, but did not follow up on Albright's disingenuous statement of her partial multilateralism – 'Just because you can't act everywhere doesn't mean you don't act anywhere.'

99. On the Clinton administration's stage-management of the event, and the frustration of other news networks at CNN's exclusive coverage, see Howard Kurtz, 'CNN Alone to Air Town Meeting on Iraq Policy', *Washington Post*, 18 February 1998. In light of the disastrous perform-ance of the Clinton officials, one of the administration's motives for choosing this single network may well have backfired: 'Iraqi President Saddam Hussein and his aides are known to watch CNN.'

100. 'Showdown with Iraq: An International Town Meeting', *CNN*, 18 February 1998.

101. Walter Goodman, 'Critic's Notebook', *New York Times*, 21 February 1998; David L. Marcus, 'Top Officials Take Heat at Iraqi Forum', *Boston Globe*, 19 February 1998; Michael Elliott, 'Cheers and Jeers', *Newsweek*, 2 March 1998.

102. For an overview of the Ohio State meeting, and its significance for the formation of policy on Iraq, see Alterman, *Who Speaks for America?*, 1–4.

103. Bruce Clark, 'Middle America Reserves Judgment on Use of Force', *Financial Times*, 21 February 1998.

104. Elliott, 'Cheers and Jeers'.

'THE NEXT AMERICAN CENTURY'?

FIN-DE-SEATTLE

In the first months of 1999, commentators in the US began to turn their eyes towards another American century, grounding their vision in an upbeat assessment of the present and recent past. In the years since Henry Luce's 1941 essay, the United States had faced down the forces of totalitarianism and communism, winning the Cold War and still leaving time for a decade of neoliberal 'globalisation' – a process which consolidated the US victory across the globe. Bill Clinton's 1999 State of the Union address suggested that the US had made great progress towards preparing the ground for 'the next American century'; other Americans shared his optimism, seeing few obstacles to US domination of another hundred years of world history.[1]

As some of the more influential US commentators prepared their millennial musings at year's end, however, they were rudely interrupted by an unexpected source of protest. Earlier in the year, the World Trade Organisation (WTO), the umbrella organisation for international trade negotiations, had decided to begin a new round of talks in Seattle. The city happily accepted the challenge of hosting the conference, but various dissenting groups announced throughout the year that they would make Seattle the focus of protests against the WTO. These groups represented a wide variety of interests. Environmentalists saw the WTO as a leading force behind global climate change and the circumvention of environmental standards, especially in the developing world. Labour advocates charged the WTO with exploiting low-wage workers in other countries. US unions carried their personal grievance that the low-wage economies encouraged by the WTO in developing countries had taken manufacturing jobs from American workers. Development groups protested over the issues of Third World debt and systemic global poverty, accusing the WTO of encouraging free trade even as the gap between poorer and richer countries widened further.[2]

These groups had many things in common. They were mostly based at the grassroots level, and depended on local organisers, often brought together by innovative technologies like the Internet. They were well-organised, and understood both the issues before them and the need to build coalitions (and public support) to effect change. Most profoundly, however, they represented ideas and values which were largely excluded from the political mainstream in the US, Europe and much of the rest of the world. Amidst the talk of the free-market revolution, or its 'centrist' variant, the so-called 'third way', there was virtually no room in political debate for these emphases on the protection of the global environment, the need for good working conditions and a livable wage, and the problem of global economic inequality. Although the WTO was merely the forum in which politicians and business leaders would discuss a new round of trade liberalisation, these protesting groups correctly realised that the Seattle meeting would gather together many of those primarily responsible for the planet's most pressing inequities. Even before the WTO delegates began to arrive, the press billed the meeting as 'the battle in Seattle', a rare moment in which the leaders of the global economy would come face to face with organised and intelligent opposition.[3]

To the apparent surprise of the Seattle officials and the Clinton administration, which had organised the WTO convention, the protesters disrupted proceedings from the first day of the meeting. On Tuesday 30 November, tens of thousands turned out to march in the streets, to form human chains around buildings at which WTO events were scheduled to take place, and to register their complaints about the WTO and the injustices of the international economy. WTO delegates were marooned in their hotel rooms, unable to move freely around streets filled with protesters. The police, realising that the opening day of the conference was descending into chaos, began to employ more draconian tactics against the vast crowds. Unarmed protesters were dispersed with tear gas, concussion grenades and even rubber bullets. The police fought running battles through the streets, struggling to overturn the vast numbers of marchers, who simply regrouped after each gas attack and began to march once more. The scenes of protest and repression were beamed throughout the US and around the world, presenting a striking contrast to the generally upbeat tone of the Clinton administration on economic issues. In the midst of a spectacular American economic boom, an estimated 35,000 protesters gathered in Seattle to reject the president's line on the global economy.[4]

The president himself made a typically contradictory contribution to the meeting. Arriving late on Tuesday night, the president prepared for his address the next day by instructing the Seattle authorities to impose martial law, and to seal off an enormous area of downtown Seattle from anyone without WTO credentials.[5] With the National Guard instructed to take up positions on Seattle's streets, the president travelled to a lunch meeting with the major international delegates, and spoke of his sympathy for the protesters he had just excluded. Condemning the small minority (estimated in the dozens by virtually all observers) who had committed acts of violence, Clinton went on, inexplicably, to praise the thousands of others who had choked on the tear gas of the police the previous day:

> But I'm glad the others showed up, because they represent millions of people who are now asking questions about whether this enterprise in fact will take us all where we want to go. And we ought to welcome their questions, and be prepared to give an answer, because if we cannot create an interconnected global economy that is increasing prosperity and genuine opportunity for people everywhere, then all of our political initiatives are going to be less successful.[6]

Clinton, the master politician, may well have taken this line in the hope of advancing his vice-president's cause with the US labour unions, especially with a view toward the 2000 presidential election.[7] Moreover, his tolerance of the protesters was obviously made easier by the careful exclusion of those same protesters from the city on the day of his speech. However, the angry response of some delegates and business leaders to his comments suggested that his modest remarks had worried his audience of governmental officials and corporate representatives. Given the complete breakdown of relations between the angry crowd and the angry WTO delegates, was there any hope for a reconciliation of the two? And if this preliminary meeting had aroused such passionate opposition and such large crowds, did Seattle represent a precedent for the expression of popular opinion through direct action, rather than via a political system largely funded and controlled by elites?

The story of what happened in Seattle is worthy of closer examination, not least because many of the commentators we met in the last chapter have tried to take over this story for themselves, or to frame the issues as best they can to alienate the protesters from the millions of Americans who saw the demonstrations on television or in the newspapers. Jeffrey Garten, writing in *Business Week*, actually warned his readers in advance of the conference that Seattle 'is likely to be the scene of a big test for global capitalism'. With impressive inventive skills, Garten depicted the forces of global capitalism as weak and threatened, and portrayed the non-governmental organisations (NGOs) and protest groups as the oppressive force in the battle for public opinion:

> While governments and chief executives bore the public and the media with sterile abstractions about free markets, NGOs are sending more nuanced messages sensitive to the anxieties of local communities around the world. At the same time, they are preparing sophisticated strategies to influence television networks, newspapers, and magazines. There is plenty of evidence of NGOs' growing clout. In recent years, they have changed the policies of global corporations such as Nike (over treatment of workers abroad), Monsanto (over genetically engineered products), and Royal Dutch Shell (over environmental issues).... If Washington and Corporate America don't move decisively, NGOs could dominate public opinion on global trade and finance.[8]

To many readers, these examples of NGO pressure might seem positive contributions, a proper public scrutiny of corporate interests. For Garten, however, these modest achievements portended the broader submission of business to public pressure, an outcome which led to the hysterical suggestion that NGOs might find ways to influence an international media which is securely in the hands of some of the world's largest corporations. Even the readers of *Business Week* found Garten's warning hard to handle, complaining in subsequent correspondence that his 'surreal' vision merely proved that, rather than an 'open world economy', the 'one thing the world needs is open political processes.'[9] Garten's article was useful, however, in showing the anxiety of financial elites about the kinds of questions raised by protests in Seattle, and their effects on a broader base of public opinion.

Fareed Zakaria, ministering to the readers of *Newsweek*, acknowledged after the protests that Seattle had been a 'fiasco', an 'unmitigated disaster'. However, his editorial defended the international economy and the current mechanism of global trade in equal measure. Conveniently ignoring the fact that inequalities between rich and poor nations have increased massively in recent decades, Zakaria suggested that the 'downtrodden' people of the Third World were clamouring for the WTO and its many instruments of trade liberalisation. Moreover, Zakaria tried to indemnify the WTO from any responsibility for implementing minimum standards on labour conditions, wages and environmental concerns. 'There are other methods, treaties and organizations aimed at pursuing these worthwhile goals', he announced sophistically, as if trade and social conditions were mutually exclusive. The final weapon in his arsenal was to accuse the protesters of hypocrisy in their complaints against the WTO:

> The demonstrators claimed to be acting in the name of democracy.... But, of course, not one of these organizations is in any way accountable to anyone. Most of them represent small and narrow interests that have been unable to build mainstream support for their demands. The truth is that labour unions, environmental activists and other activists are trying to impose regulations through the WTO that they were unable to persuade the United States Congress to accept.[10]

Apart from the obvious hollowness of this charge, given the participatory and extremely democratic structure of many of the protesting organisations, there is something rather absurd about Zakaria's pique. Hailing the WTO's commitment to democracy just weeks after it voted to admit China as a full member seems rather hollow; as does the shrill boast that protesters cannot obtain the backing of a United States Congress which was, at the end of the twentieth century, more dependent on lobbyists, campaign finance and corporate influence than at any other time in American history.[11] Instead of questioning the efficacy and reliability of these putatively democratic processes in American life, Zakaria simply smeared the protesters who'd chosen to deliver their message in Seattle rather than in Washington, DC.

Predictably, the most irate commentator on Seattle was Thomas L. Friedman, whose own bible of globalisation, *The Lexus and the Olive Tree*, had hardly predicted this kind of popular uprising in the US. Friedman actually needed two editorial columns in the *New York Times* fully to expectorate his bile at the protesters – 'Senseless in Seattle', and the sequel, 'Senseless in Seattle II'. Friedman could hardly contain his anger: 'Is there anything more ridiculous in the news today than the protests against the World Trade Organization in Seattle? I doubt it.'[12] Friedman's tactics were rather different from those of Garten and Zakaria, however: his telling of the Seattle story cast the protesters as late-twentieth-century Luddites, opposing neither global inequality nor labour exploitation, but the idea of trade between nations itself.[13] This enabled Friedman to reach some odd conclusions about the protesters' motives and methods:

> What's crazy is that the protesters want the WTO to become precisely what they accuse it of already being – a global government. They want it to set more rules – their rules, which would impose our labor and environmental standards on everyone else. I'm for such higher standards, and over time the WTO may be a vehicle to enforce them, but it's not the main vehicle to achieve them.

Since Friedman refused to imagine a 'globalised' world in which standards of pay, labour conditions and environmental impact are regulated and improved, he couldn't recognise the protesters as truly international in their vision; nor could he understand why they would target the WTO, the body which supposedly regulates global trade, if the notion of regulation in and of itself has been demonised. His editorial pieces were notable for their complete inability to accept the protesters' terms, or to consider their mere presence in Seattle as valid. For Friedman (as for Garten and Zakaria), the job of the WTO is to destroy environmental or social standards which bar free movement of goods and money, even if the consequence is a rush to the basement by governments and employers, eager to produce the cheapest products regardless of their effects on workers and on the environment.

Friedman's initial editorial, written in the heat of his anger, seemed unusually intemperate and rude. In his follow-up, he acknowledged that his 'environmentalist allies' (translation: former environmentalists who now work for corporations) had suggested that 'my criticism of the protesters in Seattle was too broad-brush'.[14] Rather like Bill Clinton, Friedman offered the vague idea that the WTO could be 'opened up', although he undercut any radical implication here by simply noting that it had 'no need' to be secretive in its deliberations.[15] Friedman's willingness to open the WTO to scrutiny was tied to a crucial companion tactic, concerning the agenda of the protesters in Seattle. The protesters had argued that standards on labour, wages and the environment should be guaranteed internationally. Friedman, on the other hand, contended that the customer should determine such things – if customers were sufficiently vexed by low wages abroad, or by the environmental impact of a corporation's activities, they should organise *ad hoc* protests and change policy by their actions at the cash register. In the meantime, free trade would continue to define the global economy and environment, with only intermittent interruption from the occasional *cause célèbre* of consumer groups.

Many objections to Friedman's solution come to mind. In the first place, corporations hardly publicise many of their abuses or cost-cutting exercises, and the notion that 'consumers' will learn of these abuses from a corporate-controlled media seems optimistic at best. The television and newspaper coverage of the Seattle events frequently suggested that the protesters were enemies of any kind of trade, and that a high proportion were engaged in violent activities during the protests. Conversely, journalists were often uncritical of the Seattle police department, even after pictures of tear-gassing and the firing of rubber bullets had reached the newsrooms. In the midst of the street protests and the 'riot-control' measures, Lou Waters of CNN concluded an interview with a Seattle police spokesperson with a cheerful sign-off: 'Good luck to you out there today.' Given this kind of soft-pedalling, it seems fanciful to suggest that corporations or governments are overly worried that the media will amplify the message of Seattle's protests to a wider public.[16]

Moreover, 'consumers' in the richest countries possess far more disposable income than citizens of poorer countries, and this wealth entitles them to a much greater influence in any market-based regulatory system.[17] Regulation by consumer would amount not to democratic control, but to the foundation of a one-dollar, one-vote principle at the heart of the world's political system. Should the fate

of the majority of the world's people depend entirely on the consumer preferences of a small minority in Western countries? According
to Friedman, undoubtedly. Finally, the impact of industry and energy
consumption on the global environment is measured in climatic
changes over decades, even centuries. Although most scientific experts
agree that the planet is headed towards disastrous climate change, the
effects of this change will be overlooked by governments and individuals unless they are compelled to take a long view. Many consumer decisions are extremely short-term and fickle, and the notion
of basing environmental policy on such immediate concerns as cheap
fuel prices seems extraordinarily short-sighted as one views the
environmental problem from a broader perspective.[18]

The idea of regulation, then, seems absolutely necessary to combat the environmental and human disasters which loom in the coming century. Friedman, however, anticipated this thinking in his
editorial, and reanimated an old demon to forestall these ideas:

> Too many unions and activists want the quick fix for globalization: just
> throw up some walls and tell everyone else how to live. There was a
> country that tried that. It guaranteed everyone's job, maintained a pro-
> tected market and told everyone else how to live. It was called the Soviet
> Union. Didn't work out so well. In the end it probably did more damage
> to its environment and workers than any country in history.[19]

Behind the protests in Seattle, then, lay a simple choice: rampant
globalisation on Friedman's model, or a submission to regulation
which could only lead back towards communism and Soviet tyranny.
In Garten's warnings about the power of NGOs and popular protest,
Zakaria's arguments that protesters were undemocratic because they
couldn't afford to lobby the US Congress, and Friedman's explicit
incarnation of the Red menace, the same message was apparent: at
the end of the twentieth century, the only alternative to unfettered
capitalism, with all its admitted faults and inequities, was communist
terror; and so there was really no alternative at all.

Although we should refrain from passing definitive judgement on
the six decades since Luce's 'American Century', we can hardly avoid
observing that the battle against communism has been a constant
theme in American politics throughout this period; and that political
debate even today, more than a decade after the Soviet Union's

collapse, is conditioned by the supposed threat of socialism or communism. Although the US government has intervened heavily in its economy throughout this period, particularly in the support of military industries and through corporate tax relief more generally, the suggestion that the US should regulate the economy more closely to guarantee minimum standards of health, education and income has been anathema to generations of politicians and ideologues. Moreover, the spread of neoliberal ideology in the past two decades has imposed this thinking on countries around the world, to the point where the American political and economic philosophy has itself become highly dogmatic, even fundamentalist. The automatic equation of unregulated capitalism with freedom, and of government intervention with communist oppression, has persuaded an entire generation that the inequities and problems of our world are irresolvable, even as those inequities and problems worsen across the globe.

An arrogant 'globalism', which upholds this single model of world development, has achieved near-total consensus in Washington; the sheer weight of evidence contradicting its claims, however, has forced the occasional insider to dissent from the general view. A few days before the events in Seattle, the chief economist of the World Bank, Joseph Stiglitz, resigned from his post. Stiglitz, an academic economist who had served in the Clinton administration and the World Bank throughout the period of Clinton-led neoliberalism, was hardly a socialist; however, his departure was linked to his sense that the American commitment to neoliberalism, faithfully implemented by the World Bank, had become politically and morally untenable.[20] In his 1999 report on Russia, which criticised the US and the IMF for their advocacy of 'shock therapy' (and which was seen by many as responsible for his exit from the World Bank), Stiglitz had addressed this point directly:

> One deeper origin of what became known as the 'shock therapy' approach to the [Russian economic] transition was moral fervor and triumphalism left over from the Cold War. Some economic cold-warriors seem to have seen themselves on a mission to level the 'evil' institutions of communism and to socially engineer in their place (using the right textbooks this time) the new, clean, and pure 'textbook institutions' of a private property market economy. From this cold-war perspective, those who showed any

sympathy to transitional forms that had evolved out of the communist past and still bore traces of that evolution must be guilty of 'communist sympathies'. Only a blitzkrieg approach during the 'window of opportunity' provided by the 'fog of transition' would get the changes made before the population had a chance to organize to protect its previous vested interests. This mentality is a reincarnation of the spirit and mindset of Bolshevism and Jacobinism.[21]

Not surprisingly, this kind of talk made Stiglitz very unpopular in Washington. Although Stiglitz was, according to the *Financial Times*, 'personally friendly' with the new US Treasury Secretary, Lawrence Summers, 'Mr. Summers had to look after his constituency on Wall Street'. The financial media speculated that Stiglitz had actually resigned under pressure from his boss, James Wolfensohn; and, indirectly, at the behest of Summers, who controlled Wolfensohn's pending reappointment as World Bank president.[22] Regardless of the extent of American involvement in Stiglitz's resignation, his departure from the World Bank removed another opponent of the Washington Consensus, and cleared the way for a resumption of the Clinton administration's global mission, to 'level the 'evil' institutions' which stand in the way of the final triumph of market 'freedom'.[23]

PROSPECTS

In the four chapters of this book, we have explored the problem of US relations with the rest of the world from different perspectives. In the first chapter, we considered the emergence of an American economic perspective which has shaped the rest of the world, especially through the institutions of the World Bank and the IMF. In the second chapter, we looked at the relationship between the US and the UN, the fickle American respect for international law, and the inconsistent and occasionally disastrous US engagement with post-Cold War peacekeeping. In the third chapter, we analysed the military strategies of the US in the decade since the USSR's collapse, the encouragement given by the US government to its largest defence industries, and the actual consequences of American military action in Iraq and Kosovo. Finally, in the fourth chapter, we examined the various perspectives and theories of US policymakers, and the context in which decisions on foreign policy action (or inaction) are reached and justified. Having traced these recent developments, we can only conclude that the US has created and fostered a world in which inequality and injustice are either encouraged or harboured, and in which efforts to address systemic inequities and looming crises are deterred by American military or economic power.

Although the world is more closely linked than ever before, inequality between richest and poorest has reached record levels. This has created a paradoxical and dangerous situation – the disenfranchised and oppressed are better able to identify and understand the forces ranged against them, even as political power around the world is increasingly concentrated in the hands of wealthy individuals and corporations who deter any alternative to the global economic order. Inevitably, protests against the present system will continue, manifesting themselves in the kind of direct action witnessed in Seattle, or in acts of violence against wealthy elites in the US and elsewhere. Less certain is the response of the US to these protests. As the Seattle demonstrations made clear, democratic protest against the onward march of global capitalism is hardly compatible with 'free trade' or capital liberalisation – one day the WTO delegates were trapped in their hotels, as the protesting crowds marched through the streets; the next, the delegates moved freely, and the crowds were held back by martial law. Although the defenders of the status quo will make every effort to distract from or to circumvent these confrontations, the complaints of protesters will eventually force governments to make a choice: should capital or people be allowed to move freely? What price is worth paying for the preservation of the existing order? As one commentator observed, the US will probably seek first to 'globalise' this problem by sending the WTO back to developing countries for its meetings, where a more draconian police strategy raises fewer eyebrows.[24] But given the risk of an informed minority in the US mobilising similar protests within American borders, it seems likely that the US government will have soon to choose its loyalties and to act upon them.

Perhaps it's not surprising that we are left at the end of our enquiry with the same distinction made by Henry Wallace in 1942 – between another 'American century' and the prospect of a period of international cooperation and, where necessary, regulation. Despite the globalisation of the international economy in the past three decades, political and military power remains firmly with the United States, which pays lip service to internationalism but which has shown little respect for any international organisation, with the possible exceptions of the WTO, the IMF and the World Bank. Although the US may be able to preserve its domination of global affairs for many more decades, the trends that we have been tracing – in economic, political and military development – suggest that concerted opposition may arise to American actions, and that this opposition may not necessarily manifest itself in a simple military threat, or restrained political protest. A genuine and firm commitment to the United Nations would go a long way towards inoculating the United States (and the world) against these dangers, and would at least remove the international perception that the US conducts its affairs with an arrogance matched only by its self-regard.

A major change in US policy would, of course, entail a deeper American engagement with its recent history, and a reassessment of the stakes and the meaning of the US battle with communism in the decades of the Cold War. As Joseph Stiglitz warned, US policy-makers have interpreted this battle in a simple framework of good and evil, a perspective which has encouraged triumphalism, complacency and a kind of political inflexibility which bodes ill for the coming century. Political and economic regulation is easier than ever before, given the interconnectedness of the planet and the growing number of shared problems which threaten every nation. The prospect of such regulation, however, seems impossibly distant. If the twenty-first century is to be less bloody and destructive than its predecessor, the US will have to use its enviable resources and power to redistribute wealth, raise living standards around the world, and to place political and environmental needs ahead of economic gain. In practical terms, this would entail the restructuring of organisations like the World Bank and the IMF to allow for debt cancellation, and the protection of essential services, like health and education, from 'market forces'. Just as the IMF currently defines the structural make-up of many of the world's economies, it must in the future ensure that minimal standards of public service provision are guaranteed to everyone. In the past, efforts to underwrite these essential services have often failed under the pressure of globalisation – countries have tried to improve their own conditions, only to lose trade to other countries which undercut them with cheap labour, minimal benefits and an eviscerated public sector. In the twenty-first century, the US must use its power, influence and wealth to establish these standards around the world, and must compel its mighty corporations to respect them as the foundation of a future, more equitable global economy.

The principal obstacles to these changes in American policy are familiar and, many commentators would argue, inevitable − self-interest, freedom of the individual (and of the corporation), the difficulty of ensuring cooperation on a global scale. However, if the US maintains its present course, there is a serious danger of increased inequality, violent unrest and environmental catastrophe. Beneath the triumphalist rhetoric of the 'American century' reside a series of unpleasant, even disastrous visions of the decades before us. The challenge for American politicians and the American people is to see these visions even in a moment of American predominance, and to avert them by directing US power towards social and economic change around the globe, rather than the narrow pursuit of American interests.

NOTES

1. Clinton administration officials had referred to the 'next American century' as early as 1996 − see Anthony Lake, 'Defining Missions, Setting Deadlines', address delivered at George Washington University, Washington, DC, 6 March 1999. Bill Clinton chose the phrase as the peroration of his 1999 State of the Union address, delivered before Congress, 19 January 1999. Pundits also employed the phrase − see Mortimer B. Zuckerman, 'A Second American Century', *Foreign Affairs* 77, no. 3 (1998): 18−31.

2. For overviews of the protesters' provenance and various emphases, see David Postman et al., 'Why WTO United So Many Foes', *Seattle Times*, 6 December 1999; Robert A. Jordan, 'Battle in Seattle Sent a Message', *Boston Globe*, 7 December 1999; and Todd Gitlin, 'From Chicago to Seattle', *Newsweek*, 13 December 1999.

3. On the composition and platforms of the protesters, and the innovative form of democratic action they envisaged, see Michael Byers, 'Woken Up in Seattle', *London Review of Books*, 6 January 2000. For an advance

warning of the protests, see 'Storm Over Globalisation', *Economist*, 27 November 1999.

4. For an overview and chronology of the events in Seattle, see 'Countdown to Chaos in Seattle', *Seattle Times*, 5 December 1999. On the police tactics, see Sam Howe Verhovek and Steven Greenhouse, 'National Guard is Called to Quell Trade-Talk Protests', *New York Times*, 1 December 1999. Estimates of the crowd in the press varied from around 35,000 to 50,000.

5. According to the *New York Times*, the city of Seattle 'radically changed its tactics for dealing with the demonstrators' after Clinton's arrival on the evening of 30 November, 'apparently under the strong suggestion of the federal authorities.' David E. Sanger, 'In Stormy Seattle, Clinton Chides World Trade Body', *New York Times*, 2 December 1999.

6. Remarks by the president, Four Seasons Hotel, Seattle, 1 December 1999.

7. On Clinton's tendentious (and abrupt) sympathy for the labour unions' perspective on the WTO, see Joseph Kahn and David E. Sanger, 'Seattle Talks on Trade End with Stinging Blow to US', *New York Times*, 5 December 1999. Since Clinton was effectively the midwife of the WTO, having overseen its emergence from the old GATT system in 1994, his sudden scepticism raised obvious questions about his sincerity. See Walter Russell Mead, 'Skewered in Seattle', *Los Angeles Times*, 5 December 1999. Mead noted that 'the WTO we have now is, for better or worse, the WTO that the Clinton administration designed, and administration officials once bitterly condemned the dissenters who warned of the dangers that Clinton now vainly seeks to address.'

8. Jeffrey E. Garten, 'A Sophisticated Assault on Global Capitalism', *Business Week*, 8 November 1999.

9. 'Letters to the editor' (Gerald Cavanaugh and Phillip Gordon), *Business Week*, 29 November 1999.

10. Fareed Zakaria, 'After the Storm Passes', *Newsweek*, 13 December 1999.

11. For critical perspectives on China's entry into the WTO, which was largely fêted in the US media, see Jim Mann, 'WTO Deal: Wisdom or Folly?', *Los Angeles Times*, 17 November 1999; and John Sweeney, 'Why China Should Not Be Admitted to the WTO', *Boston Globe*, 20 November 1999. On the influence of corporate cash and 'soft money' on Congressional elections, see Chapter 4 above, notes 60, 61, 68 and accompanying text.

12. Thomas L. Friedman, 'Senseless in Seattle', *New York Times*, 1 December 1999.

13. Note Friedman's contemptuous description of the protesters: 'a Noah's ark of flat-earth advocates, protectionist trade unions, and yuppies looking for their 1960s fix'.

14. Friedman, 'Senseless in Seattle II', *New York Times*, 8 December 1999. In both of his editorials on Seattle, Friedman sneered at Green campaigners who live in the 'old world' of direct action – and praised

the new breed of environmentalists–cum–consultants who, according to one of his 'allies', Paul Gilding, 'understand that the market, and global integration, is now king'. Gilding resigned as head of Greenpeace International in 1993, complaining that the organisation wasn't sufficiently interested in working with corporations. He then established himself in Sydney, Australia as an environmental consultant to big businesses, including BP Australia, DuPont and Monsanto. For details of his career change, see Donna Shaw, 'Foes Become Former Activist's Clients', *Philadelphia Inquirer*, 13 June 1997; and Sharon Bender, 'Through the Revolving Door: From Greenpeace to Big Business', *PR Watch* 6, no. 3 (1999): 1–4. Gilding is something of a regular in Friedman's columns; with no apparent irony, Friedman uses Gilding's Australian environmental consultancy in an earlier column to demonstrate the usefulness of the Internet – without which, as Gilding observes, 'you just couldn't operate a global business from here'. Friedman, 'Honey, I Shrunk the World', *New York Times*, 12 September 1999.

15. Friedman, 'Senseless in Seattle II'.
16. For an account of the influence of corporations on the media, see Chapter 4 above, notes 80, 81 and accompanying text. For an overview of media distortions in the coverage of events in Seattle, especially the tendency to portray the protesters as enemies of trade *tout court*, see 'WTO Coverage: Prattle in Seattle', a report by Fairness and Accuracy in Reporting (FAIR), 7 December 1999. Lou Waters offered his encouragement to the Seattle police in his interview with Christie Lynne-Bonner, 'CNN Today', *CNN*, 1 December 1999.
17. For a useful elaboration of unequal distribution of income and unbalanced patterns of consumption between richer and poorer countries, see United Nations Development Programme, *Human Development Report 1998* (New York: Oxford University Press for UNDP, 1998), 25–30, 45–60. The *Report*'s authors note that global inequality has become much more pronounced in recent decades: 'In 1960 the 20% of the world's people who live in the richest countries had 30 times the income of the poorest 20% – by 1995, 82 times as much income.' Ibid., 29.
18. For further and recent evidence of the threat of climate change, and attendant environmental catastrophe, see Konstantin Y. Vinnikov et al., 'Global Warming and Northern Hemisphere Sea Ice Extent', *Science*, 3 December 1999; and William K. Stevens, 'Arctic Thawing May Jolt Sea's Climate Belt', *New York Times*, 7 December 1999.
19. Friedman, 'Senseless in Seattle II'.
20. Louis Uchitelle, 'World Bank Economist Felt He Had to Silence His Criticism or Quit', *New York Times*, 2 December 1999.
21. Joseph E. Stiglitz, 'Whither Reform? Ten Years of the Transition', paper prepared for the Annual Bank Conference on Development Economics, Washington, DC, 28–30 April 1999, 22–3.
22. Nancy Dunne, 'Knives Out in Washington for a Free Spirit', *Financial Times*, 25 November 1999.

23. Critics of Stiglitz, and boosters of the Clinton administration's export of neoliberalism, lined up to suggest that Russia actually needed much more neoliberal medicine, and that the problems could have been avoided by 'quicker liberalisation'. See Anders Åslund, 'Russia's Collapse', *Foreign Affairs* 78, no. 5 (1999): 64–77; and Martin Wolf, 'Transition Proves Long and Hard', *Financial Times*, 10 November 1999.
24. Marc Cooper offered this droll remark: 'After this week's Battle in Seattle, one thing is definite: The next World Trade Organization confab will be held in some place like Singapore or Jakarta.' 'Teamsters and Turtles', *Los Angeles Times*, 2 December 1999.

INDEX

Import-substitution industrialisation (ISI), 39n
India, 122
Indonesia, 122, 129, 131, 201, 217
International Criminal Court, 61, 64, 68–73
International Monetary Fund: advocacy of structural adjustment, 11, 13–14; and Africa, 21–3; and Asian financial crisis, 35; and debt crisis, 10; future role of, 244–5; gold sales of, 23; and loans to Mexico, 15, 18–21, 47n; and a 'new global architecture', 35; and Russian 'bail-in', 33, 241; US influence upon, 3, 4, 10, 35–6, 194, 244
International Relations (IR), academic theories of, 183, 189–90, 194–7, 220–21n
International Trade Organisation, 4
Iran, 5, 41n, 70, 120–22, 129, 141, 152
Iraq: allies with US in opposing International Criminal Court, 70; attacked by US (post-1991), 69, 115, 140, 142–5, 147, 151–2, 156, 194, 215–18, 243; early US support of, 129; effect of sanctions on, 142–5, 151–2, 156, 169–70n, 194, 204; as enemy of the US, 120–21, 127, 212; invasion of Kuwait and Gulf War (1990/1), 60, 74, 94, 115, 118, 119, 120–21, 123, 139–45, 150, 179, 182, 207; and US public opinion, 215–18, 243
Isaacson, Walter, 208, 232n
Isolationism, 63, 70, 138, 149–56, 203
Israel: buys political influence in US, 201; occupation of Palestinian territories, 140–41; opposition to International Criminal Court, 70; recipient of US military aid, 129, 135, 141; as US ally, 120; and weapons of mass destruction, 122

Jackson, Jr., Jesse, 25, 50n
Japan, 199
Joffe, Josef, 185
Johns Hopkins University, 181
Johnson, Lyndon B., 6
Jordan, 200
Jordan, Vernon, 45n
Jubilee 2000, 22

Kaplan, Robert D., 191–2, 223n
Kennan, George, 96n
Kenya, 153
Keynes, John Maynard, 3, 7, 10, 11
Khobar Towers bombing, 153
Kissinger, Henry: academic, corporate and government careers of, 197; and Anthony Lake, 204–5; bombs Laos and Cambodia, 204; destabilises Chile, 101n; and international relations theory, 195–6; and NATO expansion, 125–7; and the 'poor Henry' argument, 101–2n; praises Huntington's Clash of Civilizations, 192; views on Russia, 26, 125–7, 191
Korea, 65, 120–22, 127, 162n
Kosovo: debates in the US over, 146–7, 171n, 187–8, 204, 208–10; expulsion of civilian population, 147–8; fast-food interpretation of (Thomas Friedman), 187–8; and Kosovo Liberation Army (KLA), 146; and manipulation of the media, 207–8, 230n; and US tactics, 149–51; war in (1999), 115, 119, 145–51, 207–10, 213–15, 243
Krauthammer, Charles, 48n, 157n, 178–9
Kurds, 131, 141–3, 217
Kuwait, 139–43, 144, 145

Lake, Anthony: 'pragmatic idealism' of, 204–5; and Presidential Decision Directive 25 (PDD-25), 81, 83; and Presidential Review

Participating Organizations

Both ENDS A service and advocacy organization, Both ENDS collaborates with environment and indigenous organizations, both in the South and in the North, with the aim of helping to create and sustain a vigilant and effective environmental movement.

> Damrak 28–30, 1012 LJ Amsterdam, Netherlands
> Phone: +31 20 623 08 23   Fax: +31 20 620 80 49
> Email: info@bothends.org
> Website: www.bothends.org

Catholic Institute for International Relations CIIR aims to contribute to the eradication of poverty through a programme that combines advocacy at national and international level with community-based development.

> Unit 3 Canonbury Yard, 190a New North Road,
> London N1 7BJ, UK
> Phone: +44 (0)20 7354 0883   Fax: +44 (0)20 7359 0017
> Email: ciir@ciir.org
> Website: www.ciir.org

Corner House The Corner House is a UK-based research and solidarity group working on social and environmental justice issues in North and South.

> PO Box 3137, Station Road, Sturminster Newton,
> Dorset DT10 1YJ, UK
> Phone: +44 (0)1258 473795   Fax: +44 (0)1258 473748
> Email: cornerhouse@gn.apc.org
> Website: www.cornerhouse.icaap.org

Focus on the Global South Focus is dedicated to regional and global policy analysis and advocacy work. It works to strengthen the capacity of organizations of the poor and marginalized people of the South and to better analyse and understand the impacts of the globalization process on their daily lives.

> C/o CUSRI, Chulalongkorn University, Bangkok 10330, Thailand
> Phone: +66 2 218 7363   Fax: + 66 2 255 9976
> Email: Admin@focusweb.org
> Website: www.focusweb.org

Inter Pares   A Canadian social justice organization, Inter Pares has been active since 1975 in building relationships with Third World development groups and providing support for community-based development programs. Inter Pares is also involved in education and advocacy in Canada, promoting understanding about the causes, effects and solutions to poverty.

  58 rue Arthur Street, Ottawa, Ontario, KIR 7B9 Canada
  Phone: +1 613 563 4801   Fax: +1 613 594 4704

Third World Network   TWN is an international network of groups and individuals involved in efforts to bring about a greater articulation of the needs and rights of peoples in the Third World; a fair distribution of the world's resources; and forms of development which are ecologically sustainable and fulfil human needs. Its international secretariat is based in Penang, Malaysia.

  228 Macalister Road, 10400 Penang, Malaysia
  Phone: +60 4 2266159   Fax: +60 4 2264505
  Email: twnet@po.jaring.my
  Website: www.twnside.org.sg

World Development Movement   The WDM campaigns to tackle the causes of poverty and injustice. It is a democratic membership movement that works with partners in the South to cancel unpayable debt and break the ties of IMF conditionality, for fairer trade and investment rules, and for strong international rules on multinationals.

  25 Beehive Place, London SW9 7QR, UK
  Phone: +44 (0)20 7737 6215   Fax: +44 (0)20 7274 8232
  Email: wdm@wdm.org.uk
  Website: www.wdm.org.uk

TANZANIA
TEMA Publishing Co Ltd
PO Box 63115
Dar Es Salaam

ZAMBIA
UNZA Press
PO Box 32379
Lusaka